Visions of Beirut

Visions
of
Beirut

The Urban Life of Media Infrastructure

Hatim El-Hibri

Duke University Press   Durham and London   2021

Designed by Drew Sisk
Typeset in Portrait Text by Westchester Publishing Services
Library of Congress Cataloging-in-Publication Data
Names: El-Hibri, Hatim, [date] author.
Title: Visions of Beirut : the urban life of media infrastructure / Hatim El-Hibri.
Description: Durham : Duke University Press, 2021. | Includes bibliographical
references and index.
Identifiers: LCCN 2020042291 (print) | LCCN 2020042292 (ebook)
ISBN 9781478010449 (hardcover)
ISBN 9781478010777 (paperback)
ISBN 9781478013020 (ebook)
Subjects: LCSH: Mass media—Social aspects—Lebanon—Beirut. | Mass media—
Political aspects—Lebanon—Beirut. | Mass media and culture—Lebanon—Beirut. |
Beirut (Lebanon)—In mass media.
Classification: LCC DS89.B4 E43 2021 (print) | LCC DS89.B4 (ebook) |
DDC 956.92/5043—dc23
LC record available at https://lccn.loc.gov/2020042291
LC ebook record available at https://lccn.loc.gov/2020042292

Cover art: Pan American Airlines map (detail), 1960s, exact date unknown. Photo
courtesy of Belal Hibri (2010). Illustration by Drew Sisk.

CONTENTS

Arabic terms have been translated and transliterated using a simplified version of the *International Journal of Middle Eastern Studies* conventions. For Arabic names and place-names, I have followed the most common English transliterations.

ACKNOWLEDGMENTS

If it is true that books are never really finished, you just stop working on them, then it must also be true that you never really start writing a book: you are given countless gifts of kindness and intellectual generosity, which you eventually turn into words on a page. I have to first thank my mentors at NYU—I couldn't have asked for a better guide than Marita Sturken, a giver of incisive feedback on the most versions of this book of anyone. Helga Tawil-Souri demonstrated what it is to be a colleague and mentor, which made her insights and humor all the richer. Ella Shohat remains a deep inspiration, and an example of an interlocutor in the form of doing close readings. I am also grateful to Brett Gary, who first suggested the idea to pursue a doctorate. In my time at the department of Media, Culture, and Communication, I had innumerable conversations with Nick Mirzoeff, Arvind Rajagopal, Arjun Appadurai, and Allen Feldman, whose comments shaped the formative stages of this project. I was also fortunate to be in the company of Naomi Angel, Jamie Berthe, Song Chong, Travis Hall, Marissa Kantor-Dennis, Kari Hensley, Sarah Stonbely, Nadja Millner-Larsen, Kate Brideau, Kouross Esmaeli, Tamara Kneese, Elizabeth Patton, Carlin Wing, Robert Wosnitzer, and Jacob Gaboury. Scott Selberg and Wazhmah Osman were and are a solid rock and a safe harbor.

May Farah's comradeship has spanned the gap from graduate school to my first job at the American University of Beirut. I was fortunate enough to work closely with Nabil Dajani, Greg Burris, and

Sara Mourad in the media studies program there. My colleagues in the department were all exemplary, especially George Azar, Habib Battah, Nora Boustany, Sari Hanafi, Anaheed Al-Hardan, Rima Majed, Toni Oyry, Sylvain Perdigon, Nadya Sbaiti, Livia Wick, and Maysaa Kobrosly. I am also grateful to the patient listening and incisive feedback on this project at transformative stages from Adam Waterman, Anjali Nath, Samhita Sunya, Lisa Hajjar, Ira Allen, Omar Dewachi, Sami Khatib, and Patrick McGreevy. Kirsten Scheid's friendship, guidance, and deep understanding of Lebanon were of tremendous help; she was also kind enough to give permission for the use her photos. Additional thanks are owed to the welcoming space of the Center for Art and Humanities Mellon Faculty Fellowship, and to Reem Joudi and Rami Deeb for their work as research assistants.

Since I came to George Mason, Jessica Scarlata's mentorship, friendship, and encouragement have been tremendous. I am also grateful to Amal Amireh, Johanna Brockman, Tamara Harvey, Jessica Hurley, Yasemin Ipek, Alex Monea, and Stefan Wheelock. Libby Anker, Matthew Scherer, Bassam Haddad, and Noura Erakat have gone above and beyond as friends and interlocutors.

Marita Sturken, Helga Tawil-Souri, and Jessica Scarlata read a complete draft of the manuscript, which was greatly improved because of their comments. The feedback of the two anonymous reviewers was generative, and they have my thanks. I couldn't have asked for a wiser or more generous editor than Courtney Berger. She and Sandra Korn have been the best kind of colleagues, and their efforts directly improved this book.

In the fall of 2019 I had the privilege of being a visiting faculty fellow at the Center for Advanced Research in Global Communication at the Annenberg School for Communication at the University of Pennsylvania, where I finished revising this manuscript. I am very grateful to Marwan Kraidy, Marina Krikorian, and Clovis Bergère for all of their companionship and support. I also owe special thanks to Padma Chirumamilla, Giang Nguyen-Thu, Ergin Bulut, Fernanda Rosa, and Stanislav Budnitsky for all the inspirational conversation.

There are many people to whom I spoke about this project who have requested anonymity but to whom I am grateful, and I owe thanks to more friends and fellow travelers than the names that appear here. Bassile Khoury's good humor and careful management of the cartothèque at IFPO were a tremendous help, as were the staff of Assafir's archival collection. Mona Fawaz shared her deep knowledge and insight at crucial junctures. I am grateful for numerous conversations with Omar Al Ghazzi, Michael Allan, Narges Bajoghli, Hiba Bou Akar, Paula Chakravartty, Sabine El Chamaa, Rayya El Zein,

Ghenwa Hayek, Yasmine Khayyat, Kristine Khouri, Niko Kosmatopoulos, Peter Limbrick, Munira Lokhandwala, Laura Marks, Fouad Marei, Heather O'Brien, Lisa Parks, Tarik Sabry, Deen Sharp, and Nadia Yaqub. Leena Akhtar, Karron Karr, Jerry Salame, and Andy Tank have each been the most incredible friends. The Arab Image Foundation came through with a last-minute digitization request. I owe special thanks to Tarek El-Ariss for his unflagging support, camaraderie, and guidance over many years. Belal Hibri shared in the trials of this project in all its different stages, and took many of the photos that appear in the pages that follow.

My deepest debts are to three people. My parents, whose exceptional support and encouragement are an entire lifetime of thanks. Most of all Tania, whose fierce intellect, patience, and love had maybe the deepest impact of all.

Any errors and flaws remain my own.

Media start us in the middle of things. In this way, they are not unlike events—large and small, personal and political—that assert themselves through the everyday. By the time we are aware that something is an event, it tends to already be in motion, to have accumulated a momentum whose directionality has only just become perceptible. When I visited Beirut late in December 2006, I was already aware of the sit-in demonstration organized by Hizbullah, the Lebanese political party and militia. The group had emerged in the 1980s during the Lebanese Civil War (1975–90), at the nexus of Shi'ite social movements that predated the start of the conflict, and with backing from post-revolutionary Iran. Hizbullah had fought a war with Israel in the summer of that year, which the party termed a "Divine Victory." They denounced the standing government, organized by an opposing political bloc affiliated with Western and Saudi interests, as not representing the true interests of all Lebanese. The call for protests came soon after. When I visited the sit-in demonstration that resulted, it had been ongoing for the better part of three weeks, and had effectively shut down large portions of the historic city center, and also the site of Parliament. The area had been badly damaged during the Civil War, and in the early 1990s was placed into the hands of a private company for development.

The atmosphere that prevailed that night was a stark contrast with what the heavily policed space was typically like—oriented exclusively to high-end shopping, luxury apartments, banks, and government offices, and empty when compared to other parts of the city. Major thoroughfares were closed, people smoked hookahs in parking lots converted to gathering spaces, and informational booths set up by the party and its allies had been established in Martyrs' Square, a large open space that was an important historical site of protests seeking a national stage (as it had been just a year earlier). Street vendors—ordinarily not allowed in the neighborhood—sold street food, party-branded memorabilia, coffee, and cotton candy from carts and impromptu stalls. While taking in the disruption to the typical order of things, I soon noticed another modification to the space. The demonstration's organizers had set up large screens near the Parliament building and at Martyrs' Square (where there was also a stage for nightly performances), onto which was projected Al Manar, the television channel affiliated with Hizbullah. What was striking about these screens was that on more than one occasion, what appeared both on screen and in the space was live coverage of the demonstration *at* the demonstration. I was eventually able to figure out where the on-scene and on-screen reporter was by walking around and glancing at the screen while keeping a lookout for the lights of the camera crew.

The circularity of such an image was part of what initially stood out, because of the novelty of seeing the *mise-en-abyme* created on location, particularly as it was a spectacle of public disruption harnessed to the agenda of a major political party. The demonstration, operating in this key in its initial weeks, capitalized on perhaps the most made-for-spectacle part of the city. It occupied a square that had been both city center and protest center since the late Ottoman era, albeit in the incarnation taken by postwar neoliberal construction with all its nostalgia for the French colonial style. This experience left me with questions that have led to this book. What history of images in and of the city might contextualize this event? What role have images played in attempts to manage, shape, and contest the spaces of Beirut? If the visual vectors of that night drew attention to the act of looking itself, how might these specificities offer a perspective on how media condition urban space and everyday life? What is the context in which these images, and media infrastructural conditions, make sense? This book grapples with these questions so as to investigate contemporary visual culture, and the role of infrastructure in shaping how that public and that space were brought into being. It gives an account of shifting topologies of power, and of contingent techniques and infrastructural alignments as they congeal in Beirut's radius.

Infrastructure, Incompleteness, and Mediation

Our ability to grapple with the political stakes of infrastructure depends on a precise understanding of its spatial and temporal qualities. This is in turn a question of the entanglement of urban space with the images that animate it. The opening paragraph of Edward Said's *Orientalism* discusses commentary by a French journalist about the damage done to downtown Beirut in the first years of the Civil War. Said shows how this expression of regret reflected an outsized fascination for the East, which in turn produced a very particular kind of disappointment in the place itself.[1] Such imaginaries clearly continue into the contemporary moment. Yet alongside this cultural register, there is a less examined media history of techniques of visualization in support of endeavors such as urban planning, real-estate investment, and military surveillance. The history of the space of the city—fundamentally bound up in the politics of the creation of its geographic outside and periphery—is also historically intertwined with the media infrastructures that circulate such images. Considering the uneven and contested nature of visual culture from Beirut allows a productive perspective on the politics of the circulation of images. It may often be that infrastructure is defined by its overlooked place in everyday life—not noticed within our daily rhythms and media habits because of its continuous, smooth functioning. The aesthetic experience of infrastructure may encourage a common-sense view of it as a finished and distinct thing, or even a sublime totality. But in places like Lebanon—as it is in many parts of the Global South[2]—the everyday is itself defined not by whether water and electrical cuts may hypothetically happen, but by how predictable those cuts become.

There is an incompleteness intrinsic to infrastructure, a spatiotemporality that requires maintenance sometimes beginning before construction is even completed, and which perhaps by definition is always ongoing. Embarking on infrastructural projects can have a certain evidentiary utility for elites who wish to perform development—wherein the completion of public works is secondary to the exchanging of money and favors.[3] Yet infrastructure would seem to be defined by its essential incompleteness—not simply in the sense that roads also crumble in wealthy neighborhoods or the metropole, or that life persists unevenly in imperial and neoliberal ruination. The study of infrastructure from the perspective of maintenance and repair has allowed for a sense of the politics of its temporal duration, and of modifications that take place within its path dependencies.[4] This incompleteness can be mobilized toward ends that are sometimes less obvious and more politically ambiguous.

A similar perspective emerges if we trace the spatiotemporal relations of mediation itself—or, as I explore in chapter 3, the relationship of multiple, conflicting visual vectors allows an eventful understanding of visual culture. If infrastructure is the relation between things—which is itself something like a definition of mediation—then many kinds of mediation are also incomplete. To investigate mediation means to consider the verb form of media, or, those processes that media do. Considering mediation in Beirut brings the incompleteness of infrastructure to the foreground. The contradictions of incompleteness appear there in ways that can be dramatic, mundane, or mundane in their drama.

Mediation is not simply circulation in the way that walking or driving are—although mobility and technology have been intertwined since long before GPS. The study of media infrastructure gains a great deal from the insight that the term *communication* used to include transportation in its ambit, attending to the particular forms that mobilities take.[5] Not all kinds of mediation are about movement in space, even if it is defined by a differential relation between mobility and circulation. If infrastructure is a system, it is one that is greater than the sum of its machines, in that it implies a set of relations that are an ongoing process of dispossession, accumulation, and contestation. Attending to incompleteness does not mean all is free-flowing contingency and contestability, just as Stuart Hall once argued that the political has no guarantees.[6]

Infrastructure is an elastic concept, gathering numerous and sometimes quite disparate things together. Some approaches to infrastructure emphasize the forging and remaking of the terms of citizenship, as people only partially served by the state negotiate rights that are not automatically granted. Other approaches stress the sensory formations and aesthetic experience of infrastructure—or at least, those parts that people experience either directly or indirectly. The study of infrastructure, of which the study of media infrastructure is one kind, has grown rapidly in the past decade. Parks and Starosielski (2015) highlight what the study of media gains by attending to infrastructure, or even more interestingly, by adopting an *infrastructural disposition*.[7] They argue for a critical approach premised on a relational understanding of the political economic and social formation of media industries and technologies.[8] Larkin's (2013) examination of the relationship of anthropological study and infrastructure draws attention to its world-making politics (or techno-politics, if one wishes). He offers a useful working definition:

Infrastructures are matter that enable the movement of other matter. Their peculiar ontology lies in the facts that they are things and also the relation between things . . . what distinguishes infrastructures from technologies is that they create grounds on which other objects operate, and when they do so they operate as systems. (B. Larkin 2013, 239)

The stakes for the study of infrastructure, here, are in the modes of relation they create—a useful starting point from which to consider mediation. As Peters (2015) would have it, an infrastructural understanding of media directs one less to the history of specific devices than to the sociotechnical relations that constitute the conditions of possibility of human community. Peters proposes a daring conception of media—not so much as environments but as elemental processes, opening our understanding of human communication to a wilder set of potentialities. Debates in anthropology and geography link the politics of infrastructure to the transformation of everyday life in urban contexts, and to the conditioning of the senses and movement.[9] Rather than distinct disciplinary boundaries, these approaches are better understood as having a shared scholarly inheritance, traceable to the modernist (or Marxist) concern to understand a world set in motion. Critical study of infrastructure can not simply ask what is materially below the surface of culture and everyday life, but should offer insight into the spatial processes of power.

The politics of the contestability of infrastructure—the sovereignties, relations, and modes of circulation that it enables—are better understood when we center incompleteness. Rather than infrastructure as a thing or thing-like assemblage, the politics of mediation require attending to the specific nature of the systems infrastructure is made to embody. The state of continuous breakdown of power, water, road, internet, waste, and even broadcast infrastructure in Lebanon lend themselves to understanding the rhythms of incompletablity. The frustrating and debilitating experience of infrastructural incompleteness and failure can make completeness seem like the sweetest of dreams, or a sign of investment in the conditions of possibility for collective life.[10] In Lebanon, access to even the most basic necessities (much less those social services ordinarily the province of the liberal welfare state) is for many a function of their proximity to political parties and leaders, divided by sectarian affiliation in its neoliberal incarnation. Even harsher precarities come into view if one considers the differentials of citizenship in Lebanon from the perspective of how they affect foreign domestic workers and Syrian refugees, whose labor has been a cornerstone of the Lebanese postwar economy.[11]

An Infrastructural Approach to Visual Culture

Rather than trace a single line of determination—as when culture is thought to be the emanation of institutions or sociotechnical systems—I take an infrastructural approach to visual culture, which also brings into question those modalities that purposefully go unseen. To develop a critical approach adequate to Beirut requires attending to the particularities on the ground, but also contending with the narrative frameworks that position visuality in modernity. W. J. T. Mitchell (2002) once called for an analytical move from the "social construction of the visual" to the "visual construction of the social," a move he later clarified requires a departure from the essentialism and ocularcentrism of the notion of "visual media."[12] This insight explicates that looking is a kind of social and cultural practice, and is as informed by ideas and debates about what it means to see or present the self (as in portraiture) as any other.[13] To draw out the co-implication of visual culture and media infrastructure requires an analytical shift—from close readings of images, texts, and devices prefigured by disciplinary inquiry to also considering visual relations themselves. As Mirzoeff (2011) has demonstrated, for as long as systems of domination structure ways of seeing the world, there will be a need to invent new and reactivate old ways of seeing each other that affirm other possible communities, equalities, and intimacies.

Mirzoeff draws on Rancière's conception of the political, which juxtaposes the consensus view of the social imagined by the powerful with a radical break from an existing order, created when those who have no part begin to enact equality within conditions of inequality. Rancière (1999) contends that a true rupture from a political order is not simply the aggrieved or disenfranchised articulating demands for inclusion and visibility, but a fundamental contestation of the terms under which community is constituted—what he calls the distribution of the sensible.[14] The understanding of dissensus implied here is not simply an antagonism of competing worldviews, or a simple bid for recognition, but a rejection of the inequality implied by the public ordering of who may speak and how they should do so in order to be sensible.[15] To dominant historical configurations, dissensus appears as disordered movement, unruly bodies, or just rebellious noise.[16] Against the oversight of the slave overseer, the imperial cartographer, and the counterinsurgent, there is the actuality and possibility of countervisuality, which is to say, the claiming of "a right to look" against the political order and for equality. Against liberalism's promise of inclusion and recognition, or notions of politics as a settling of accounts, this conception opens up the possibility of a decolonial rejection of the foundational violence that inequality presumes and visually reenacts.[17]

Thinking of visual culture in this vein makes attention to infrastructure and incompleteness much more valuable. It makes it possible to reconsider ways of being overlooked by overseers. Most critical vocabularies of visibility and invisibility are attuned to the politics of not being seen or being made seeable, or the ethics of witnessing. Much of the media of everyday life oscillate between spectacle, mundane and ambient sensory experience, and corporate and state surveillance. These familiar forms can lead one to misrecognize what I refer to as modalities of concealment. A state of concealment can be said to exist when a tactic (or more commonly, a combination of tactics) deliberately keeps a person or place from appearing to an opposing force. It isn't the camouflage but the visual modality of the camouflaged vis-à-vis the verticality of the drone.[18] To conceal is to attempt to remain unseen or undetected, or to keep secrets selective. Concealment is both an infrastructural modality and a relatively noncommunicative relation that can be said to exist when these tactics function according to plan. In some conditions, concealment of its material form can even enable the functioning of infrastructure itself. It is not (primarily) a feature of a text amenable to hermeneutical approaches, but the mode of mediation of an undisclosed underground communications bunker. It isn't the visual mode that results from the collective occupation of Tahrir Square and the training of cameraphones and global news agencies on it in the Arab Uprising, but rather, when protestors would on occasion run and hide from the police down side streets so as to gain spatial advantage. It is also just as easily utilized by the powerful and the state as by the freedom fighter and dissident.

To push the concept of dissensus a step further, one might say that its supposedly sudden appearance (to a police order) is a sign that somewhere else, unseen or ignored, there are ways of communicating and moving that remain undetected or unregistered. To understand these modalities, consider two different historical examinations of the systematization of light in modernity. Browne (2015) interrogates how lantern laws in colonial-era New York City enabled the surveillance of black, indigenous, and mixed-race bodies by requiring any such people over fourteen years of age to carry a light if outside after sunset. This enforced visibility at night, which as Browne shows was of a piece with the codification and documentation of the right to travel, was part of the racial surveillance of urban mobility.[19] In the city that became the heart of twentieth-century empire and an important northern node in the making of racial capitalism, there appears an attempt to make people shine a light on themselves so as to aid in their subjugation. Browne explains how this in turn led to the development of social worlds that crossed boundaries of class, gender, and race, and between both the free and enslaved, forging community under the surveillant gaze and in the daytime: an adaptation to the legal provision for harsh corporal punishments for those caught without a light at night.

A related development was the systematization of street lighting. As Schivelbusch (1995) shows, the installation of street lighting in European cities was an inextricable part of the creation of modern urban policing. The preindustrial urban night was darker not simply in degree but in kind, and Schivelbusch shows how the creation of street lighting—like the electrical grids that came after—was part of a reconfiguration of the relationship of modern states and citizens. Rather than self-identification in the form of a handheld light (a requirement in many European cities in the early modern period), the illumination of the street displaced the act of self-identification and surveilling others to the state. Before streetlights became systematically implemented and bright enough to fill the urban landscape, one person could extinguish their lantern so as to gain the tactical advantage of comparative darkness.[20] Schivelbusch suggests a rather direct relation between the installation of the infrastructure of public lighting and the monopolization of coercion and policing by the state. The initial outcome was that when the streets got brighter, it became both very symbolic and practical to smash lanterns.[21]

These two examples each open modern systems of light to differential relations to power. If, in the first example (Browne), the visual culture of a racialized urban space is regulated by individual self-identification, in the second example (Schivelbusch) the urban space as a whole is transformed to be more readily watchable. These examples each resound with the incompleteness of infrastructure and the (im)mobility it fosters. These examples can also be taken as evidence of the importance of remaining hidden to the politics of urban space. Electricity and electrification in Lebanon and Arab countries of course have their own uneven history.[22] Yet while lanterns can be said to cast light, they are also different from phenomena like live television and its promise to see at a distance. They are also unlike the broadcast of the Hizbullah protest at the protest in that, rather than a contestation of and regulation by light, Al Manar (which can be translated as "the beacon" or "the flame") exemplifies the degree of influence that the party has in Lebanon, even as its broadcasts are in no small way part of a contestation of a global visual culture that it frequently describes itself as contesting. Rather than an interruption of or defection from the capitalist order, or a subversion of televised spectacle— what Wark (2013) describes as the "disintegrated spectacle"[23]—the Hizbullah sit-in demonstration constituted a much more mundane demand for a bigger part of a system of rule it is basically compatible with. If we consider the visual relations of the event—the patterning of modes of attention, the assertion of collective experience, the performance of making political claims to space—it is also the forging of spatial linkage at multiple scales (in the city, during the national and regional nightly news hour, for a variety of transnational audiences). However, when Hizbullah's Secretary General Hasan Nasrallah gives speeches of this type in the era after the 2006 war, he only rarely appears at the location of the event in person and never with advance warning, out of reasonable concerns for security. The infrastructure of live satellite broadcasting can enable and depend on a kind of hiddenness while on air.

Although concealment is not the same thing as Rancière's conception of dissensus, the two do have some similarities at a certain level of abstraction: both imply a potentially open-ended, noncommunicative antagonism, and both emphasize that the police order of the social is already a way of overlooking those kept in place.[24] They also both have an ambiguous tactical relation to recognition as a goal unto itself. The refusal of the politics of recognition is one whose utility has been discussed in indigenous critique.[25] In some situations, being overlooked employs a queer aesthetic opacity that defers or refuses recognizability on normative terms.[26] Concealment should not be equated with any one technique, as this would mistake the action for the visual tension or broader field that it is in tension with—sort of like mistaking the technology for the outcome. Concealment is better understood as a mode of mediation—one defined by historically and materially specific confluences of agentive action and infrastructural formation. Concealment is also something other than "opacity" and its relationship to the ethics of "transparency"—which has not always been a self-evidently desirable political relation (transparency of the self to itself, to the state, to society, or of the state to society).[27] In the contemporary moment, concealment and attitudes toward those who seek to remain concealed are in tension with a historically specific configuration of individual privacy, state secrecy, and techniques of targeting. Public demands for state transparency dovetail with communication infrastructures that are both leaky and (almost) always on.[28]

While the forms of concealment investigated here are primarily those of infrastructure and not of subjectivity per se, the two are linked. This book's primary focus on the visual field is not a suggestion that concealment is essentially visual, and study of its sonic history would surely deepen our understanding of it. Concealment is a phenomenon that requires critical attention not because of an inherently emancipatory potential, although it does undermine an easy faith in the power of posting truth to power. As I explore in chapters 3 and 4, concealment structures the visual formations of Hizbullah's guerrilla tactics in both war and protest, and has an ambiguous politics in itself. Hizbullah's mobilizations usefully demonstrate the overlooked presence of concealment's relation to media infrastructure.

The concept of the distribution of the sensible suggests that the part who have no part have always spoken out even if they remain policed, and specifies enacting equality in the here and now, not in the yet to come. Yet the state of affairs in post–Civil War Lebanon is not only one of political polyphony (multiple actors who vie with, over, and against the government) but one fully articulated within geopolitical competition between regional and global powers. This is true at various levels—from the multiplicity of broadcast institutions associated with rival political parties and geopolitical blocs, to the "resistance" idiom that comes to characterize the manufactured bipolarity of the contemporary period.[29] Lebanon demands a refined conception of dissensus, so that the duality of intelligibility/unintelligibility, and the capitalist system that it is a part of, can grapple with situations in which multiple groups (and the political right in particular) adopt the language of opposition. All too often, it becomes possible to conflate partisan geopolitical disagreement with dissensus, and to mean "resistance," with a positive normative connotation attached. Doing so potentially obscures the dynamics by which political actors may contest the distribution of the sensible on one level, but leave it untouched on another. As many people around the world long ago figured out, the enemy of my oppressor who is the enemy of equality is not inherently my friend.[30] Any political party that seeks to increase their share of a system that by definition generates inequality, and reduces politics to a game of elite or ethno-religious mutuality and competition, should be understood to already be a part of the problem. The political binaries expressed in the Hizbullah and Future-led blocs are preeminent examples of status quo politics papered over by the veneer of partisan bickering.

Lebanon, TV, Arab Media

This book's chapters each interrogate the historical interrelation of a range of cultural forms with the politics of managing and shaping the spaces and people of Beirut. Much like its neighborhoods, charities, and legal systems, the political economic structure of Lebanese television is inseparable from the contradictions of sectarianism. Sectarianism is a political order in which parliamentary seats, key government posts, and personal status law are divided along ethno-religious lines. It is a crucial factor shaping the nature of political contestation over the state, and a defining feature of the media land-scape. Like other misfortunes of racial capitalism, sectarianism should always be that which needs explanation and never the explanatory framework, lest one mistake the transactions of power for inevitability. The distinctly mod-ern messiness of forging sectarianism into a political framework is a process whose fundamental nonsense is continuously and periodically retooled and refinanced, covered over with blood and legal precedent, and discursively rearticulated to suit geopolitical reconfigurations of state and non-state ac-tors. Sectarianism in Lebanon—particularly the organization of violence along ethno-religious lines—was a response to the awarding of rights and protections on the basis of group affiliation as part of the Ottoman *tanzimat*, or modern-ization plan.[31] Rather than an age-old story, it is one no older than the mid-nineteenth century.[32] Rather than a pre-modern phenomenon originating in theological dispute, it is specific to the form that secular political structures took, in this case, under pressure from European powers to protect the rights of Christians. The outcome was that battles for dominance and position pro-ceeded at pace, and the consolidation of political power meant cutting new lines through communities on the basis of ethno-religious group belonging, culminating in a series of massacres of Maronites and Druze between 1858 and 1860.[33] Local elites, Ottoman reformers, and European notables initially strug-gled to make sense of the scale of violence inflicted on previously mixed neigh-borhoods and villages, resulting in the deployment of some 6,000 French troops in 1860 (one of the maps that resulted from this expedition is discussed in chapter 1). Beirut's rise to prominence can also be dated to this period, im-pacted by the arrival of those fleeing violence in the mountainside and the transformation of the region by its integration into new economic flows.[34]

The origins and contemporary formations of sectarianism bear a biopo-litical logic, and it has always been a gendered and sexed form of subjec-tification and rule. As explored in the chapters that follow, this requires a feminist critique of the patriarchal order it depends on.[35] Infrastructure, ex-amined here in terms of the processes of mediation and the normativity of shaping space, is one whose biopolitical horizon is akin to the erection of scaffolding—enabling, debilitating, and abandoning particular forms of life and interrelation.[36] Making sense of the biopolitical requires that one turn to a historically contingent understanding of governmental techniques, pro-vocatively developed in Foucault's later work. As Collier argues, Foucault in the late 1970s stepped back from epochal and totalizing claims, a move away from a concern "with a single line of biopolitics that links diverse elements as if through a kind of inner functional coherence. Instead [Foucault] draws a much clearer system of correlation, and provides a vocabulary for describing how . . . they are brought into a relationship, but remain heterogeneous" (2009, 90).[37] Rather than utilizing the same approaches as his earlier work, applied to an "age," it becomes possible to engage in an analysis of what Collier dubs a "topology of power." This reading allows for an empirical investigation of specific governmental forms, without a totalizing claim that reflects a very partial understanding of the colonial metropole. This reading also requires a step back from those conceptions of technology that imagine sovereign power as a quasi-theological, ultimately thanatological force—the Heideggerian technological inheritance that informs many conceptualizations of biopolitics.[38] Instead, one might consider how infrastructure is an incomplete process with biopolitical implications, which has always already been premised on the racial (or ethno-religious) structures of colonial modernity.[39] What this book gives is an historical account of the governmental logics of making space visible, and the intertwining of this process with the biopolitics of population management.

Sectarianism is a framework that is adaptable to regional and geopolitical adventurism, and divides such as the Muslim/Christian split that defined the Civil War can fall away when others gain momentum, such as the Sunni/Shi'ite split fanned by the US invasion of Iraq in 2003 and the ongoing conflict between Saudi Arabia and Iran. Sectarianism is best understood as a mode of organizing social and political life, and one that is spatially and infrastructurally constituted. As Nucho (2016) argues:

> Infrastructures are the channels through which the activity or process of sectarianism is produced in specific instances as opposed to other modes of differentiation. . . . Just as channels and infrastructures serve to create spaces of connection and conjoined action, they also serve to differentiate, subtract, or reroute people and things. (206, 5)

Rather than an immutable outcome, sectarianism is a process as incompletable as the temporality of infrastructure and the nature of urban life—and one reproduced through and by contingent formations of resource provision, the arrangement of neighborhoods, political access and protection, and the production and distribution of media.[40]

In most Arab and many postcolonial states, the history of television can often be told as a story that begins with strong state control of broadcasting institutions, which then face either a wave of privatization or challenge to their monopoly beginning somewhere in the 1980s. The emergence of distinctly transnational and neoliberal political economies in more recent decades has led to new configurations of local and regional production and distribution, with national frameworks challenged or projected outward in new counter-flows.[41] Much like the state, broadcasting in Lebanon began in the colonial period and was run as a semi-private commercial endeavor prior to the Civil War, was coopted by militias during that conflict, and was then remade in the shape of a regional market with the emergence of satellite broadcasting in the 1990s. Unlike Egypt, for example, there is no strong Lebanese tradition of a developmental state producing programming in service of forging a national consciousness and educating a modern citizenry.[42] Radio began in the 1930s as an effort by French Mandate officials to counter the presence of Radio Berlin on the airwaves in Lebanon and Syria.[43] By comparison, British Mandate authorities granted radio a more central role in the administration of Palestine, where it created separate Hebrew- and Arabic-language services within listening distance.[44] Radio in Lebanon continued to be a field of contestation, between states in regional competition and among internal actors during periods of crisis—particularly in 1958, when militant factions started their own stations.[45] Given the proximity of nearby countries such as Syria and Egypt, it was possible for listeners in Lebanon to tune in to signals originating in nearby countries.[46]

Domestic television broadcasting began as a private endeavor with the granting of a non-monopoly license to two businessmen, with La Compagnie Libanaise de Télévision (CLT) beginning service in 1959. A second private station, Télé-Orient, was granted a license and began service in 1962, with additional backing by the US ABC network. In this regard, Lebanon was unique among Arab states in terms of its broadcast history prior to the Civil War, a condition that combined with a relative degree of press freedom—the 1962 press law granted official freedom of the press, but with ambiguous language around "endangering national security," "insulting heads of state," or "inciting sectarian unrest."[47] These two stations would continue to broadcast after the outbreak of the Civil War in 1975, but would be combined to form Télé-Liban in 1977, under government control but with joint public-private ownership.[48]

The Lebanese state was only intermittently able to exert any degree of control over the airwaves during the fifteen years of the Civil War. The political fragmentation of the period meant that broadcasting primarily became the province of militias, and any with the means and desire to put out a signal did so. The availability of inexpensive, low-power solid-state radio transmitters (with relatively limited range) made it so the airwaves were populated by as many as 150 stations, oftentimes broadcasting on the same frequency.[49]

Television broadcasters proliferated, some of them operating on a commercial basis. As television required comparably more expensive equipment and a greater degree of technical sophistication, it primarily became the province of the better-funded militias. One of the best examples of these is the Lebanese Broadcasting Corporation (LBC, affiliated with the Christian Lebanese Forces militia and formed with support from American televangelist Pat Robertson's CBN),[50] which began operation in 1985 and continues to define the Lebanese media landscape. The proliferation of illegal and militia broadcasters created an unusual ratio of channels per person, and a cadre of people with some degree of experience in the media and advertising industries. It also transformed the nature of the television-viewing public—one in which the nature of programming and the language spoken was premised on a more intimate appeal to audiences. LBC's mode of televisual address was premised on seeming closer and more relevant to contemporary audiences—less formal Arabic, and more appeals to the overlapping and gendered categories of consumer and citizen.[51]

The Taif Agreement, named for the Saudi town in which they were brokered in 1989, brought an official cessation to the armed hostilities of the Civil War, but reinforced the logic of sectarian politics. The agreement ordered all militias to disarm save for Hizbullah, which was granted official recognition as a resistance force aimed at ending the Israeli occupation of southern Lebanon. Taif also set the regulation of the broadcast spectrum as a key priority, as the crowded broadcast spectrum featured many overlapping signals.[52] This resulted in the 1994 Audio-Visual Media Law, which created the National Council of Audio-Visual Media and set out to reduce the number of terrestrial broadcasters by several orders of magnitude. This in turn led to a licensing war, the winners of which resulted in a pattern of ownership that reflected the clout of private interests, and perpetuated the logic of sectarian "balance." Future TV (owned by Hariri), NBN (then a prospective station owned by Speaker of Parliament Nabih Berri), LBC, Murr TV (owned by the deputy prime minister), and Télé-Liban were the initial crop granted licenses. As Al Manar (which began transmission in 1991) was granted an exception, Télé Lumière (which mainly broadcasted Catholic religious programming), was also granted a license to avoid an imbalance of domestic "Muslim" channels. The scarcity of funds and underlying political irresolution led to a media system perpetually prone to crisis and in need of patronage.[53]

The end of the Lebanese Civil War roughly coincided with the end of the Cold War, and the advent of popular viewing of satellite television in the region—inaugurated by CNN's coverage of the first US war on Iraq.[54] The Arab

League had formed a consortium in 1976 with the aim of launching communication satellites, the first of which became operational in 1985. MBC (based in London, a key urban hub for Arab media) began free-to-air broadcasting in 1991.[55] As a consequence of signing a peace deal with Israel in the 1970s, Egypt was a late signatory to Arabsat, which allowed Saudi Arabia to become a dominant shareholder.[56] The coincidence of Saudi funds, a Lebanese television industry in flux, and a burgeoning Arab-speaking viewership accidentally created the conditions for an outsized role for Lebanese broadcasters in the new terrain of satellite television.[57] Despite the historic centrality of Egyptian film and music in Arab popular culture—which also constituted an important feature of Lebanese television content during the Civil War—Egyptian networks would never attain the same kind of prominence. An explosive growth of channels would follow, and with the satellite footprints of Eutelsat and Hotbird falling across the region, any overly simple description of the television landscape as "Arab" requires qualification.[58] Al Manar would branch out into satellite coverage in 1997, although as I examine in chapter 3, it would only ever have a tenuous grip on satellite bandwidth.[59] For example, it was booted off of Arabsat in 2016 for Hizbullah's continued military support of the Assad regime. Although nominally independent from Hizbullah, the station has always been operated by senior party members, like the many other media organizations affiliated with and financed by the party. If the social experience of television reflects its uneven adoption across public and private spaces, then like other Lebanese channels, Al Manar's programming tends to reflect an awareness of its audience that focuses on quite local concerns, but staged with a sense of a transnational or global audience in mind.[60]

Examining Al Manar's tenuous place in Arab media and global visual culture allows for a unique perspective on the visual constitution of political order, and how the city and its infrastructure are themselves also shaped by imaginaries populated by a belief in the power of images to do things. Similarly, the maps and aerial photographs of twentieth-century urban planning allow a critical understanding of how the visualization of Beirut has been an important part of the production of its spaces. The sit-in that began in December 2006 was the first Hizbullah event that I had attended, but not the first time I had seen Al Manar. When my family began making regular visits to Lebanon in the late eighties, everyday media life for me entailed a fairly typical middle-class Sunni Beiruti relationship to television (inextricably related to power cuts and videocassette rentals, but not much "political programming" allowed when I was younger). Centering this inquiry in Beirut allows for a situated understanding of global visual culture, as cities congeal spatial processes that extend beyond the borders of municipalities, nation-states, and regions.[61] The study of media in the Arab world has often profitably examined the politics of everyday lived experience of which media are a part.[62] More recent work has contextualized everyday life in terms of the urban soundscapes that constitute it.[63] This book adds to this work a critical understanding of the role of images in governmental processes, and exceptional events like wars and protests.

The question of urban form and/as media, images, screens and the city, and television in the home, are preoccupations of media studies this book shares.[64] I examine the relationship of infrastructure and televisual liveness, attending to the linkages created between different spaces, and the televisual as one part of the visual culture of an event. As Brunsdon (2018) argues, the domesticity with which postwar British television was associated made decolonization into an intimate experience—one that she theorizes prompts a comparative study of the relationship of television and the city, and which can clarify the relation between particular cities, genres, and aesthetic and narrative conventions. Brunsdon argues that the fictional cities found on television explicate the history of the medium's relationship to its metropolitan counterparts. This book takes up some of these concerns in Beirut, examining the relationship of televisual liveness and the city. White (2004) likens live televisual forms to Gunning's (1986) conception of the "cinema of attractions" characteristic of early film. Her conception of televisual liveness, which "solicits the attention of spectators by displaying visibility for its own sake" (85), decouples liveness from a necessary link to catastrophe, and looks closer at the quietly factual, such as C-Span and weather channels. White also argues that thinking in terms of a television of attractions can lead to a more precise understanding of replayed footage captured live at exceptional events, arguing that "these *recorded* images, as attractions, are historicized, rather than enlivened, by the processes of narrativization which are brought to bear on them" (2004, 85).

The politics of mediation require attending to the nature of the systems infrastructure is made to embody and enact. The state of continuous breakdown of infrastructure in postwar Lebanon can facilitate understanding the rhythms of incompletability, and problematizes normative conceptions of infrastructure as a finalizable totality. In the face of discussions of circulation, Doreen Massey's ever-insightful comment is to think not from the perspective of the man on the plane flying overhead, but with the woman "waiting in a bus-shelter with your shopping for a bus that never comes" (1994, 163). Not all reduces to capital, and not all that results from its processes is movement and placelessness.

Plan of the Book

The four chapters that follow each examine an economy of images, focused on one particular type of image. The first chapter centers on maps, engaging with critical cartography and urban history. The second examines how images of before/after have shaped the postwar urban and media landscape, and draws links between the literatures on media and the city, and corporate film. The third chapter engages more explicitly with theories of mediation, verticality, and war, centered on Al Manar's live satellite broadcast. The fourth chapter examines the Hizbullah Mleeta Museum of the Resistance, and engages with debates on the relationship between religion and media. The methodological orientation of this book is primarily to archives (in the city) and a range of cultural forms—corporate films, aerial and satellite photographs, live broadcasts, real estate advertisements, and urban planning documents. I supplement this with selected interviews with architects, urban planners, journalists, finance professionals, satellite television installation technicians, and tour guides. Many of them spoke off the record, and all in their capacity as professionals in their respective fields. Walking with the city—at different times of day and night over many years, in both a pointed and a more aimless manner, helped open my understanding of the place to skepticism about my own habituations. The first part of the primary research for this work was completed over the summer of 2009 and the first half of 2010. The second part was conducted from the summer of 2014 through the spring of 2017, when I was at the American University of Beirut.

Chapter 1 dwells in the cartographic archive in Beirut, and traces attempts to manage the shape of the city as evidenced in cartographic practice. While mapping is almost unavoidably a trope or metaphor of knowledge-making understood as spatial mastery,[65] my inquiry is into the contingencies revealed by the lives of maps. The chapter digs through the roughly seven decades from the creation of Lebanon as a distinct territorial state administered under the French Mandate in 1920, through the decades of state-led development in the post-independence period, and through the damage-assessment studies conducted during the Civil War. This chapter unfolds the relationship between the projects and technical practices that generated maps, and the spaces of the city they both anticipated and were shaped by. Although centered on Beirut and the archives found there, the chapter also attends to the influence of French counterinsurgency and urbanism on the Mandate period, as well as that of mid-century planning and development economics in the decades after. Raymond Williams (1973) once asserted that cities often attain a sense of coherence via their relationship to an outside. This chapter traces a Beirut influenced by a countryside drawn increasingly into its political orbit, even if that constitutive outside remained inconsistently mapped. Maps remained important to operations of power in the years after, but the following two chapters, which deal primarily with the decade and a half of the postwar period, shift focus to two other media forms.

The official end of the Lebanese Civil War in the early 1990s roughly coincided with the fall of the Berlin Wall, a new exuberance in the global financial industry, and the introduction of digital systems into mainstream cartographic and architectural practice. This confluence of factors shaped a context in which visual forms became key to postwar construction, and so chapter 2 examines the proliferation of before/after images in this period. A before/after image consists of a shot of a damaged building or street transposed with an illustration of a space-to-be (and later, a photograph of work completed). The chapter examines how before/after images came to play a critical role in the financialization of postwar construction. I understand financialization here to be a distinct tendency within capitalism whereby economic activity and even everyday life comes to bear not just as a logic of accumulation over time, but also tethered to the more specific scale and volatile needs of speculative investment.[66] The before/after image was instrumentally pressed into the service of attracting financial investment in a future prosperity that was imagined to be inevitable, but also imminent to attachments to the proposed urban futurity. Much of the chapter focuses on how the before/after image was deployed by Solidere, the private company established by Rafiq Hariri, the on-and-off prime minister for the first decade and a half after the Civil War. Solidere was given control of the badly damaged central district, repeating a political logic of spatially and politically cantonized projects, drastically reducing the scope and institutional framework for comprehensive national recovery.

The Solidere project cannot be taken as the whole of the city for a number of reasons—chief among them being that it wasn't even the only major postwar construction project. Thinking of it as equivalent to the whole of the city occludes the very real disparities created by such projects' nomination of a specific part of the city for intensive investment and work. I argue that the before/after image, often understood in terms of the temporal sequence "before/after destruction or trauma," also has a second form in many post-conflict societies—an image of "before/after construction." Postwar Lebanon remains awash with uneven memories of past wars.[67] The problem might not be an official state of "amnesia" about the past, which in the first decade or so of the post–Civil War period became the central contention of liberal imaginaries and their conception of memory. Rather, the before/after image speaks of a more fundamental loss of ability to imagine the future as leading to anything but future war and ruination, entangled in real estate schemes. I argue that the before/after image presents itself to an ideal viewer I term a citizen-investor—a problematic figure traversed by the gendered inequalities of Lebanese citizenship, and tied to a financialized imaginary. The first two chapters examine two different dimensions of the role images have played in the making of the contours of the city, examining how images and imaging technologies became important to technical and financial expertise, and how these even come to inform public debate.

These two chapters establish a context in which the political polarization of the post–Cold War era (and the inauguration of the US War on Terror) can be more readily interrogated. When placed in this context, Al Manar's position on the ground and in the televisual sphere during the 2006 war and sit-in demonstration later that year come into sharper focus. In chapter 3, I analyze the politics and aesthetics of infrastructure by tracing the conflictual relationship between processes of live mediation—principally broadcasts, surveillance feeds, and concealment. While concealment is briefly discussed in the first chapter's recounting of aerial reconnaissance in the Mandate, the politics of this modality are more fully theorized in this chapter. I examine concealment's formation in guerrilla hit-and-run videos, drone-camera footage, the cultural imaginaries of the channel's resilience in the face of aerial bombardment, the jamming and hacking of the signal, and guerrilla attacks staged for live broadcast. These phenomena demonstrate the crucial role of concealment in the biopolitics of war and its visual culture. The chapter closes by returning to the sit-in protest mentioned above, tracing the visual geography of speeches made by Hizbullah's Nasrallah, increasingly made via live feed from an undisclosed location. The chapter analyzes how these two events are constituted by quite different forms of concealment.

If the third chapter endeavors to understand the role of live mediation and concealment within an event, chapter 4 examines what happens when the infrastructure of concealment is decommissioned and turned into a tourist attraction. The Mleeta Museum was opened on the tenth anniversary of the Israeli withdrawal from most of the country because of Hizbullah's efforts. Set on a mountaintop not far from the border with Israel and with commanding views of the nearby countryside, the museum transforms the site of an underground bunker into a public exhibit. It is necessary to step outside of the immediate boundaries of the city to make sense of the contradictions generated by the concentration of political economic power in Beirut, and to make sense of the history of concealment. The museum was opened in a moment when the party had become a powerful player in the Lebanese parliament. This was also a moment when the party had found new footing to make claims to speak in the name of the national interest, but before the opening rounds of the militarization of the Syrian Uprising. With a cinema hall that screens a film about the party's official history, a flower garden with decommissioned weaponry, and the inevitable gift shop, the premise of the museum is the public staging of a space originally kept secret. I examine how the museum embodies a contradiction internal to the creation of communicative spaces that are constitutively oriented to an outside. It is designed around the embodied experience of masculinized fighters, and rooted in the patriarchal voice of authority also discussed in chapter 3. Mleeta also expresses the contradictions of geopolitical conflict within contemporary capitalism—an ordering of memory in the language of "Resistance" with a capital "R," where it becomes possible to be anti-Israeli and even make a rhetorical claim to an inheritance from third world anticolonialism, but only in commodified form. In Rancière's language, one might say that much like Al Manar, there are kinds of political disagreement that do not amount to dissensus from a ruling order.

If media start us in the middle, then perhaps, by examining media, it becomes possible to understand how the conditions of possibility for life are cut short in uneven fashion and the future foreclosed. If the map is not the territory but part of a mediated reality that it performs, then it follows that media infrastructure is not a schematic but a set of ongoing relations. Although the incompleteness of infrastructure implies that other worlds are possible, this should not be taken as a sign that all is easily remedied. Practices such as concealment are already utilized by the forces of militarist intensification, although perhaps for this reason, it becomes even more important to look to a decolonial horizon.

The horrific explosion at the port of Beirut on August 4, 2020, occurred during the final stages of this manuscript's preparation. As I was unable to incorporate it, my hope is that the account that follows may add to our understanding of the period that came before.

The Social Life of Maps of Beirut

The Lebanese National Archive is located on the fourth and fifth sub-level of a converted underground parking garage in a commercial building in the middle of Hamra, the popular neighborhood in Beirut named for its main street. The building's mezzanine floor is home to a video poker arcade, and next door to what was once the Piccadilly movie theatre, whose entrance was converted into a retail space long ago. The office is on the tenth floor of that same building, a strikingly ordinary space.[1] This particular archive serves as a general repository, and also collects the documents of now-defunct or superseded government agencies, such as those of the short-lived Ministry of Planning (1940–45). With limited ventilation, no precise climate control systems, and beset by power cuts, the storage space accumulates dust, mold, and car exhaust. The archive is shaped in a direct and material fashion by the space whose history it presumably secures. It is easy to quip that the archive is in and of the space, and the space is in and of the archive, and that mapping is part of urban planning. It is another matter to trace how the production of space folds back into the official processes by which the city is known and seen—to "stay with the trouble" of the map.[2]

This chapter focuses on roughly the first seventy years of the history of the mapping of Beirut since the formation of Lebanon as a distinct political entity, from about 1920 to 1990. I consider mapping and related media practices as traces of past attempts to shape the spaces of the city. One common critical gesture is to say that the map is not the territory—that the representation of space is inaccurate, or the God-trick of the top-down view distorts the truth on the ground. In this line of thought, the cartographic misrepresentation of lived social complexity was a kind of techno-epistemic violence that aided the colonial process of drawing borders and putting groups of people together in combinations that suited the needs of the Great Powers. The line on the map becomes a territorial line, and the drawing of that line appears as the most important moment in the mediation of space. The spatial outcomes of the governmental technology are read off of the map, and hegemony appears to be automatic and assured. This familiar critique is easily made, particularly of the kind of paper maps that were based on data that at the very least were collected at a previous moment in time. Critiques of cartography, and critical cartography, have likewise asserted that the relationship between maps and the spaces they represent are better understood to exist in a kind of recursive process whereby both shape each other—that maps are a part of how space is produced and managed by modern states, but the most interesting parts of the story are riddled with ambivalent outcomes.[3] What if one were to take this insight a step further, and examine maps as indelibly a part *of* the space, and that the history of the mediation of a city is inseparable from the gaps and patterns found in archives of maps *in* the space?

At the risk of repeating the nationalist fixation with early maps of the territorial body of the state, consider the map displayed at the entrance to the offices of the Lebanese National Archive during my visits in the spring of 2010 (figure 1.1). The original topographical base map was produced in 1862, as part of the French intervention into then–Ottoman Syria by Napoleon III under the pretext of protecting the Christian communities of the area following news of massacres between Druze and Maronites.[4] The military expedition was accompanied by a cartographic team, and a scientific contingent headed by the Orientalist and theorist of nationalism Ernest Renan.[5] This version of the map indicates that later revisions were made in 1913 and 1915, and depicts borders that might seem unfamiliar to contemporary sensibilities—for example, a narrow peninsula juts out into a blank eastern sector to include Damascus. The map also features a table that details the ethno-religious makeup of the population of different geographic districts. To critique this map, one might decry the colonial episteme and racial worldview that the map is a symptom of. This map in particular played no small role in arguments supporting petitions for a distinct Lebanese state. Maps have certainly played a crucial role in articulating colonial and anticolonial nationalist imaginaries alike.[6] However, reading a

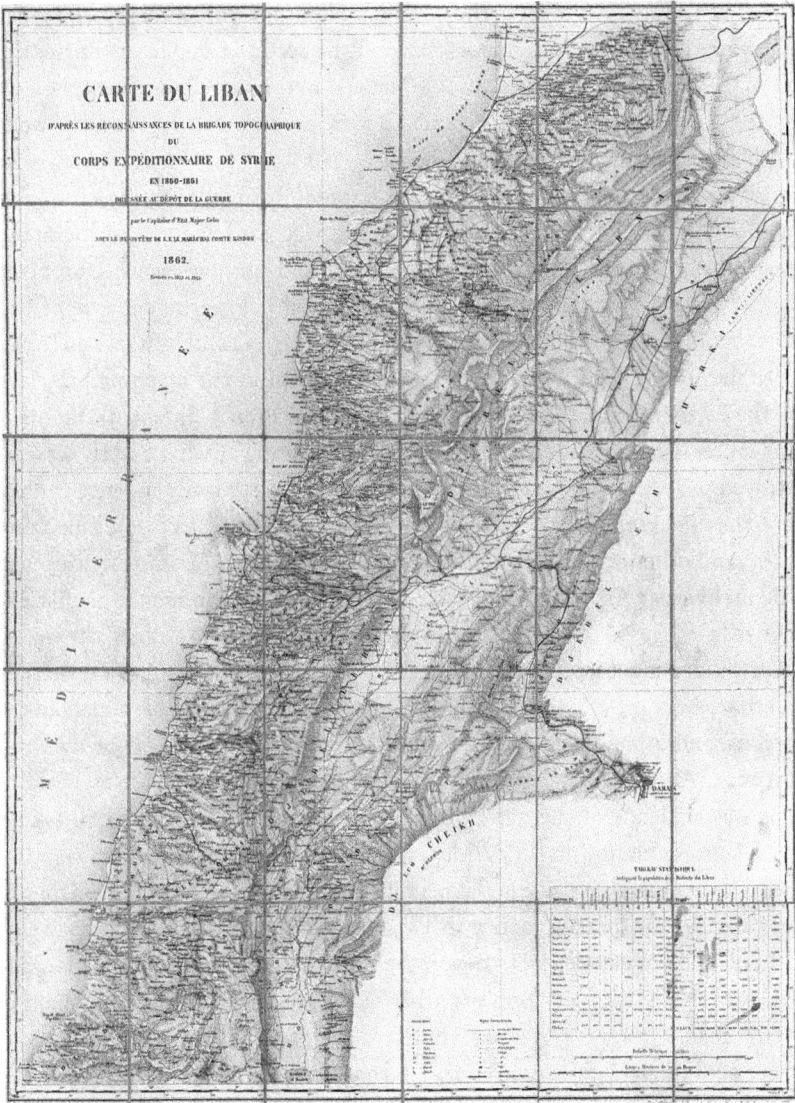

Figure 1.1 French expedition map, 1862, revised 1913, 1915.

map in this way risks missing the more mundane governmental practices that the varieties of mapping support. Beyond the realm of public discourse, the primary work done by many kinds of maps is in the more mundane sphere of state bureaucracy and governmental strategies, which do a great deal of work without persuading the general public.[7]

This chapter tells the story of maps found only in archives in Beirut, and dwells on the holes that the history of the space has left in its cartographic record. A different kind of story could be told by investigating archives elsewhere—in Istanbul to delve into the period before the collapse of the Ottoman Empire, or the US national archives near Washington related to the intrigues of the Cold War. To give a total account of the mapping practices of the French Mandate would require visiting the French diplomatic archives in Nantes, particularly to gain clearer understanding of what exactly was destroyed or lost in the messy shuffle between Lebanese independence in 1943 and the final French departure in 1946. A comparative project would examine maps and other documents pertaining to French North African territories in the archives at Aix-en-Provence, tracing the profound influence of that experience on the Mandate territories with greater precision than is attempted here. Such a move could yield interesting results, beginning with a reflection on the geography of colonial archives. My focus is on the maps, aerial photographs, and urban plans of the city in the city, in what can only be a partial account. At the risk of an anthropomorphism, I examine the lives of these maps as evidence of the nature of the mediation of space in the remaking of urban circulation itself.[8] While cartographic design encourages treating the map as though it possesses a metaphysical coherence, I examine mapping as a contingent spatial practice and system, often very resource-intensive in nature, and typically part of a governmental attempt to solve a particular spatial problem.[9] This story is in part that of key individuals who were charged with the task of surveying and planning the city and its future, which is also a story about maps left unused and plans that retroactively justified unplanned development. Some of these are men (some of whom have underappreciated relationships to women) who commonly appear in histories of urbanism and urban planning in Beirut, such as Camille Duraffourd, Ernst Egli, Raymond and René Danger, and Michel Écochard.[10] What we gain from seeing the city and those who mapped it from the perspective of the maps is a critical sense of the micro-practices of different regimes of power that saw fit to attempt to shape the city. Doing so allows for a clearer grasp of this practice of mediation and later visual modalities such as live television, unfolding the uneven and contingent relationship of maps and their spaces.

The present chapter examines this social life of maps from the emergence of Lebanon as a distinct entity in 1920, through the end of the Lebanese Civil War in 1990. The next chapter examines the postwar period, which saw the introduction of digital cartographic practice and the structural relationship that it bore to the financialization of postwar construction in the city. As I will explore in greater depth in chapters 3 and 4, these attempts to shape the city by making images of it are defined by acts of concealment, and by the spaces outside the city, particularly in South Lebanon. From the perspective of the maps in Beirut, there are three main periods: the Mandate, the first three decades of the independent Lebanese republic, and the damage assessment and anticipatory planning exercises conducted during the Civil War. These three periods can be distinguished by the distinct types of projects undertaken, but also by a fair degree of continuity in cartographic technique and some recycling of personnel. The Mandate period was defined by two key projects: the introduction of a cadastral system, and the emergence of master planning of the city. Both of these projects sought to perform a break with the Ottoman past, and were traversed by the contradictions and limits of Mandatory rule. Mapping in the first decades of the Lebanese state was defined by a series of attempts to redesign the city in line with the imperatives of national development, generating a range of thematic maps and zoning plans. Mapping in the third period primarily consisted of studies undertaken during brief bouts of relative calm in the Civil War that sought to track increasing levels of devastation to the city, whose recovery was increasingly thought to entail more comprehensive levels of intervention, particularly in the city center.

While these three periods can be distinguished by broad shifts in the kinds of governmental practices that produced maps, they also bleed into each other at every level. Mandate officials trained Lebanese counterparts, particularly in the military, and the maps they produced formed the grounds for the damage assessment exercises conducted during the Civil War. Despite the French imperative to perform a fundamental break with the Ottoman past, the two regimes are best understood as having a great deal in common.[11] The archives in Beirut are most complete beginning with the French period; with a few exceptions, most of the Ottoman maps were either taken back to Istanbul or have succumbed to the passage of time.

The archives in Beirut index the twentieth-century historical development of technologies of mapping and related media forms such as aerial photography, but in a manner that is punctuated by their quite local and national formation.[12] These archives register this history, and demonstrate how making images such as these were an integral part of the formation of the city and its infrastructure. These images reveal the contingencies of major attempts to remake the space, and the relations of mobility and visual circulation that continue to inform the contemporary moment. Although all the maps and documents that are discussed here are from archives in Beirut, how and why they were made requires following the circulation of expertise beyond the city. Cities are always defined by those landscapes imagined as their margins, and a forgetting of those "outsides" that shape them. To make sense of maps in and of Beirut requires following a broader circuit of expertise, and in the Mandate period, particularly from French North Africa to the Levant.

Mapping in the Mandate (1920–1946)

There were two primary objectives that drove mapping activity in the Mandate period, leaving a deep legacy on the processes of visualizing the city in the later part of the century. The first was the creation of a comprehensive cadastral system, and the second was the implementation of city- and nationwide infrastructural and urban planning projects. This also involved the creation of state agencies to coordinate them, and an evolution in expert discourse. These objectives were extended unevenly beyond Beirut, and were informed by the political tensions that resulted from the contradictions of the violence of Mandate rule. Remaking the city was thought to require new socioeconomic legibilities, meant to facilitate the rationalization of space and the governability of its inhabitants. The dovetailing of urban planning theory and practice with counterinsurgency constituted a crucial part of how and why maps were made, and requires examining the relationship between aerial photography, land surveying, and cadastral mapping in particular. It is now well established that the French experience in Morocco formed the backdrop against which Mandate rule was based, as well as a key talent pool that the newly formed regime drew from.[13] Hubert Lyautey was a vital cog in the machine of colonial administration, linking Lebanon and Syria to Rabat and the Rif, and to the rest of the circuitries of expertise within the French empire.

Lyautey began his military career as cavalryman in Algeria, followed by a transfer to Vietnam, where he met Joseph Gallieni. Gallieni became a mentor of sorts to Lyautey, and encouraged him to formalize his thinking on the role of military occupation in the social management of colonies. Gallieni is often remembered for his contribution of the *tâche d'huile* concept to counterinsurgency theory.[14] This cartographic metaphor refers to the way in which a drop of oil spreads gradually across the surface of a paper map, and with enough time and drops, covers it entirely. The re-uptake of French counterinsurgency by the United States in the era of the War on Terror would rearticulate these spatial tactics as the three steps "clear, hold, build."[15] Lyautey believed that the task of controlling territory in which the native inhabitants prove hostile to the occupier could be accomplished more efficiently through a combination of social and economic policies, and the occasional exercise of overwhelming military force. This combination was thought to induce a willingness in the occupied to accede to the presumably civilizing process of colonial subjection. When Gallieni was appointed governor of Madagascar, Lyautey would follow him to serve as chief of staff.[16] The expertise in coercion circulated not only between colonial offices within empires but also between empires. Officers working in American, British, and French campaigns to repress or extinguish "unrest" often learned from and praised each other.[17]

Lyautey was assigned to the governorship of the Moroccan protectorate in 1912. His time in this post was formative for what he dubbed "pacification strategy," and he went on to publish a number of articles on the subject. As with his mentor Gallieni, the ability to manage colonies is presented as a spatial problem, with a solution that was a calibrated admixture of brutality, cartography, and socioeconomic reorganization. Lyautey held a measured contempt for the policies he saw employed earlier in Algeria. For one thing, he saw few things as foolish and futile as the idea that its peoples could ever be made into Frenchmen. The racial intimacy of such a mode of governance was to his mind both distasteful and a misapprehension of how to manage territory, populations, and culture. Rather than approach the cities as tabulae rasae, Lyautey championed partnering with local elites via a version of a context-sensitive approach. Inadvertently paralleling some later critics of empire, he had few positive things to say about the practice of urban and military planners in Paris drawing up grid systems which were then air-dropped into Algeria with little reference to existing social and urban formation, or military occupations such as that of Algiers in 1830, which led to the city's devastation.[18] For Lyautey the political technologies meant to secure counterinsurgency objectives and durable colonial occupation were those of militarized urban and socioeconomic reform, but were thought to work more efficiently via a kind of sensitivity to "traditional culture."[19] Lyautey believed this was best implemented via the creation of divisions between modern and traditional quarters within cities, and the creation of transportation infrastructure connecting rural areas to urban administrative centers, and then commercial interests to ports and the metropole.[20] This also presumed a rigidly patriarchal social hierarchy modeled on the military, in which a superior governing class ruled their inferiors.[21]

As the administrative capital of the newly created Lebanese territory and nation-state-to-be, Beirut assumed a key place in both the cadastral survey and comprehensive urban planning. These two projects, both of which were thought to require the creation of precise geographic knowledge, were also implicated in a new geometry of cartographic knowledge and geographic claim-making. Space was to be managed from a centralized bureaucracy, and maps would be stored at a physical distance from the spaces they depicted or anticipated; this much replicates the geographical metaphysics and expertise of colonialism more generally.[22] Beginning in the 1920s, aerial photography also played a key role in the creation of a new visual and temporal relationship to space—unlike topographical surveying, photographic reconnaissance could be performed over much larger areas in relatively less time. The view from above, which had long structured modern imaginaries of the city,[23] was hesitantly adopted to play a more time-sensitive role in colonial administration and surveillance.[24] Aerial photography came to regularly support the process of map production in this period, but typically was used to supplement pertinent details such as land use and elevation data gathered through survey work. The production of aerial photographs for the purposes of increasing map precision was far from a complete process, limited by both technical limitations and cost.[25]

There are two primary components of a cadastral system: a registry that records the ownership and legal status of parcels of lands, and land use maps that present the exact shape and location of the parcels and buildings in question. These two components imply a system of private land ownership (often understood to be individually rather than collectively owned), and detailed survey work to establish fixed boundaries for parcels of land. The degree of precision demanded by cadastral maps and the privatization of ownership they supported could not be achieved with aerial photos and photogrammetric technique alone.[26] The principal objectives were to reorganize the social system of land ownership so as to be compatible with the need to levy taxes on individual land owners, to facilitate the creation of a real estate market, and to bring agricultural production in line with industrial levels of production in a manner that would not fundamentally challenge local elites. This goal also left its mark on the division of mapping activities between state agencies post-independence—the military's geographic department produced topographic relief maps, a shifting array of governmental and consulting agencies produced urban plans, and a special division of the Ministry of Finance (and some cases, individual municipalities) produced cadastral maps. Camille Duraffourd, the French officer who designed the cadastral system and oversaw its implementation

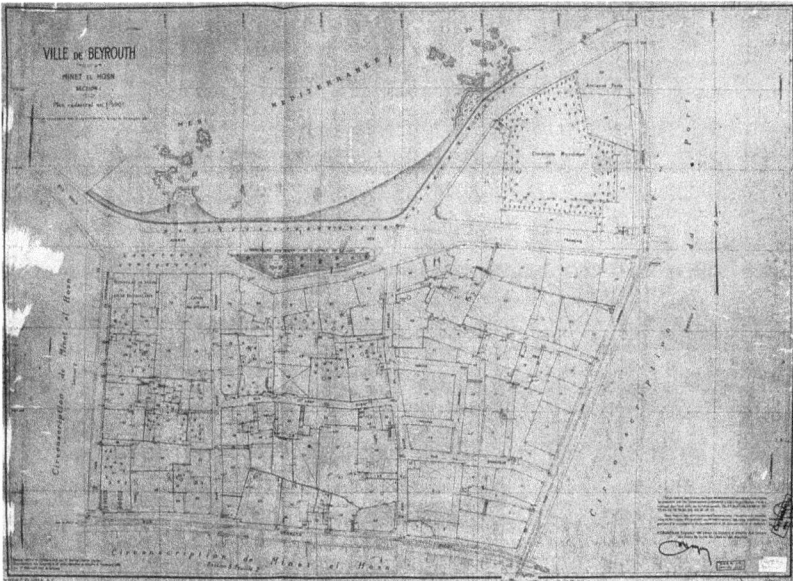

Figure 1.2 Cadastral map, Minet El Hosn, showing area near the port and the former Yugoslav embassy, 1931. Photo courtesy of Belal Hibri (2010).

in the 1920s to 1940s, embodied Lyautey's imperative to account for "local specificity" in colonial rule. Duraffourd's application for the position highlighted his previous experience in Istanbul and familiarity with Ottoman legal codes, and therefore the knowledge of how to transform them into a form legible to French systems of land use and taxation.[27] Many of the original cadastral maps are now lost, and it is difficult to know with certainty which were intentionally destroyed to keep them from falling into Vichy hands and which were simply lost in the chaotic handover from the French to the independent Lebanese government. Many were also undoubtedly returned to France.[28]

The maps of Beirut were primarily done on a 1/500-meter scale, with survey work beginning in 1923. This work proceeded with some interruptions in the first few years, prior to the establishment of more vigorous military control. For example, the cadastral map of the Minet El Hosn district near the port (figure 1.2) was produced in 1931 based on survey work done in 1930. This map bears a number of significant qualities. The dark blue coloration marks it as a blueprint—a term which originally referred not to architectural plans per se, but to the ferro-prussiate salts used to stain an exposed paper surface in a one-off printing reproduction process. After the drafting of an original, copies of a map could then be produced as needed. By the late 1920s, the reproduction process—from exposure to drying—could be handled mechanically.[29] This specific copy of the Minet El Hosn map had two stamps placed on it by CERMOC and then IFPO.[30] It also bears the signature of Duraffourd, one that appears on every cadastral map from this period that I found. Despite the gradual introduction of mechanical and later photomechanical processes to the drafting and reproduction process, the older tradition of maps drafted by hand in this period can still be felt. Not coincidentally, the maps archive at IFPO contained an original 1938 edition of Erwin Raisz's seminal *General Cartography*, alongside a copy of Paul Vidal de la Blache's *Principles of Human Geography*, which the archivist proudly told me were originals from the Mandate era. The presence of these two texts is telling: the latter resonates with the influence of Lyautey's interest in regional and local specificity; the former is the first cartography textbook to be widely used. Raisz was known for having a distinctive drafting style, a recognizable hand from the last period before automation and photomechanical processes would largely eliminate this visible trace of the body of the draftsman (an almost exclusively male profession in this period).

This particular map mentions that it was produced as part of the land reform effort of the states of "Syria, Lebanon, and the Alawites"—notably, the French authorities considered the latter as candidates for a separate state. The map also notes the location of the Yugoslavian embassy and credits a "Mr Melnikoff, Chef de Brigade" with conducting the survey work. In fact, it was a team of Russian survey engineers that was hired to carry out the surveying work for most cadastral maps, paid per square meter of land. Gallina Alexandrovna Duraffourd, who would manage her husband's real estate endeavors and was also Russian, made the connection.[31] One of the team's most recent projects had been in the recently created Yugoslavia, another multi-ethnic and multi-religious society formed into a nation-state following the breakup of the Ottoman Empire. This is no small coincidence, and reflects the concern to generate maps that could handle what were presumably the unique challenges posed by multi-ethnic societies. The commissions set up by the League of Nations to establish the territorial basis for new nation-states after World War I (such as Yugoslavia) sought to create territorial units that would be ethnically compatible with the emerging international state system, a project shaped in no small way by the eugenicist concerns underpinning US immigration policy at the time.[32] To lend credibility to their claims, the commissions also employed the methods of ethnographic cartography, a discipline whose attempts to pin people to locale often became a fraught endeavor. In truth, this segregative biopolitics was formative of racial, ethnic, and ethno-religious systems. This world-defining violence—a core feature of many programs supported by the liberal humanist call for "coexistence" and "tolerance"—aimed to manage populations by shaping their relations, defining the manner in which collective rights could be voiced, and occasionally, wholesale geographic transfer.[33] Part of the motivation for the American contingent in the commissions was to calibrate the US intake of immigrants from countries perceived to be of lesser racial stock. This was not a direct basis for the delineation of Mandatory Lebanon, which had its own complex relationship to legal categories of whiteness and Arab American advocacy in the United States,[34] and to French policies related to what was imagined as the proper regulation and modernization of multi-religious societies.[35] This map reflects an attempt to make space conform to the territorial exigencies of the emerging system of nation states, but is also part of a cartographic welding of populations into distinct groups whose interrelation could be managed within purpose-made spaces.

The cadastral system came with the advantage to the state of being a centralized form of bureaucratic knowledge, displacing the location of knowledge and expertise from local officials.[36] In addition to performing a technical and bureaucratic break from the Ottoman *defter-khane* registry, this reform was a crucial part of the project of replacing the *musha'* system of semi-feudal land ownership over the course of the 1920s. Rather than the peasant cooperative system, land ownership would be transformed to facilitate land taxation and the capitalization of a private real estate market, and also encourage the growth of industrial-scale agriculture suitable for international markets, a key goal of Mandate reform. It is important to note that although the design of the cadastral system itself wasn't finalized until 1926, preliminary and survey work had begun three years prior. Duraffourd established the Torrens land registration system, named for a colonial administrator in Australia, as the basis for the Lebanese one. The Torrens system made it so that the land itself (rather than deed of title transfer) would need to be registered via a licensed surveyor, introducing a degree of transactional simplicity and facilitating the creation of an active real estate market of the kind sometimes fostered in colonies with regimes of land expropriation.[37] The use of fixed-point and absolute triangulation allowed the precise definition of the boundaries of individual plots of land—an innovation that allowed the identification of land with property rights, and property rights holders.[38] The creation of a system of private property was imagined to help create rational economic subjects of the kind needed for modern nationhood, who would also comply with the French authorities and their local partners.

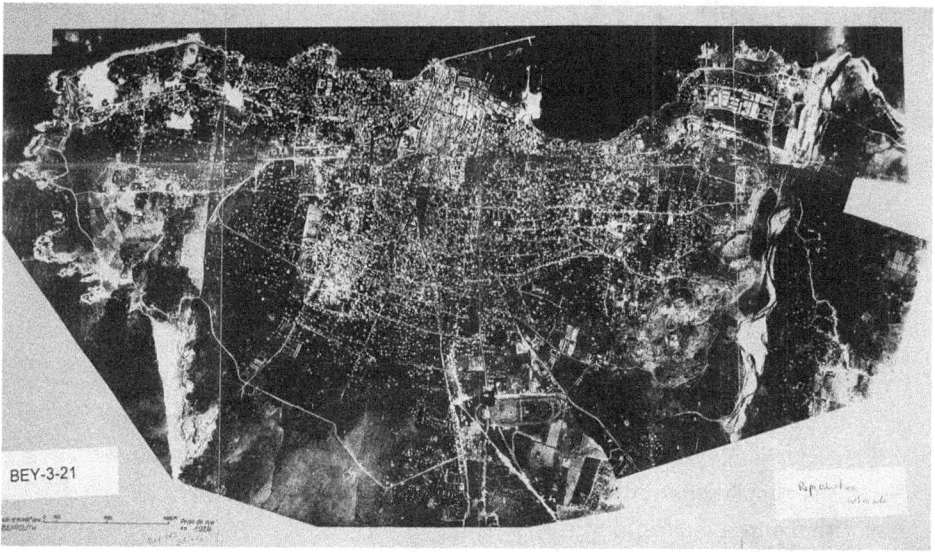

Figure 1.3 Composite aerial photograph, 1926. Photo courtesy of Belal Hibri (2010).

There are many stories that could surely be told about the implementation of the Lebanese cadastral land survey, which was at its most detailed degree of completion in Beirut, at its greatest degree of incompletion in the south of the country, and met with fierce and sometimes armed resistance in different places and times. The survey workers, and the agricultural and tax reform that they were meant to support, were not always given a warm welcome. To the extent that the survey and the progress it was said to herald coincided with the Great Depression, even the technical superiority of the system was called into question.[39] Aerial photographs such as the one in figure 1.3 were typically used to compare the accuracy of survey measurements, but could also be used to locate changes on the ground to be noted on updated maps. French cartographers in this period would project light through a photographic diaposi-tive onto an existing map, superimposing two temporal moments that would be reconciled in a newly updated map—an early precursor of the before/after image discussed in the following chapter.

This particular image is a composite of a number of photographs into a larger one—a photomosaic produced through extensive optical recalibration to fit the slight differences between images together into one. The photographs were taken in 1926, the year the cadastral survey began in earnest, and at the time of the first mass revolt against French rule. The image tells of the

CHAPTER ONE

aerial policing of urban space, and of the investment made by some in images promising the power of an all-seeing eye from above.[40] The pacification strategy of the Mandate held that nationalist rebellions could be best contained by rooting out their supposed origins in cities, which were thought to have a command center relationship to rural areas. However, the spatial character of the revolt involved a great deal of organizational strength in the countryside. Urban neighborhoods deemed unresponsive to modernization's appeal to rational self-interest would have to be shown that it was in their interest to comply so as to avoid aerial bombardment. The most extensive urban bombing campaigns were conducted in Damascus and not Beirut, and some villages in the countryside were bombed in their entirety.[41] In this destructive calculus, the instructional value of overwhelming force was understood to have a specifically modernizing effect on not-yet-modern communities and their nationalist sentiments. The inculcation of willingness to submit to or at least partner with colonial authorities became the measure of the ability of local subjects to demonstrate the capacity to recognize their own self-interest, whose teleological end point was the capacity for self-rule. The supposed ungovernability of the colonized becomes the justification for new and harsher forms of managing life itself.[42] British officials championed similar if not more aggressive tactics in Iraq, arguing that as a direct form of communication delivered in a distinctly modern and spectacular form, the aerial bombardment of civilian areas would leave a great impression on Arabs in particular, and was therefore more humane in that it would more quickly bring rebellions to heel.[43] The violence of liberal conceptions of rule and modernization are revealed in particularly gruesome fashion in such episodes, leaving deep marks everywhere in the colonial record.[44]

While the novelty of airpower was supposed to have a modernizing effect on presumably premodern Arab sensorial schemas, the actual outcome was the introduction of a different spatial and temporal dynamic to revolt. If the aerial photomosaic can be taken as part of the technological underpinning of military practice, the nature of this practice is specific to reconnaissance— meaning an individual sortie to create timely information in visual form, often for the purpose of enabling direct and accurate targeting. Putting the camera on the plane promised to increase the vertical distance for observation, and decrease the time between detection and militarized response. There were two primary ways that the Arab Revolt exploited the limitations of this visual force vector. The first is in the guerrilla tactic of dispersing upon detection by the visual and acoustic conspicuousness of the plane. By the time intelligence from a reconnaissance mission could be made actionable, encampments could be moved. The second tactic was the direct targeting of reconnaissance aircraft, which seems to have been frequent enough that guerrillas developed a tactical manual detailing the best ways to do so. Rebel groups even learned how to mimic the French surface-to-air signal patterns so as to deceive pilots into flying lower and slower, thereby making themselves into better targets.[45] This was more than just a possibility or ironic detail, and is better understood as an animating factor in the historical logic of this moment. When French efforts to rescue the personnel from an aircraft downed in Jabal Druze took a particularly heavy-handed approach, the outrage that it generated decisively accelerated the revolt as a whole.[46]

Airpower primarily played a supporting role in combat in Lebanon, but given the mastery of space suggested by this aerial photomosaic, it might seem easy to read the life of the image as one leading directly to effective targeting. Aiming artillery is like the cadastral registry, in that it requires a precise understanding of topography. Rather than a directly visual relation, the gunner requires the ability to precisely plot relative position, elevation, and other variables such as weather. The prototypical situation presumes that a line of sight does not exist, and instead relies on calculations based on topographical maps.[47] As maps such as these didn't exist until much later in the Mandate period, artillery fire during the revolt was often inaccurate by definition, a deficiency that the French compensated for by just firing more munitions.[48]

The revolt was interpreted by Mandate administrators as evidence of the recalcitrance, ignorance, and fanaticism of local populations, who were mired in a sectarian game that led to partisan refusal of the benefits of the social and economic improvements of modernity.[49] It was also interpreted in France and elsewhere as the failure of the policies utilized to date, or even as evidence of the futility of the attempt to create self-governing entities in the region. This did not, however, lead to an increase in funding for Mandate territories per se, as even those in France who supported the overseas empire did so with varying levels of enthusiasm, with many in favor of the endeavor being self-financed.[50] As Lyautey's influence waned, new variations emerged around his basic formulation—that urban elites could be played off of their rural counterparts, and that modernizing cities were key to their economic development, which in turn were key to winning the support of the native populace. Remaking spaces also implied the reordering of social relations in ways that rendered them more amenable to biopolitical management. When violent coercion failed to produce sufficient demonstrations of reason (equated with submission to willingness to enter into partnership with authority), part of the answer wound up being a reorganization of space and circulation itself.

Part of the growth of Beirut in size and importance (both material and imaginary) during the late nineteenth and early twentieth centuries involved a broader reorganization of economic flows through the port to transportation networks in the interior and to points further east. This required substantial infrastructural development, notably the creation of the Damascus highway and expansion of the port to accommodate shipping traffic.[51] The district near the port had been symbolically important for the Ottoman regime that the French sought to supplant. As the seat of the Mandate government, the neighborhood was slated for special attention meant to demonstrate the superiority of the new regime. The process of remaking the space was meant to perform a temporal break with what came before. As is often the case when a logic of security underpins the reordering of space and movement, a dual purpose came into effect. The first of these was the need to foster modes of circulating people and goods deemed economically desirable by reorganizing movement within the city, and establishing guidelines for future urban growth. Put more specifically, the aim was to remake the space and its economy to be in line with interests that would seek to minimize undesirable events and subjects prone to misconduct—traffic accidents, protests, vandalism, and in this case, the expression of political solidarities and socialities that did not seek colonial recognition. The second purpose can be detected in the way that these spatial forms could also facilitate the rapid deployment of police and the display of military capacity. The modernizing project was imagined to make the people and its spaces governable.

The decade or so that followed the quelling of the 1924–26 revolt saw a reinvigoration of efforts to generate comprehensive plans for cities, requiring the support of cadastral mapping. Urban planning was thus reenlisted for social and economic reform, which were understood to also be military goals. In addition, like in many post–World War I contexts, the military technology of aerial photography (with its attendant techniques of photogrammetric calculation, photo-triangulation, and photo-interpretation) came to play a crucial role in the generation of cartographic information for urban planning.[52] The technique of aerial photography would have a deep impact on conceptualization of urban space in the humanities and social sciences, first felt in this period and deepening after World War II. Visualizing space in this form lent itself to conceiving of the urban as a malleable social totality, a conception which can be found in the thought of midcentury thinkers and practitioners in fields ranging from architecture to philosophy to ethnography and urban planning. The aerial view even played a fundamental if often overlooked role in the work of Marxist thinkers such as Henri Lefebvre, albeit one that fostered a critical perspective on the production and transformation of urban space as a historical totality.[53]

In the relatively stable years in Beirut after the Arab Revolt, the Mandate turned its efforts to systematic urban planning.[54] In 1929 Duraffourd drafted a feasibility study titled *Bayreuth en Cinq Ans* (Beirut in Five Years), the first in what became a series of master plans for Beirut. Prior to this point, comprehensive city planning had been more limited.[55] Based on what it projected as future growth, the plan issued recommendations of how best to link municipal codes to a desired modern social consciousness, and the kind of urban milieu that could support it. City planning also took into account new forms of desirable movement within and out of the city—not simply connecting the port to the Damascus highway, but also guiding the relationship between new automobilities and an improved road network. Driving from the city to mountain towns and vacation homes or ancestral villages was an activity that emerged in the interwar period, and quickly became a definitive part of the lives (and gendered anxieties) of middle-class and elite Beirutis, and those of tourists.[56] Duraffourd's 1929 study formed the basis for the 1932 *Plan Danger*, created by René and Raymond Danger. It linked economic strategy, public hygiene, architectural form, and transformed social consciousness in a single visualization of a possible future. This second plan was couched in a language of transforming unclean, backward urban lives fostered by the current state of the city, and carried a reformist preoccupation with creating proper hygiene and circulation by bringing uncontrolled growth in line with a uniform plan.

As was common in French Beaux-Arts planning circles at the time, the Danger brothers rejected the notion that town planning could be a solely technical affair divorced from aesthetic considerations, or that it could impose standardized forms that didn't take local social life into account.[57] They detailed a five-year construction plan that would have implemented a building code and created public spaces, gardens, and an upgraded sanitation system. As seen in one section of the plan (figure 1.4), it also sought to make other infrastructural improvements to accommodate commercial interests—such as making additional improvements to the road network near the port area to connect it to both the highway to Damascus and the city center nearby. The Danger brothers' consultancy, which counted plans for Aleppo and Damascus in its portfolio of projects,[58] was also part of a broader injection of Beaux-Arts classicism into urban planning and architecture in former Ottoman cities. Their approach emphasized a "contextual sensitivity" that fell across a modernity/tradition axis—in that universal progress meant rupture with the Ottoman past, but in a manner that abhorred standardization. It is perhaps of no

Figure 1.4 Section of the Plan Danger, at what was once the urban frontier, 1931. Photo courtesy of Belal Hibri (2010).

surprise, then, that the Danger brothers began their career as survey engineers, with their overseas careers starting in Morocco. They first came to work in the eastern Mediterranean (on a plan for Izmir) on recommendation by Lyautey to the Kemalist state; on their first visit to Beirut in 1929, they would highlight the preservation of the Achrafiyeh neighborhood as a key long-term goal.[59]

The *Plan Danger* would remain officially unapproved in 1932, but formed the basis for two successive plans; 1932 was also the year that the Beaux-Arts-trained architect and urbanist Michel Écochard, then a fresh graduate, arrived in Damascus, and in the following years to Beirut. Écochard's career would track with and inform key strands of the planning of the city for decades to come. Écochard's original stint in the Mandate overlapped with Duraffourd by less than a decade, as the latter would pass away suddenly in 1941. He left his mark in the technical design of the cadastral system, his signature on its original maps (figure 1.5), and his name on a street in the Ain El Mraisseh neighborhood. Mrs. Duraffourd was able to steer their affairs so as to make a fair amount of money on the emerging real estate market.[60] The seaside villa originally owned by the Duraffourds and used as a guesthouse (on the Corniche also constructed during the Mandate), was torn down in 2010 to make

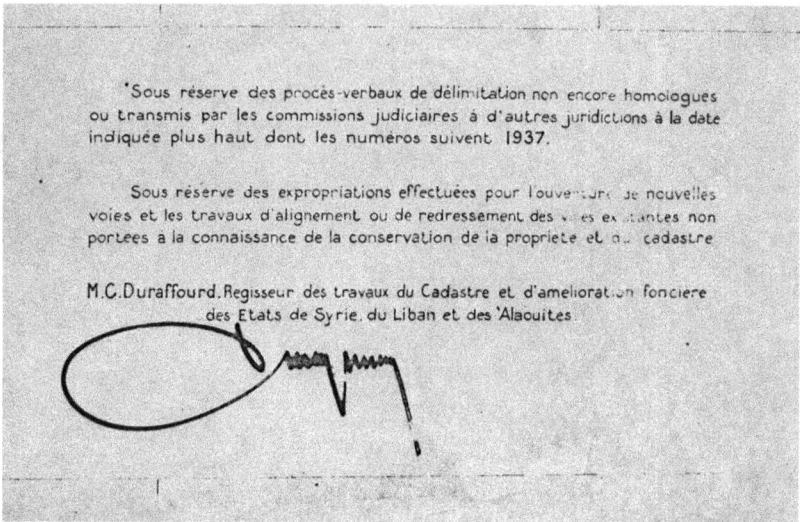

*Sous réserve des procès-verbaux de délimitation non encore homologues ou transmis par les commissions judiciaires à d'autres juridictions à la date indiquée plus haut dont les numéros suivent 1937.

Sous réserve des expropriations effectuées pour l'ouverture de nouvelles voies et les travaux d'alignement ou de redressement des voies existantes non portées à la connaissance de la conservation de la propriété et du cadastre

M.C.Duraffourd. Regisseur des travaux du Cadastre et d'amelioration fonciere des Etats de Syrie, du Liban et des 'Alaouites

Figure 1.5 Detail of signature, cadastral map of Mazraa, 1937. Photo courtesy of Belal Hibri (2010).

way for the high-rise luxury apartment buildings that emerged in that phase of overdevelopment.

The overlapping careers of Duraffourd and Écochard are indicative of how the management of urban space was conceived, and the changing techniques and forms that the visualization of the city and urban planning would take. Écochard's career was punctuated by a series of public laments about lost chances to deal with what he saw as the burgeoning problems of uncontrolled urban growth, itself fueled by the kinds of real estate speculation that Mandate reforms made possible. Écochard worked as a correspondent for the Danger brothers' firm, and was instrumental in drafting the first master plan for Beirut. The plan specified the appropriation of quite significant amounts of land by the state to fulfill the recommendation of creating green spaces and public gardens, leading to opposition by elite families and interests. The plan ultimately remained unapproved.[61] This early experience would only reinforce a liberal humanist perspective embodied by Écochard—that Beirut's problems stemmed from centuries of Ottoman misrule and social stagnation, which shaped a historical trend toward over-concentration in the city center that would only worsen if left unchecked.

The realignment of political economic order and state formation during the Mandate would create a crucial contradiction. At the same time that social processes were brought into governmental purview and rendered with increased precision on paper, the resulting political formation would double back onto the planning efforts themselves. If there is a single episode that materializes this contradiction most succinctly, it would be the creation of a Place de l'Étoile in the city center modeled on the one in Paris. The semi-failed attempt to remake the space illustrates the conflicting interests and desires at play even at the high point of colonial rule. The star-shaped square, along with the rest of the transformed city center, became a physical embodiment of the tensions inherent to the dual impulse to preserve architectural forms and "traditional" ways of life deemed to be valuable "heritage," but also to improve society and economy through rational planning. This binary formed the political underpinnings of the Mandate regime, which as a matter of policy and expediency partnered with political, religious, and commercial elites. In fact, Duraffourd and Écochard were both known for the painstaking efforts they took to document and understand local architectural forms and ways of living in place, which they understood to be valuable traditional forms that should be left undisturbed to the greatest extent possible (meaning, while still rendered governable). For example, Écochard's first assignment while at his Damascus post was to conduct an archaeological study of old baths, an experience that he presumed gave him special insight into the inner geometries of "Arab civilization."[62] The implied periodization, in which the Eastern/Islamic past falls into darkness before being superseded by Euro-modernity, conveniently creates a teleological arc in which the *mission civilisatrice* determines the line between local "tradition" to be preserved within modernization, and also creates career opportunities.

The creation of the Place de l'Étoile, like the remaking of the rest of the city center, was based on *Bayreuth en Cinq Ans* and was the most ambitious project of the Mandate. The plan was in part informed by an attempt to anticipate and guide the transformations occurring in the city, driven by new property relations and economic networks.[63] The plan would replace part of the old street plan nearby with the straight lines of a grid of streets named for conquering generals such as Allenby, Foch, and Weygand. The square itself would feature a new clock tower located not far from the Ottoman clock tower. It was also in sight of the Grand Serail, the former Ottoman military barracks turned courthouse, which became the headquarters of the French High Commission, and after independence, the prime minister's office. The clock was to be set to reflect Paris instead of Istanbul standard time, supplanting one of the key interventions by the sultanate meant to reinforce the modernity of the relation between the provinces and the imperial center.[64] The project encountered two key obstacles—local resistance to the appropriation of land to complete the seven arms of the star, and limited financial support for the project due to the pressures of the Depression-era economy, which did not help requests for increased funding from France. To achieve the effect of a star whose arms radiate out from the square meant cutting seven streets through the existing urban fabric. To do this, the project would have had to expropriate land held by both Christian and Muslim *awqaf*—the civil-religious institutions implied by Mandate law that held land in a trust on behalf of a sectarian group.[65] It would have also have had to cut through part of a historic market. After a number of intense rounds of negotiation, the French authorities reached a compromise with the religious and merchant elite who objected loudly to the prospect of losing land.[66] The result was a star with five and a half arms instead of seven. The contradiction of the five-and-a-half-armed Place de l'Étoile is one that concretizes the frustration of planning efforts to make the spatial formation of the city conform to visual order and design, what T. Mitchell (1988) identifies as the modern remaking of the built environment to align with ordered representational forms.

A similar contradiction can be found in the gendered politics of circulation in the spaces of the city. Mandate efforts to secure the city in the later 1920s and early 1930s involved upgrades to the street system intended to facilitate policing and speedy troop movement. Since the late Ottoman period, the city's central axis was bisected by an avenue running from south to north to the city center, allowing for rapid deployment from a nearby barracks to the administrative buildings located there. The Mandate would widen this avenue, facilitating the movement of both *gendarmes* and commercial traffic headed for the port. In this period the military also began creating land-use maps of the entire city that detailed the location of individual buildings, reflecting the ontology of cadastral mapping's concern for individual ownership of property. It was also on this basis, however, that *awqaf* were able to lay claim to space and ultimately to block the refashioning of the square. Although the technique of the cadastral map and the legal and economic system that it enabled were adopted, not all of the spatial forms of the Mandate were achieved, in this case primarily because of the quid pro quo arrangements and partnerships with local elites that the regime depended on.

However, the Mandate government's policy of partnering with and strengthening existing political and religious elites also created new social tensions with the new economy and social mobilities it depended on. More and more women worked outside of the home and participated in labor unions. In addition, a larger contingent of women from rural areas circulated between rural areas and potentially unfamiliar neighborhoods in the city. The gendered anxieties that shaped nationalist and other political movements that emerged in the 1930s involved a particularly gendered street violence, a characteristic also found in French policing practices.[67] In the manner of patriarchal structures in need of self-reaffirmation, the youth clubs of the new political movements favored public demonstrations of the virile masculine bodies they asserted would win national independence and safeguard the nation's honor (figured as a female body). Many of these newly formed movements, such as the Phalange party inspired by Franco and the Spanish fascist movement, were organized along explicitly sectarian lines. The same streets created for the theater of troop movement became the optimal venue for group calisthenics, parades, and other performances of synchronized bodily discipline. Mainstream public discussions of citizenship at the time tended to treat women as subjects in need of protection and regulation by their male kin. This is despite, or perhaps because of, the prevalence of and even leading role of women in the labor movement, whose place in the Lebanese socialist movement and communist party were not always uncontested or welcomed by their masculinist counterparts. Working-class women's militancy, particularly in the south, often worked against the pressure created by sectarianism for people to articulate their demands and resolve their differences within its divisions.[68]

If the Mandate ushered in new mapping techniques and institutions, a reorganization of the relationship between visual and spatial forms, and a sharp increase in the sheer number of maps produced, then from the perspective of the life cycle of the maps themselves, the end of the Mandate was an extinction event of sorts. The destruction of maps in the 1940s and before the final departure of French forces in 1946 certainly outpaced production. It is difficult to know with certainty why specific gaps in the archive exist, or what specific reasons led to the destruction of which maps and aerial photos. The importance attached to rendering space legible so as to make it manageable, productive, and targetable also meant that maps were often destroyed so as to ensure they wouldn't fall into the hands of opposing military advance, particularly by Vichy forces during the Anglo-French clash during World War II.[69] Large numbers of maps were undoubtedly also lost in the messy handover between when independence was officially declared in 1943 and the actual departure of French forces in 1946. Many were taken back to France, some remain in rare pockets of preservation in municipal offices, and still others exist in archives in Beirut that are more difficult to access—such as older cadastral records in the Ministry of Finance or the military's Geographic Affairs division.

The Early Republic (1946–1975)

The post–World War II and post-independence periods roughly coincided in Lebanon, and were accompanied by the life cycle and geopolitics of state-led development planning. This periodization should by no means be taken to be an epochal or historic break, but rather one where older and local priorities were renegotiated in a new context. Generally speaking, the push to implement state-led planning initiatives and their elite renegotiation established a pattern of interaction—between formal planning and informal development, and socioeconomic and political exclusion—that would be an important dimension of postwar planning as a whole.[70] Although 1943 is marked on official calendars as the year Lebanon gained independence, the story told by maps suggests that 1946 is a better date to mark the beginning of the country's nominally sovereign status over its own techniques of rule. For example, city maps of Beirut dated as late as 1945 indicate the "Service Géographiques du F.F.L." (Forces Françaises du Levant) as their producers. The French military didn't depart until 1946. The first decade or so after independence was marked by very similar cartographic techniques and visual language, and maps produced as late as 1957 indicate the names of the same officers as during the Mandate. The actual draftsmen and surveyors responsible would probably have been Lebanese. The use of local draftsmen was a common colonial cartographic practice as they typically were paid much less, and, in the case of protectorates and Mandates, were seen as a way to tutor local subjects in the technical dimensions of modern statecraft.[71] While many of the techniques, institutions, and actual experts carried over into the first decades of independence, the kinds of projects that generated maps of Beirut were quite different, reflecting the rise of midcentury development discourses, the shifting location of Lebanon in regional Cold War allegiances, and transformations in cartographic practice. Other than the kinds of maps produced in support of the administrative work of municipalities and ministries, some of the most important projects in the years prior to the Lebanese Civil War were the master plans for Beirut of 1951 and 1963, and the nationwide state-commissioned study by IRFED (Institut de Recherche de Formation et de Développement). The differing priorities of and tensions between the IRFED study and the work of Écochard reveal the politics of mapping Beirut in this juncture.

In the interim between independence and his return to Lebanon in the early 1950s, Écochard assumed the post of director of town planning in Morocco, which he held from 1946 to 1952. He had been an active member of the modernist-functionalist CIAM group (Congrès Internationaux d'Architecture

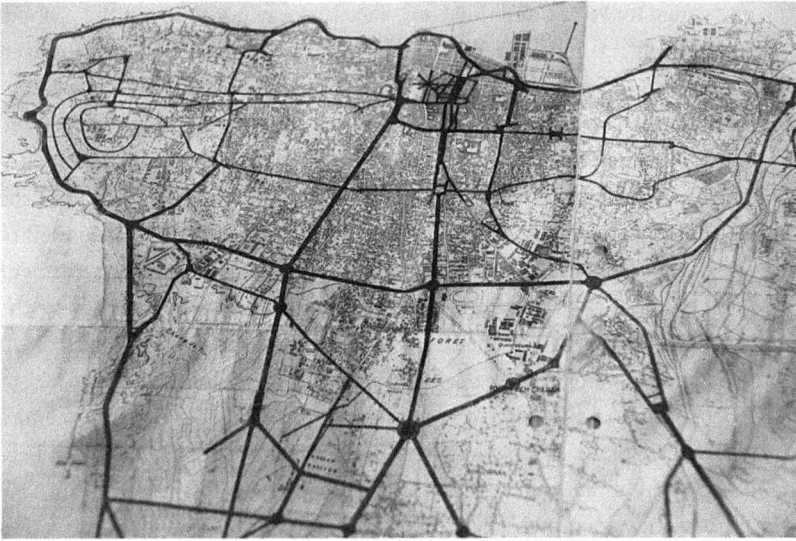

Figure 1.6 From the Egli plan, 1951. Photo courtesy of Belal Hibri (2010).

Moderne) since the early 1940s, a commitment that found expression in his response to the rural exodus created by Lyautey's interventions in cities such as
Casablanca. As noted by Rabinow in the opening of *French Modern* (1989), the
mass housing projects that Écochard envisioned as the appropriate response
were shaped by the CIAM school, but as a result of a conflict with the priorities
of private interests were only ever half implemented. Following his resigna-
tion, Écochard established a private practice based in Paris. When Écochard
returned to Beirut as a consultant, he was welcomed back by an increasingly
professionalized urban planning milieu.[72]

In 1954 the Beirut municipality officially approved a master plan drafted by
Ernst Egli, largely based on the one Écochard had drafted many years earlier.
The plan was primarily confined to a street and traffic circulation plan, and
did not address key issues such as city zoning (figure 1.6).[73] The plan made
provisions to connect the city to a highway system running the length of the
country's coastline, which Écochard had conceived as early as the 1930s. When
viewed alongside the military land-use maps of Beirut that preceded the Egli
plan, it almost gives the impression that it was produced by taking the most
up-to-date land-use map and just superimposing a modified road system on top
of it. This impression echoes a common way of critiquing cartographic logic,
which, like other modernist forms, imposes an unfeeling geometric order detached from lived realities onto a place—or conversely, valorizes the vision of

the draftsman for seeing and ordering space in a way not mired in the particularities and political contingencies that bend it into its current form. However, doing so takes the aesthetic form at face value, and tends to assume rather than explain the more uneven relationship between the space on the paper and the space of the city. More interesting is an account of the multiple modes of mediation that constitute maps, and the very pointed contestation of the future shape of the city that they are a part of. The Egli plan responded to the rise of development planning, and to a rising tide of nationalist sentiment in which the question of how to integrate the capital city with the rest of the country became a central concern. The comparatively limited goals of this plan would also soon be superseded by a key shift in planning ideology.

The election of Camille Chamoun to the presidency in 1952 represented the ascendance of a political strain that sought a closer alliance between Lebanon and the United States, Britain, and France—and against the Pan-Arab movement and its connection to the Soviet Union. Part of the motivation for doing so was to assuage fears, especially among entrenched private interests, that Lebanon would become engulfed by a politically dominant Syria, and the Pan-Arab nationalist tide more generally.[74] The US involvement in the Middle East was guided in no small measure by the twinned concerns of securing oil economies and containing Soviet influence.[75] The ascendance of modernization theory, and its self-assured optimism about the superiority of the American way of life, provided a framework to extend influence to newly independent countries in the guise of technical aid, and in ways that left an indelible mark on Cold War social science.[76] The policy of the US Army Corps of Engineers at the time was to form mapping agreements with all countries not aligned with the Soviet Union, ostensibly in support of agricultural and industrial development, but with the added benefit of leading to increasingly precise US military maps.[77] The project of containing Communist and pro-Soviet sentiment found expression in policies that sought to intervene in spaces of poverty. Maps were also an integral communicative form in the ideological battle between the superpowers, and as Truman's famous Point Four Program became the Technical Cooperation Administration, maps of the world and region became routinely produced to highlight what kinds of aid were going to which countries.[78]

One of the outcomes of this alignment of mapping and mid-century modernization that left a trace in the Lebanese National Archive is the US Operations Mission in Lebanon, or USOM/L. It was at this time that Beirut was transforming into a key node in the financial networks of the postwar regional oil boom. This transformation was further bolstered by the flight of capital from

THE MIDDLE EAST AND AMERICA

From earliest civilization — which probably began in the Middle East — the kind of life man leads has been determined largely by the land on which he lives. Man, seeking to make the land and the elements work for him, learned to divert the water from the streams to irrigate his fields. He built strong houses for protection against storms. He tamed the camel, the goat, the cow, and chickens. He selected the best fruit and vegetables and grew them for food. He discovered the sciences of medicine, of mathematics, of navigation. Through the ages the best ideas were passed on to other men. Europe and the West copied the East and applied the ancient learning to the new environment. America, the newest land to be settled, was able to draw upon the accumulated knowledge of the Middle East, of Europe, of the Far East. America was settled by men and women from all nations who knew these things. Because there were few people in America at first, and because the country was large, it was necessary to develop machines to do some of the work. These new machines — tractors for plowing, drills for digging wells, trucks for taking the crops to market — are new centuries. By applying the ancient sciences, by continuing to adopt new ideas from the people of every land, and by making new contributions to learning, Americans have been able to develop a high standard of living.

The presence of American technicians in the Middle East is, in a sense, a repayment by a young nation for the contributions from the old. It is a continuation of the great interchange of knowledge between men.

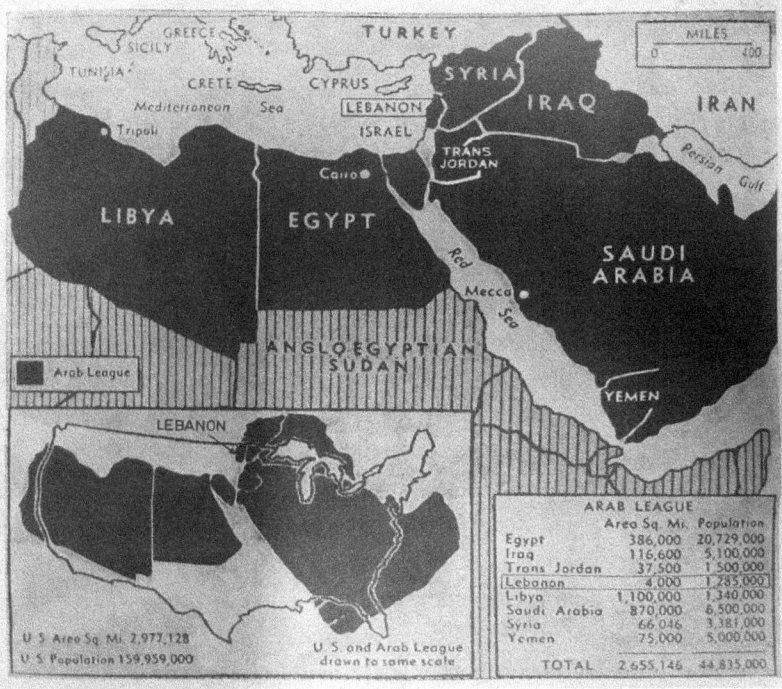

GREECE · SICILY · TUNISIA · CRETE · CYPRUS · TURKEY · SYRIA · LEBANON · ISRAEL · IRAQ · IRAN · Mediterranean Sea · Tripoli · TRANS JORDAN · Cairo · LIBYA · EGYPT · SAUDI ARABIA · Red Sea · Mecca · Persian Gulf · ANGLO-EGYPTIAN SUDAN · YEMEN · Arab League · LEBANON · MILES 0 400

ARAB LEAGUE	Area Sq. Mi.	Population
Egypt	386,000	20,729,000
Iraq	116,600	5,100,000
Trans Jordan	37,500	1,500,000
Lebanon	4,000	1,285,000
Libya	1,100,000	1,340,000
Saudi Arabia	870,000	6,500,000
Syria	66,046	3,381,000
Yemen	75,000	5,000,000
TOTAL	2,655,146	44,835,000

U.S. Area Sq. Mi. 2,977,128
U.S. Population 159,959,000
U.S. and Arab League drawn to same scale

Figure 1.7 From the US Operations Mission to Lebanon booklet, 1955.

Arab countries fearing nationalization, or displaced from Palestine by the establishment of Israel.[79] It was also facilitated by the implementation of banking secrecy laws that effectively shielded accounts from government oversight.[80] It was in this context that the Chamoun government sought American support for development.[81] The USOM/L was set up to provide technical assistance in five areas—agriculture, education, health and sanitation, transportation infrastructure, and natural resource management. The presence of the USOM/L in the 1950s should be understood as part of a broader context in which a number of recently decolonized countries sought to participate in a transnational circulation of development expertise, particularly if adopting their recommendations curried favor and aid.[82]

In 1955 the USOM/L published a booklet that gave a summary of its efforts, circulated primarily to officials in Washington and Beirut. It had both English and Arabic editions, and was also intended for economic elites in Beirut. The booklet presents its mission in grand civilizational terms, in which the historical progression of humanity can be measured by an advancing technical domination of nature. The booklet's introduction tells a grand world historical narrative in which "Man" domesticates animals, tills the land, and learns the art of irrigation, leading inexorably to the rise of Western science and the taming of the empty but fertile American wilderness by the robust ingenuity of the melting pot, and culminating in the high living standards of the contemporary moment. The first pages of the booklet include a map (figure 1.7) of newly drawn Middle Eastern states,[83] with a table of figures comparing the populations and surface area of the United States and Arab League nations. It describes the nature of the exchange as such: "The presence of American technicians in the Middle East is, in a sense, a repayment by a young nation for the contributions from the old." The genealogy of American exceptionalism is presented as extending even further back than Ancient Greece, and returning in a friendly global embrace.

Visual forms also played a central role in the implementation of projects aimed at the general population, and labor training and public health programs alike relied on the method of screening educational films. Industrial training films, considered to be a cost-efficient way to demonstrate new methods to the public at large, were also procured in large quantity. The booklet makes mention of a sizable film library.[84] The sanitation program (organized into urban and rural divisions) claims to have shown films related to hygiene and public health to 10,340 people in the eighteen-month period prior to publication, linking the management of population to both individual practices and the creation of broader systems targeting whole communities.[85] The postwar challenges of modernizing public health and the new risks of disease endemic to global circulation were often imagined to have a cinematic solution.[86]

I found the USOM/L booklet by accident, stuffed into one of the many folders of the IRFED development project in the National Archive. IRFED, founded and led by the Dominican priest Joseph Lebret, conducted what was by far the largest, most comprehensive study and development program in this and maybe any other period in Lebanon's history. That the USOM/L booklet was tucked inside of an IRFED folder is an almost too on-the-nose allegory for the changing political forces in Lebanon, the differing roles that planning and development took within their administrations, and the way that a new regime of cartographic knowledge and planning expertise can fold what came before into itself. The political crisis of 1958 escalated into a series of clashes between opponents and proponents of Pan-Arab nationalism, bringing Fuad Chehab to the presidency. The former military commander was seen by many in Lebanon as having a relatively neutral position in relation to bitter regional and sectarian political factions. Chehab believed that a state-led project of national unification could remedy the political fractures and economic exclusions of sectarianism, but that such a project would require a stronger centralized state. This approach to social and economic policy made him unlike any other Lebanese president. His experience in the military had exposed him to the uneven geography of inequality in the country, a problem that had played a key role in the unrest that brought him to power, and that he understood as being his task to ameliorate. As part of the Chehab administration's reorganization of the state apparatus pertaining to urban planning, a new Directorate of Town Planning in 1959 (later renamed the Directorate General of Urbanism, tasked with coordinating plans for municipalities) was created, and the Higher Council for Urban Planning in 1963.

The political unrest that brought Chehab to power interrupted a study being done by the architect and planner Constantin Doxiadis. In 1957 the USOM/L, in conjunction with Chehab's predecessor, had commissioned Doxiadis Associates to develop a national housing program. Doxiadis was often a favored US partner for Cold War projects, as the approach of his "science of ekistics" aligned with the American objective of remaking cities to mitigate the political discontent that was believed to sprout into pro-socialist sentiment in urban slums and informal settlements throughout the developing world.[87] *Ekistics* was a term of Doxiadis's own coinage (and name of a journal that he founded), which referred to a science and philosophy of urban planning and geography that imagined its foundations to logically extend from geometric principles, the properties of the natural environment and human nature, and the need to re-anchor modern urban experience in local tradition. Other than leveraging his former work with the Greek ministry of reconstruction into contracts from American institutions, Doxiadis's approach was useful in its alignment against "improper" urban mobilities that led to the exposure of the presumably apolitical masses to radical political movements and Soviet infiltration.[88] The study conducted by Doxiadis featured an extensive photographic survey of Beirut and its growing slums, and of much of the rest of the country. Aerial survey was a key component of Doxiadis's totalizing vision of society and space.[89] Among the plan's recommendations were a slum clearance project, mass housing development in Beirut and other cities damaged by a recent earthquake, and a new seat of government outside of the historic city center. The study also proposed the construction of a number of new urban centers on the outskirts of Beirut proper. Given Doxiadis's targeting of "trouble areas" inhabited primarily by Shi'ites and Muslim Palestinians, the recommendations had socioeconomic implications that, if implemented, would likely have activated a sectarian politics.[90] This attempt to bring in a prestigious outsider to put a neutral face on highly political recommendations was stymied by the armed conflict of 1958, an event bound up with the social conditions the plan was meant to resolve.[91]

The Doxiadis study also recommended a full social and economic survey of the country, to more precisely manage the synchronization of country and city, and more urgently, to anticipate and guide future urban development. Soon thereafter, IRFED would conduct a similar survey. Chehab sought to publicly distance his administration from the explicitly pro-American stance of the Chamoun presidency, and sought to build a national consensus through a development program that would remedy the problems of inequality. A friend of Charles de Gaulle, Chehab commissioned IRFED in 1960 to assist with his plans for national development. From the perspective of the lives of maps and plans of Beirut in the post-1958 period, Écochard and IRFED represented two quite different kinds of governmental expertise. The starkest differences between the two can be found in their perspectives on planning for Beirut, which are better understood not simply as the contrast one might expect between a development agency and an architect-urbanist, but as also indicative of the shifting priorities and needs they were commissioned to address.[92] Although both plans warned of what they saw as the dangerously uncontrolled and under-regulated growth of the city and its informal suburbs, they did so in very different registers. It was very much the case that private interests and real estate speculation had almost always either coopted or out-maneuvered the state bureaucracy.[93] For example, critics at the time characterized state planning efforts, such as the updated Building Code of 1954, as simply retroactively sanctifying what had already happened in (or to) the city. One can often find among frustrated urban planners the more nuanced insight that mapping and planning are a recursive social process.[94] Just as Chehab's attempts to curtail economic inequality and its articulation within the sectarian political system were met with opposition, the recommendations detailed by both the IRFED study and the Écochard plan would be stymied by the landed elites of Beirut.

In his early career as a clergyman, Lebret was influenced by the engaged charitable work of the Social Catholic movement. This experience with rural community activism in France informed his interest in economic development, particularly what he dubbed the "human economy" of an area. This approach emphasized strategies that centered on including the poor and marginalized groups in broader national development programs, an effort that presumably countered the irreligious influence of communist movements.[95] Lebret became involved with the organization Economie et Humanisme, and directed a number of development studies in Latin America in the 1940s, most notably in Brazil and Colombia. In 1958 he founded IRFED with the objective of bringing together like-minded reformers and technocrats around the idea of "harmonized development." This perspective placed the individual as the central subject of concern, who was understood to be in need of insulation against the social fragmentation of modern life, particularly as found in cities. Advocates of humanized development sought to maintain and strengthen community ties, which they thought to be the remedy to this underlying problem, and which they saw as neglected by other approaches to development planning.

Summaries of IRFED's findings and recommendations were published in 1961 and 1963, the first of which elicited a great deal of debate in Lebanon. The first edition of *Besoins et Possibilités de Développement du Liban* (Needs and Possibilities of Development of Lebanon) was published in two volumes, and established rural development as a national priority, and the best solution to many urban problems as well. In a departure from debates in local planning circles, which had often given solutions for what was seen as over-centralization within the city, IRFED's recommendations aimed to de-center Beirut within a transformed national fabric. Harmonized development held that rural-to-urban (and to a lesser extent, suburban) migration was inherently linked to social fragmentation, human degradation, poverty, and political unrest. This perspective sounds as though it were informed by a reading of the Parisian experience of urban migration in the previous century, or possibly the more common mid-century view within planning discourses of an atomized mass society created by rapid urbanization. Ethnographic research in Beirut from the late 1960s and early 1970s suggests a different perspective. Rather than a mass of rural poor uprooted by their move to the city searching for work, many Lebanese who came to Beirut in this period had already secured a job, often through close ties to village, family, and community that they maintained. Although the major pre–Civil War ethnographic studies to focus on a transforming spatiality of sectarianism by Joseph (1975) and Khuri (1975) differed in their reading of the spatiality and politics of sectarian affiliation, they both indicated that economic marginalization need not necessarily imply social and political disintegration.[96] Given the central role of familial ties and connections in structuring economic opportunities, the IRFED study's recommendations respond to the sharp geographic inequalities between city and countryside, but also reflect an underlying belief in the moral gains of village life that affirms a gendered social order.

The IRFED study produced quantitative data at a steady pace, and although the IRFED team published an atlas of Lebanon in 1964, *Besoins et Possibilités* contains far more statistical charts and graphs than conventional maps. Unlike the persuasive power of an idealized futurity often associated with urban plans, in this particular moment the numerical mapping of society and economy became integral to establishing the basic snapshot on which its recommendations were based. For example, numerical tables estimating rural/urban demographic ratios were used to illustrate an unequal relationship between Beirut and other regions in the country, or comparative rates of building permits issued in the preceding decade in Beirut and Tripoli. The study's emergency plan focused on rural areas, particularly those in South Lebanon, a region historically marginalized by the Beiruti domination of national politics. Although the IRFED doctrine emphasized a comprehensive approach to national planning, the project never issued a master plan or proposal for Beirut as such. Instead, the published recommendations consist of a summary of local and regional initiatives dispersed throughout the country. This emphasis on the social unit of the local community reflects IRFED's aim of working in both top-down and bottom-up modalities.[97] These recommendations were met with heavy criticism by local architects, urbanists, economists, and Beiruti elites.[98] For example, the political economist Georges Corm would begin his career with a critique of state-led planning in the mold of IRFED.[99]

Unlike IRFED, Écochard had long-standing connections to local professional organizations and elites. The ideas underpinning his functionalist approach to planning were couched in a language that was familiar to the profession and those interests that paid attention to it. Écochard met Chehab in the late 1950s and 1960s in the course of working on commissions for master plans for the municipalities of Byblos, Jounieh, and Sidon.[100] He had of course also worked on master plans for Beirut during the Mandate. In 1961 Écochard was commissioned to develop a plan for a new administrative center to the south of Beirut to serve as a new seat of government, an idea recommended by the Doxiadis study.[101]

Écochard came back with recommendations that went far beyond this initial brief, putting forward a comprehensive plan for Beirut, its expanding periphery, and the surrounding region. Écochard's recommendations included a reorganization of traffic flow into and out of the city and a comprehensive zoning plan detailing maximum building height and square footage per apartment on a neighborhood-by-neighborhood basis. Even more importantly, and unlike IRFED, the plan included a detailed set of recommendations about how to deal with the growth of the so-called misery belt along Beirut's southern suburbs. The plan included a map illustrating demography by zone, which regulated for future density according to zoned use (leisure, residential, industrial, varieties of mixed-use) using functionalist criteria, and sought to increase the total amount of green space in the city. The new highway plan, which included an illustration presenting proposed vectors of movement with graphic arrows for explanatory purposes, would shift the flow of traffic away from the city center, linking Beirut to a regional circulation plan accommodating the coastal highway system. Écochard saw cars as a dehumanizing force invading the city, and sought to safeguard the urban fabric from increased automobile congestion by shifting it away from heavily pedestrian areas.[102] Calibrating the correct ratio of human and car density seems, in these images, to indicate a sense of the city itself as a configurable machine, echoing the perspective of the CIAM school as adapted to a city in the Global South.[103]

The bitterness surrounding the plan's public contestation, and the piecemeal way in which it was adopted and implemented, marked a major turning point in the planning of Beirut. Écochard and IRFED may have represented two different approaches to development, and two different ways of conceiving, knowing, and representing urban space, but they shared a common fate in that both plans were stymied. Écochard's plan hinged on its proposed zoning mechanics to achieve many of its key outcomes, and to function as a comprehensive and unified plan for Beirut. However, the proposed maximum building densities and minimum sizes for plots of land ran afoul of real estate interests with plans of their own. The plan also became part of a sectarian contestation in neighborhoods such as Chiyah, where some Christian parties wanted lower land values to secure lower- and middle-income Christian residents in the area against the perceived demographic threat of recently arrived Shi'ite Muslims.[104] The plan that was finally approved and implemented in 1964 stripped the study's more comprehensive recommendations down to a zoning plan only loosely related to the original (see figure 1.8). It disregarded the proposed creation of new administrative centers, greatly increased the allowed building densities, altered its mixed-use specifications, and generally flattened the plan's nuances to a series of concentric rings emanating from the historic city center. This so incensed Écochard that he publicly and angrily disassociated himself from it. Despite his vehement denunciation of the plan that was passed, it continues to be commonly referred to as the Écochard

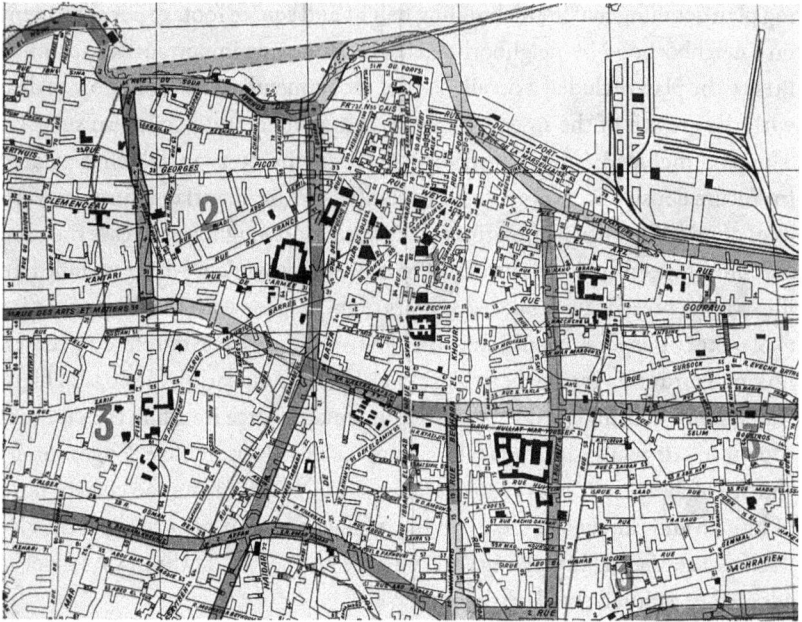

Figure 1.8 Final zoning in the modified Écochard Plan, 1964. Photo courtesy of Belal Hibri (2010).

plan to this day. Technical representations of the city can and do escape the intentions of their creators when they enter into the bureaucratic life of approvals and rejections.

The private interests that remade urban planning in the Chehab era also ultimately undid the Chehab presidency. Chehab's opponents included prominent Beiruti families, and in terms of urban planning, perhaps most vocal were Henri Eddé (related to a former president) and Assem Salaam (related to the country's first prime minister). Eddé and Salaam went on to have long careers as public commentators on matters related to urban planning and architectural preservation, particularly in the post–Civil War period discussed in the following chapter. Chehab was also widely criticized for the creation of the infamous Deuxième Bureau (of Investigation), whose politically independent status led to accusations of a lack of accountability.[105]

The last officially approved comprehensive zoning plan for all of Beirut reflects priorities that suggest that the interests of real estate speculation had the last word. The plan allowed continued industrial and slum growth in the city's southern suburbs while neglecting infrastructural investment. It also gave little provision for the Palestinian refugee camps established nearly two decades earlier, which had lasted for all but five years of the official existence of an independent Lebanese state. The effects of power can be felt in the capacity to foster some lifeworlds while excluding others—or in cities like Beirut, in how it only ever incompletely addresses some spaces, an infrastructural condition also found in other cities in the Global South.[106] The afterlife of the Écochard plan in contemporary Beirut is not always found in the enactment of its prescriptions, but in the negative traces of a "ghost infrastructure" with a legal basis that never materializes—such as in building codes that were enforced in anticipation of a state appropriation-to-come for a new road grid and peripheral highway that, five decades later, remains an unappropriated but perceptible gap in the urban fabric.[107]

The first decades after independence saw the deepening of a process in which the transformation of spaces of the city was premised on visualization, but this period was also marked by a widening of the distance between plans on paper and the city proper. The direction of this equation would be reversed during the Civil War, where early preparations for reconstruction sought to reshape the city in anticipation of maps and urban plans to come (a temporal reversal of the relationship between map and city that will be more fully explored in the following chapter), and the contestation and partial collapse of the state would make municipal map archives a valuable resource for the militias that periodically assumed control of different parts of the city after 1975.

The 1960s—so often referred to nostalgically as the "Golden Years" of national economic prosperity—were also a defining decade for growing inequality and the foiling of planning and development projects. Outside of the rarified spheres of government ministries and planning debates, a different sort of map of Beirut played an important role in the somewhat different visual domain of tourism in this period—meant to orient tourists within a city increasingly fashioned for automobile traffic and affluent international travelers.[108] The financial and real estate booms of this period were buoyed by the influx of petrodollars into Lebanese banks, but were also fueled by the articulation of the tourism industry with air travel. Tourist maps of Beirut intended for transnational circulation with airlines had abounded since at least the 1950s. The map in figure 1.9 was produced by Pan American Airways as part of a tourist pamphlet, and evokes the overlapping of the twentieth-century "golden eras" of both Beirut and jet travel. In addition to giving the location of Pan Am's landmark building in the city center, it also indicates the location of a number of bars, nightclubs, hotels, and other points of attraction for tourists of means. It is important to note that the nostalgic frame through which Beirut of this period is commonly remembered was one marked by distinct ways of circulating

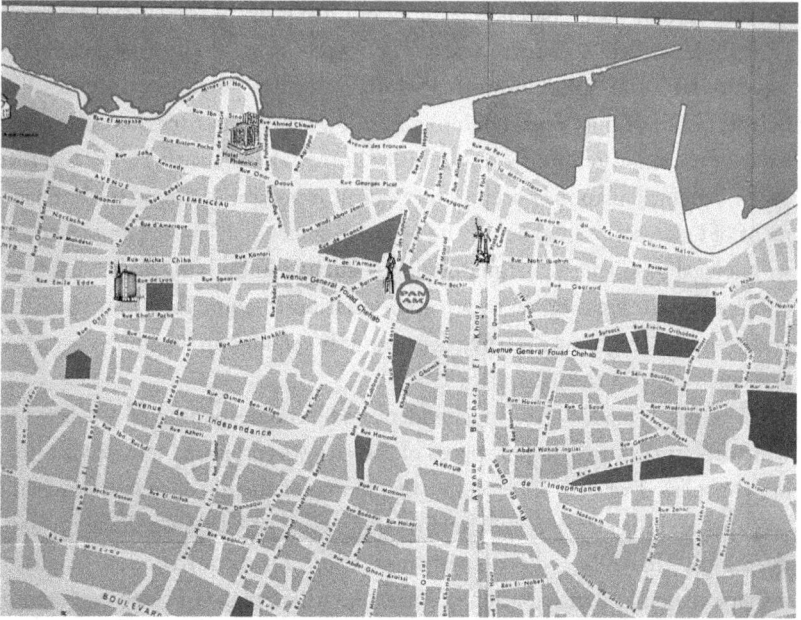

Figure 1.9 Pan American Airlines map, 1960s, exact date unknown. Photo courtesy of Belal Hibri (2010).

in and being oriented to the city—automobility linked to air travel, and the gaze motivated by leisure. Beirut came to echo in the imaginary of popular Egyptian cinema—such as the famous montage in the classic *My Father Is On the Tree* (1963), which even features a number of aerial shots of Beirut near St. George's Bay.

The aerial gaze, long an important facet of spatial imaginaries and cartographic technique, was one of several interlocking technological transformations that would shape the lives of maps of Beirut in the years to come. Chief among these long-term media historical trends were the automation and computerization of map-making and reproduction, the post–World War II quantitative revolution in cartography and geography, and the infusion of information theory, graphic design principles, and the psychology of perception into map design.[109] As the machinery (and later, information systems) required to produce maps by transferring details from aerial photos remained rather expensive, the maps that were updated utilizing these techniques were often based on those produced by the Lebanese military. Cold War aerial espionage efforts had already become fully entwined with mapping practice, even before the rise of routine satellite surveillance in the 1960s.[110]

CHAPTER ONE

The Civil War (1975–1991)

There is a common tendency to read the Civil War as the culminating episode in a long string of political failures. There is also a common tendency to critique mapping as ideology clothed in the positivist garb of neutral expertise. In this view, the colonizer and the colonial episteme draw lines on paper creating mis-formed nations and borders, in which territories fail to correspond to some more organic or cohesive collective. The dynamics of the post-colony are then described as a repetition of this original pattern, with little innovation. To the extent that this kind of argument becomes a bad habit or oversimplification, one might call it the Sykes-Picot over-read.[111] There is utility in describing messier complexities in shorthand form—and obviously, it is the violence undertaken to make reality conform to the map or plan that is actually at issue. However, this interpretation can lead to a problematic investment in the idea that a "truer" map would have been better, or could lead to a completable modern project based on ethno-national wholeness. The mismatch between cartographic representation and social realities is what is found to be at fault—a critical impulse that nominates a good object for analysis, but potentially limits our understanding of how exactly maps are or are not utilized in techniques of rule. The map is not the practices that create the territory, but the performance of the territory does often depend on a multitude of mapping practices, not all of which are about carving territorial borders.

In a similar vein, the Civil War has often been understood as having its origins in the supposed inevitability of violent conflict within multi-ethnic societies, and the ensuing violence as an expression of an atavistic return to primordial identities and religious passions that had always been lurking beneath a cosmopolitan veneer. Such thinking tends to obscure what tensions exist between specific maps and the actual territories they enumerate, the new entanglements of regional and superpower involvement in formerly colonized polities, and what is new about conflict over the nation-state. The official organs of the state are imagined as the only locus of sovereignty, obscuring other less official arrangements that may or may not be directly involved with state agencies.[112] Such thinking also tends to obscure the role of violence—particularly in its modern and infrastructural form—in producing and maintaining groups as distinct entities, but also the contingent and intertwined nature of such groups, particularly if ethno-religious belonging is thought to be the key point of differentiation.[113] It may simply be the case that modern European states (of which countries like Lebanon are thought to be failed copies) were founded on purifying violence either long since forgotten, or whose ongoing nature continues to be obscured or presented as an externality.

It would be truer to the lives of maps (at least in Beirut) to say that it is remarkable that the territory is ever made to resemble the map, which is not to say that the condition of mapping is not in need of explanation. Maps and mapping practices are better understood as traces of attempts by power to produce particular arrangements and relationships between the shape of the social and its underlying mobilities and modes circulation, and ways of relating to, understanding, and being in the space. Even when maps depict space in a totalizing mode, they are just as much the products of conflicts over space, and ways of seeing and knowing it, as the other way around. The valences of the Civil War would push this tension even further, as much of the violence was directed not just at human flesh, but at the material form of the city itself. Fregonese (2009) dubs this the "urbicide of Beirut," drawing critical attention to a type of violence directed at the level of urban space itself.[114] The geographic goals of militias during the war were many—tearing holes in buildings, securing spaces or rendering them uninhabitable, reshaping mobilities by establishing checkpoints and new urban borders, or shifting the terms of "co-habitability" divided along political and sectarian lines. Some militias also looted and destroyed government agencies and municipal archives to seize the maps they contained. Others acquired maps through contacts in the Lebanese military. Mapping can entail a kind of epistemic violence, but militias seized maps so as to improve their ability to deliver destruction of their own.

Examining the lives of maps of Beirut during the Civil War yields more insight into the relationship of techniques of visualization in attempts to generate knowledge of a city changed by the everydayness of war than into the impact of state agencies (largely non-functioning) on the space of the city. The few studies conducted in this period that generated maps shifted in focus from state-building and development from the years prior to damage assessment missions conducted during lulls in fighting. These studies were primarily framed in the language of a response to a national emergency, and were comparatively limited to plans for reconstruction. The two major efforts were the APUR (l'Atelier Parisien d'Urbanisme) study conducted during 1977–78, and the IAURIF (Institut d'aménagement et d'urbanisme de la région d'Île-de-France) study completed in 1986. Most of what is readily found of these studies in the archives in Beirut consists of the aerial photographs and photogrammetry charts that they produced. A final aerial damage assessment exercise was also conducted in 1991, after the end of the war.

The first, intense round of fighting began in 1975 and continued through the early part of 1977, after which a number of observers felt that there was a real possibility for a more lasting stability. In response to international donor pressure, Parliament formed the Council for Development and Reconstruction (CDR), and empowered it to bypass existing state bureaucracy so as to respond with urgency to the pressing matter of the damaged city. The CDR commissioned the French firm APUR to conduct a study and develop a reconstruction plan. The city's central district had been heavily damaged, and as the neighborhood was thought to symbolize damage to the possibility of future coexistence, it became the principal focus for reconstruction plans. Composite aerial photos were produced as part of this attempt to see the affected area, at a much smaller scale (1/500m). These were produced by the Lebanese state in support of the APUR study, to try to account for damage to individual buildings. However, not all damage to buildings can be usefully brought into evidence in this way. Militia violence, characterized primarily by gunfire and artillery shelling that often hits the sides of buildings, does not engage in the same vertical vector as aerial bombardment. As with cadastral and topographical mapping, precise accounting for damage to buildings and public space required additional on-the-ground surveying.

The plan that resulted from these studies was a combination of APUR's recommendations and the efforts of a local team composed of the Beirut governor and architects from the General Directorate of Urbanism (DGU).[115] It became the first legally approved reconstruction plan for Beirut, and took a conservationist approach geared toward returning the city center to its original function. The plan called for buildings to be restored rather than replaced wherever possible, and encouraged the return of the shops and businesses that had moved elsewhere. While the plan also detailed minor work to the transportation infrastructure of the area (meant to improve the flow of traffic around and into the city center), most state intervention was confined to the improvement of existing public space.[116] However, the political stability that enabled the study to be conducted was short-lived, and with the resumption of intense fighting, the plan quickly became a static record of the space in that one moment in time.

The episodic militia combat that occurred between 1978 and 1982 was bookended by intense Israeli incursions. The material and social fabric of the city went through massive transformation in this period. The so-called Green Line grew in these years, named for the vegetation that bloomed in the no-man's land of the central district dividing so-called (Christian) east and (Muslim) west Beirut. This line reflected the hardening divisions between neighborhoods, many of which also became less internally ethno-religiously mixed. The physical destruction of the city became much more widespread in this period, and included several rounds of sustained aerial bombardment by an Israeli military intent on ousting the PLO, as well the effects of a lack of systematic maintenance even in those areas not directly impacted.

The PLO and the IDF were by no means the only foreign actors in Lebanon at the time, and one can only speculate as to the true extent to which foreign agencies mapped Beirut during this particular stretch of the Civil War. For example, even though I found none of its maps in the archives I visited, Syria established a sizable military and secret intelligence network after 1982, under the pretext of maintaining stability. The Syrian presence would remain a fact of life until 2005, having received quiet approval from the United States to do so for its cooperative involvement in the first Iraq War in 1990. I did come across one US map in the archives in Beirut dating to this time—a copy of a Defense Mapping Agency map, updated in 1983 from a version originally drafted in 1978, tucked away in the IFPO cartothèque (figure 1.10). Many maps owe their continued existence to the enterprising efforts of archivists who track them down and give them a home. The continued presence of this map is emblematic of the infidelity of such documents to the intentions of those who create them. The map was printed with the instructions "Distribution limited—destroy when no longer needed," and has handwritten notes indicating what must have been locations of strategic importance—"located objects" and such. The suicide bombing of the US embassy and Marine barracks in April and October had also taken place in 1983. US forces had been stationed in Lebanon to help "stabilize" the situation following the Israeli invasion of 1982, in which the IDF had supported and orchestrated the massacre of thousands of Palestinians at the Sabra and Shatila camps by the Lebanese Phalangist militia, with US knowledge and tacit approval.[117] Neither camp appears on the Defense Mapping Agency map, although they were later targeted (along with a number of predominantly Shi'ite informal neighborhoods) for what can only euphemistically be referred to as "improvement" by Amin Gemayel, the far right Christian militia leader who assumed the presidency in 1982.[118] The exceptional powers granted to the DGU—justified by the external pressures for efficiency by international donors—had quickly turned into a legal form of population management and transfer.

The United States' partisan involvement had the inadvertent effect of making it into a target. The subsequent attack on the embassy and Marine barracks in 1983 (likely by actors affiliated with groups that were the predecessors to Hizbullah) led to an official withdrawal of the international peacekeeping force in February 1984, a withdrawal that involved no small amount

LEBANON CITY GRAPHIC 1:12,500

BAYRŪT

MEDITERRANEAN SEA

= CROSSINGS
1 PORT
2 RING
3 SODICO
4 MUSEUM
5 TAYOUNI CIRCLE
6 GALERIE SEMAN
7 HADATH-NAAATII
8 ASSAS MASALTON OF MILITARY

Figure 1.10 US Defense Mapping Agency map, with handwritten notes, 1983. Photo courtesy of Belal Hibri (2010).

of naval shelling.[119] Going by the drafting style, this Defense Mapping Agency map also seems to be the one utilized in Rayyane Tabet's artwork *How to Play Beirut*, which speculates as to the college "beer pong" drinking game that emerged in the early 1980s. While it is difficult to pinpoint the game's exact origin, the name seems to have stemmed from a bad pun on "getting bombed," reflecting the place of Beirut in popular imaginaries in the US at the time. The artwork consists of a brochure that includes a reproduction of this map, and a set of instructions on how to play the game.

Government officials took the lull in fighting in 1983 as a second opportunity to restart planning efforts for postwar recovery. A new French consultancy firm, IAURIF, was commissioned by then-President Gemayel to assist with the project. The study wouldn't be completed until 1986, and unlike the APUR study, aimed at a far more comprehensive reworking of the city and its suburbs. The IAURIF plan reflected a growing consensus that the city center would be central to Beirut's (and therefore Lebanon's) eventual reconstruction, a sentiment echoed in the publication of the book *Beirut of Tomorrow* (1983), based on a symposium organized by the American University of Beirut and the Goethe Institute. The IAURIF plan redefined the contours of the city to reflect an even balance of Christians and Muslims, based on a demographic survey conducted in this period.[120] It sought to connect the new centers of neighborhood life that had emerged within the war's modes of circulation to the city center. These were the predominantly Maronite areas of Nahr al Mawt and Hazmiyeh, the predominantly Druze Laylakeh, and predominantly Shi'ite Khaldeh. In truth, it is the activity of war and its informal policies that produce or encourage such segregation. The return to centralization was actually a confirmation of the new spatiality of ethno-religious neighborhood makeup, which became baked into plans for reconstruction even at this early stage. It was also in this period that Saudi Oger, the contracting firm that had brought billions to its owner Rafiq Hariri in Saudi Arabia, became personally involved with the question of what to do with Beirut's city center. As will be explored in greater detail in the following chapter, Oger was paid millions of dollars for demolition work in the city center. Significant portions of the city center were cleared during the war itself, in anticipation of future planning.

Conclusion

The Civil War was brought to a formal close in 1989 by the Taif Agreement, in no small part facilitated by Hariri. The agreement established a power-sharing arrangement in which a new balance of sectarian powers would be established,

Figure 1.11 Aerial photograph from damage assessment study, 1991. Photo courtesy of Bela Hibri (2010).

but leaving political sectarianism itself strengthened. All groups were to disarm save for Hizbullah, which was given official recognition by the Lebanese government as a resistance movement aimed at ending the ongoing Israeli occupation—the two countries remained officially at war. Hostilities wouldn't really wind down until the end of 1990. In 1991 a final round of damage assessment was made, in preparation for a planning effort whose reshaping of the city would be a significant break from the previous decades.

The aerial photograph in figure 1.11 was taken during this final round of damage assessment. Part of what is striking about aerial photographs such as these is the unresolvable tension that they hold, suspended in a middle point between the act of technical observation of a space, and the acts of shaping it that they support. The city below remains still and unchanged, or to put it

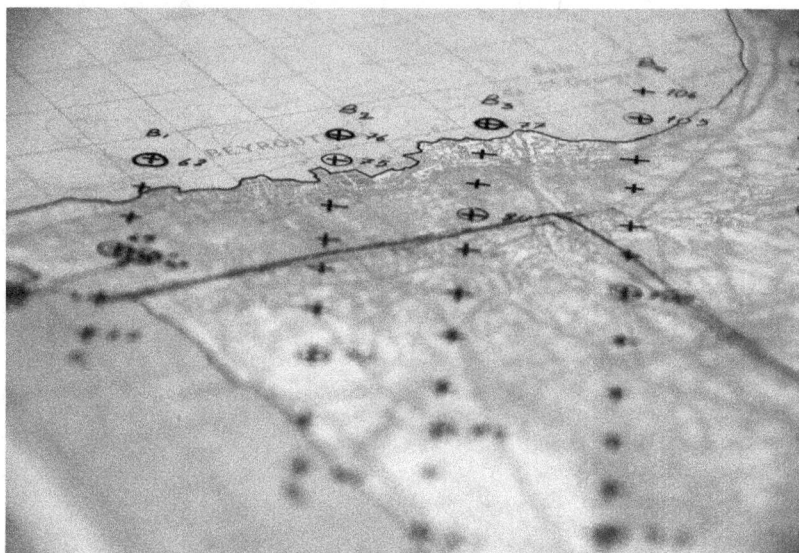

Figure 1.12 Photogrammetric key pinpointing location of figure 1.11, 1991. Photo courtesy of Belal Hibri (2010).

more accurately via Benjamin's sense of the dialectical image, there is a "then" that is a part of the "now" that is legible in such photographs of the city.[121] The photogrammetric key (figure 1.12) indicates the series of flyovers and the corresponding locations of specific shots. The photogrammetric key is of particular importance—the exact location from which each photograph was taken can be established by working back from the timestamp and the speed of the plane indicated on the photograph itself. Each point is then marked on a thin sheet of wax paper placed on top of a map of the city. In this case, the map is a 1/50,000m city map of Beirut drawn up by the French military in 1940, and subsequently revised by the Lebanese Armed Forces in 1960, reflecting the continuities and discontinuities of the practices of mapping the city.

The layering of the marked-up wax sheet on top of the map presents information as a series of overlapping, selectable layers—a process that had already become automated by the computerization of cartographic practice, and which became more widespread in the 1990s with the commercial and industrial popularization of geographic information systems (GIS). It is also remarkable that the image is an aerial photograph, reflecting a reconnaissance model of knowledge production, implying an individual and targeted action taken at a specific point in time, and a potentially large but finite series of images. The model of a constant and frequently updated stream of images produced by satellite remote sensing in the years to come would imply a very different spatial sensibility, and required not just the automation of map production but also the computerization of processing, storage, and organization of quantifiable geographic data. The postwar period had a particular appetite for technologies promising a live and direct relationship between knowing and shaping space—for infrastructures that would remake the city. While maps of Beirut would continue to play an important role in both public discussions of space and governmental techniques, maps are not a necessary visual output of digital cartography. Maps of Beirut in Beirut were given a new home, in databases that increasingly were privately owned and aimed at isolated projects, whose greater logic was the cantonization of the postwar landscape. The paper map and aerial photograph acquire the status of an artifact in media historical hindsight, making it almost too easy to project onto them the status of a bygone era in which it seemed possible to address the problems of the city as a collective.

This chapter has shown how images of the city—particularly maps, aerial photographs, and urban plans—became important to regimes of power that sought to shape the city. The genealogy of these images reflects the shifting priorities, techniques, and aims of governmental practice, which were defined by key continuities (in both form and personnel) between the colonial and post-colonial periods. In many instances, the lives of these maps demonstrate that visualizing the space so as to manage it did not always lead to guaranteed outcomes. It is important to note that many of these techniques held site-specificity as an important virtue, despite relying on visual perspectives that seemed to absent situated knowledge. It is also important to note that the advent of the verticality of the aerial gaze deployed to contend with guerrilla activity led to an early instance of concealment—which I discuss in greater depth in chapter 3. As the Civil War came to a close, the contradictions of imbuing media technology and images with the power to shape space would only deepen.

2

Images of Before/After in the Economy of Postwar Construction

> With the destabilization of the market economy, we begin to recognize the monuments of the bourgeoisie as ruins even before they have crumbled.
>
> —Walter Benjamin, *The Arcades Project* (1999, 13)

In 1990 Beirut's city center was badly damaged. The area had been a battleground marking the line between so-called east and west Beirut, the remainders of the Civil War between structures in various states of damage and disrepair. A decade later, the area had been transformed into what at the time was one of the largest privately operated real estate ventures in the Middle East. The project was and is managed by a company named Solidere, an acronym for Société Libanaise pour le Développement et la Reconstruction de Beyrouth (Lebanese Company for the Development and Reconstruction of Beirut), and a play on the French word for solidarity. The entire space was consolidated, framed as an opportunity for global investment, and turned into a financially lucrative elite venture. The decade and a half that followed on the end of the Civil War and the Cold War was defined by the deepening of local political fragmentation in tandem with regional conflict. This period was also marked by the proliferation of a type of image of a very particular temporality, in which scenes of destruction are contrasted with imagined or actual construction and repair. Images of before/after—which saturated billboards, television,

Figure 2.1 Ongoing construction with rubble and an after image on a billboard. Photo courtesy of Kirsten Scheid (ca. 1993).

film, magazines, and public discourse in Lebanon in the years after the Civil War—articulate an imaginary that has fueled the political economy of postwar construction.

The creation and circulation of these images of before/after was an important part of the forging of new circuitries of financial investment—a rarified social context where they did some of their most important work. Displaying images of the city without traces of destruction became an important practice for postwar economic recovery. Examining the variations of the before/after image mobilized by the Solidere project thus enables a critical diagnosis of how urban space, media technology, and global finance were brought together, both in Beirut in particular and in the roaring 1990s more generally. These images also reflect the postwar infrastructural imaginary, and the act of circulating them was a key part in the production of a fragmented urban and political landscape.

This chapter centers on Solidere, but it would be erroneous to equate Solidere with the whole of Beirut, or to attempt to read the spatial and economic tensions that define the city through it. To do so would be to fundamentally misread the unevenness and heterogeneity of the city, as well as the other nodes of social life within and beyond it. As a generation of scholarship has shown, the production of the spaces of Beirut cannot be gleaned from just this one project, as it is merely one part of a broader dynamic.[1] It would also be a mistake to retain a Beirut-centric optic, as this would naturalize the uneven process whereby the capital becomes a national center, and flatten its relations with other internal centers and peripheries.[2] Solidere was not the only state-sanctioned private construction project in the city, even if it did seek to occupy an outsized role in the postwar national imaginary.[3] However, focusing on the Solidere project is useful for how it dramatizes a set of visual contradictions internal to early 1990s-era neoliberal market urbanism and post-conflict societies in general, and for how it allows us to situate the image of Beirut in regional and global topologies. Yet this project is not reducible to the ideologies of neoliberal fantasists, even if it did draw inspiration from them. The company instantiated a process wherein rubble was made legible to company ledgers, and then transformed into money. The transformation of "non-productive" urban space into an investment opportunity depended on two types of imaging practice—visualization of the space so as to render it amenable to management systems, and the circulation of images of the space to potential investors and the public at large. Rubble, management, money— the diagram of Solidere. A system for increasing value that requires the whole of the space to be greater than the sum of its parts, a trick of addition multiplied by the passage of time.

Schemes to make profit from urban destruction deepened the already fraught politics of postwar memory. Indeed, fears that the nation would forget the war or fail to learn its "lessons" loomed large for many.[4] Although place and the city had featured in narratives concerning the nation in the decades before the Civil War, memory became an overtly vexed topic in 1990s Beirut.[5] Reflecting on ruins (buildings or objects) and ruination (a historical process) is of course a practice with deep roots in the modern tradition, and one that has been fruitfully examined in a number of interdisciplinary conversations.[6] Yet not all buildings and places that age, or that take damage directly from war or indirectly from the disrepair that it creates, are equally valued. The meaning of damage is something actively forged and negotiated, even made a part of the everyday. Following Gordillo (2014), describing old, crumbling, or damaged buildings and places as rubble allows a careful parsing of the tension between the social worlds that emerge after the destruction of space, and the modernist fetishization of ruins and fascination with ruin-gazing. It also allows a critical perspective on how capital values rubble and ruins differently. Beirut retains rubble and damaged buildings at its core, even if those cores are multiple, and the wars that produced them are unevenly remembered.[7] The before/after image can take a number of media forms, and played a crucial role in defining what buildings would count as unvaluable rubble and therefore would need to be cleared. The violent transformations that followed were a reorientation of how the space was typically shown and seen as well as a reorientation to how it would change over time. It is precisely the temporality of images of the city that need to be carefully parsed.

The Downtown or "Central District" of Beirut (as it was renamed) was not rebuilt after the end of the Lebanese Civil War in 1990. This is not to say that laws were not passed, schematics were not drawn, buildings were not built, and money was not invested—all of these things certainly occurred. There are two main reasons that make the idea that Downtown Beirut was "rebuilt" problematic if not incoherent. The first is the periodization introduced by the prefix "re-" in the words rebuilt, reconstructed, recovering, and other similar terms that are often used to describe the subject. Discussion of re-construction emphasizes a *discontinuity* between the formal commencement of Solidere's activities and the destruction of the Civil War, rather than its structural relation to it. As far as is credibly known, neither Solidere nor its predecessors were in any way directly involved in the militia violence of that period. However, the systematic clearing of buildings had been happening in the Downtown district as early as 1983. Oger Liban, the Lebanese branch of Rafiq Hariri's regional contracting firm, was hired for the task in a lull in fighting between 1983 and the beginning of 1985.[8] But the total rate of destruction of buildings actually escalated dramatically *after* the end of hostilities—if a third of the structures in the area were irreparably damaged by war and the neglect that it causes, then by 1993, that number had risen to 80 percent.[9] To look back at rubble is productive because of the negative relation to space that is implied—the present space is actually rubble.[10] To stand the ontology of "reconstruction" on its feet, the removal of rubble should be understood as being fundamentally continuous with the destruction of the war, and historically coterminous with the activity of construction. Solidere is a mechanism that generates and monetizes the difference between unvaluable versus venerable ruins and other forms of "heritage." It emerges from and extends the political sphere created by the war.

The second reason that the various combinations of "re-Beirut" are problematic is how they imply a definite end to the construction activities and financial and legal exceptionalities that formally began with Solidere's incorporation in 1994, and presumably will end with the completion of the project specified. However, the assemblage of technical systems, urban plans, economic models, and rubble located in Downtown are best comprehended as temporally and spatially open-ended. The idea of reconstruction is presumed on a "homogeneous empty time" in which capitalist miracles will fix the city and move history forward—often presented as a move away from the "non-Western," and the Civil War as a deviation from historical progress rather than its outcome.[11] The project is temporally open-ended in that the historic vista it occupies assumes that no past is relevant that cannot be capitalized on. Although the project itself has a formal completion date, the guiding mechanism by which economic value is created depends on a limitless future into which value will increase. The project is spatially open-ended in that while the site is located in one part of Beirut, the circulation of images and money it is premised on fostering are (theoretically) global in scope. It is also spatially open-ended in that Solidere has now diversified regionally, bringing its expertise to projects in Amman, Cairo, and the UAE. The company's slogan has changed accordingly, from "Beirut: Ancient City for the Future" in the early 1990s to the less site-specific (if more ominous) "Spaces for Life" in the early 2010s.

In this chapter I interrogate how the visual forms that animate the Solidere project were stitched into the urban fabric. Solidere demonstrates how the political, institutional, and infrastructural reorganization of the city in this period depended on a reorganization of ways of seeing that have since become ubiquitous and diffuse. The chapter is divided into three sections. In the section that follows, I investigate the context that conditioned the emergence of Solidere, and how the linkage between rubble-management-money was created. This first section examines the political and legal exceptionalities that defined the company, the two primary master plans that it released, and the public debates that ensued. The specificities of Solidere in Beirut lend insight into the work of images in attracting financial investment and affective attachment, if indeed these two dimensions are actually separate.[12] If the first section examines how the diagram emerged and how it functions, the second section turns to the visual forms that fuel it. Examining the variations of the before/after image brings into focus their implied ideal viewer, a problematic figure I call a *citizen-investor*. This figure is a native of Benjamin's dream world of capitalist progress as it came to be at the end of the Cold War and the global ascendance of neoliberalism.[13] The citizen-investor is a positionality just unmarked enough to allow for a wide range of identifications, but is constitutively bound up with a possessive relationship to the potential future earnings that can be made from manipulating urban form. You don't have to be a wealthy Lebanese man to buy in, but the citizen-investor is a way of imagining the self in a relationship to the spaces of Beirut (or images of it) that is defined by control, and ultimately reinscribes the patriarchal order that underpins the Lebanese economy and citizenship.

If the first two sections examine the role of images in the forging of a political economic order, the last section concludes by examining how those same images unravel it. Rancière reminds us that consensus is always both highly policed and contested. The political cantonization that defined the postwar period in Lebanon faltered in the mid-2000s following the killing of Rafiq Hariri on February 14, 2005. I also examine how Hariri memorialization in Beirut, as a spatial and visual phenomenon, reflected an increasingly polarized and fragmented urban fabric. The conclusion of this chapter interrogates an ontological instability in images of before/after, which present the duration of ruins and a foreclosed future in terms that make them increasingly difficult to differentiate.

As a great deal of the images and imaging processes analyzed here are a part of systems of control, a final note on sources is in order. Solidere believes that images of the results of its efforts are of great commercial value, and so requires official photography to be licensed.[14] The tight security in the area, run by the state near government buildings and private firms in the rest of the district, has only increased from the late 1990s and into the era of smartphones. As my primary concern is with images that were already public, this chapter only occasionally discusses images taken of the space before or during construction.

The Birth of Solidere

Solidere is primarily a system that generates profit by establishing and managing the interface between urban space, technologies of control, and financial circulation. More specifically, one might say it is a model for connecting rubble to global capital. The creation of the company both made the task of ameliorating the condition of the city center into a private real estate venture and ensured that the state itself would not be able to develop the institutional capacity to do so. The political system, financial investment, and novel legal frameworks that had to be put into place to make this possible were considerable. Between the Taif Agreement that brought the Civil War to an official end in 1989 and Solidere's incorporation in May 1994, a major political and discursive realignment fundamentally shaped the consensus being built. It involved the ascendance of Hariri as an intermediary between the local power structures of warlords and elites, his Saudi backers, and the Syrian presence.[15] The formation of this nominal consensus is visible in the debates that followed the public release of the Eddé and Gavin plans, named for their chief designers.

In December 1991, the standing Lebanese Parliament passed Law 117, which established the nominally legal basis for a private company to assume ownership of and construction on almost all of the land in the city center.[16] A little more than a year earlier, Fadel El Shalaq, the former head of Oger Liban, was appointed head of the Council for Development and Reconstruction (CDR), the state agency specially created to deal with the destruction of the first rounds of the Civil War discussed in the previous chapter. This move of a powerful member of industry into the leadership of a state agency meant to regulate it is a familiar one. Law 117 did not specify Solidere in particular, nor did it approve the nature of the master plan it would implement, but it did build on the idea that the existing state bureaucracy was so inefficient as to be unequal to the task at hand.[17] The CDR also came with the advantage of not having to submit its budget to Parliament for approval, shielding it even further from oversight or scrutiny. The course of events that followed from this legal exceptionality to the master plan that Solidere implemented is telling in retrospect, as the intensity of public debate that existed in this earlier period may seem distant from the polished but typically empty streets and boulevards of the first two decades of the new millennium.

Solidere has often been understood in terms of its efficacy, or in terms of the changes it effects on the makeup of the city. This is true of public and sometimes scholarly praise and critique of the project. Some of the most incisive of these public critiques linked the affective disjuncture of places damaged by the war or destroyed by demolition to a sense of futility, of lost hope for their "true" recovery. The more radical side of the public discourse in the early 1990s questioned the terms of the project itself, and instead asked what kind of city Beirut should be as a whole.[18] In fact, there was tremendous outcry against the two plans drafted for the area that were released to the public. The voices that were raised for and against the project were trenchant and passionate, and varied in kind as widely as there were investments in (and experiences and memories of) that part of the city. A senior editor at a major Lebanese newspaper in this period once said to me that for a good part of the 1990s, the reconstruction project and Solidere weren't just news, they were *the* news.[19] Opinion came from concerned citizens in general, property holders in the designated area, the political establishment, and concerned professionals (particularly architects, economists, journalists, and archaeologists). Many even contested the legality of the transfer of ownership of land.[20]

The idea of "Downtown Beirut," one of the terms used by the company and popularly to refer to the area, is a slippery one.[21] The space was actually formed by consolidating a number of older neighborhoods into the project, such as Minet El Hosn, Saifi, and Bab Idriss. Many people old enough to remember the different neighborhoods that were eventually absorbed by the Solidere

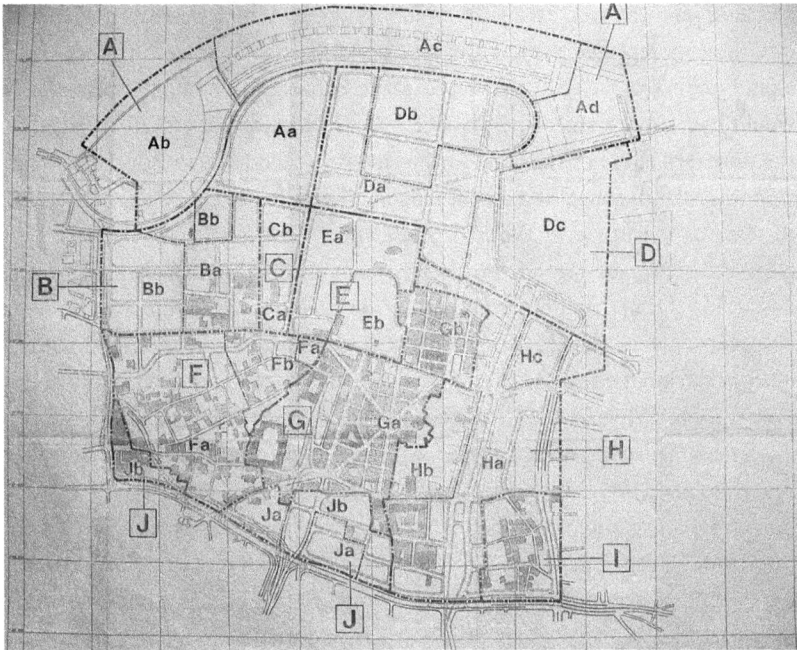

Figure 2.2 Beirut municipal zoning plan of the Solidere project, ca. 1994.

project often fondly recalled those spaces as symbols of prewar Beirut.[22] Large
sections of other nearby neighborhoods were incorporated into its area or razed
to make way for the widened ring road surrounding it, especially from Zokak
El Blat just south and Gemmayzeh to its east. Neighborhoods of course are by
no means homogeneous places,[23] but in practice the demolition of old buildings
was widely experienced by local residents and others as excessive, precipitating
further public outrage.

The first comprehensive postwar plan for reconstruction of the city center was drawn up by the multinational Lebanese architecture and engineering
firm Dar Al Handasah in 1991, some three years prior to the incorporation of
Solidere. Hariri, who had vested interest in the firm, personally commissioned
the plan. Dar Al Handasah had grown during the oil-boom years into what in
the early 1990s was one of the largest firms in the Arab world. The plan was
designed by Henri Eddé, a partner in the firm and a public figure known for
an outspoken Francophilia, and whose family had a history in the political
arena. What came to be known as the Eddé plan took the French colonial spatial sensibility embodied in the Place de l'Étoile and expanded it to the entire
area. The plan also greatly increased the architectural and urban scale of the

space. In addition to creating roundabouts and widening boulevards through-out, the plan replaced the historic Martyrs' Square with a tree-lined boulevard eighty meters wide, a full ten meters greater than the Champs-Elysées. It also would have transformed the massive makeshift landfill that had emerged on the northern shore of the area during the war (called Normandy) into a free-standing island, zoned as a new financial district featuring two towers meant to serve as Beirut's own World Trade Center. The plan spoke primarily the glass-and-steel language of the skyscrapers and buildings of the High Mod-ern period, framed by numerous large circular fountains. These were to be set along a totally new street plan, disconnected from what had been there previ-ously and from the rest of the city. The plan called for the demolition of nearly every building that had survived the war.

The images accompanying the Eddé plan suggest an elaborate staging of a space designed to be reassuringly familiar to an imagined gaze coded as West-ern.[24] The illustrations accompanying the plan depict scenes of seemingly un-interruptable leisure amid buildings that make no reference to either the city they would be a part of or the ones they would have replaced. The plan seemed to equate clearing any trace of the war with erasing that which it considered to be too local to be desirable. It replaced what was there before with a sense of blank neutrality, freed of problematic differences or political conflict, with the circulation of money and the pursuit of pleasure as the sole guiding principles. In other words, a space made ready to receive the spirit of the "end of history" discourse of the time, characterized by frictionless biopolitical (self-)manage-ment in tight accordance with market principles, with a dash of colonial nos-talgia thrown in for good measure.

Plans are futurologies as much as they aid in precipitating one particular future. They also often pull their critics into their discursive orbit as skeptics, making it so the plan and its debunking become the subject of discussion and crowding out other possible discussions. Eddé's proposal was panned by many of his colleagues, but perhaps none were as vocal as the architects and urbanists Nabil Beyhum, Assem Salaam, and Jad Tabet, who had worked in a similar mi-lieu since the days of Écochard. They attacked his plan on aesthetic and formal grounds in news articles, books, and public meetings. They roundly critiqued what they saw as an unnecessarily spectacular style disconnected from the ar-chitectural history of the city. They also criticized the street plan for isolating the area within a ring road, and failing to establish a relationship to the flow of car or foot traffic through the rest of the city and favoring an "inhuman" scale.[25]

Eddé ended up having to defend the plan in the public arena. He argued that his plan would return the city to its "rightful place" as a "cultural crossroads" in the region and even the world. Other proponents of the plan argued for it on different grounds. Fadel El Shalaq, then head of the CDR, made a case for the plan in terms of the urgency of the need of reconstruction, writing that "if we don't reconstruct the city center, it will turn into a bomb, preventing us from saying the war is over,"[26] a very deliberate choice of words. This justification was one frequently given—that the need for expedited action meant there was little time or space for debate as to the nature of the area-to-be. This urgency was also frequently described in a biological idiom—El Shalaq would later comment that bringing the commercial center "back to life" was equal to the social importance of the task, and even key to reviving the Lebanese economy as a whole.[27] Arguments for and against, coming from multiple angles, continued through the passage of the special law at the end of the year that effectively made the project a private endeavor. This equation of the recovery of the city center with that of the rest of Beirut and therefore the country as a whole was not new.[28] However, equating the social management of the nation with the economic reorganization of urban form draws a different sort of link between peace, construction, and expertise.[29] The remaking and management of social ills through a market economy have often been grasped as a security operation[30]—the health and life of the city are cast as being under threat by an impending bomb detonation that only private interests can defuse.

After the end of the Civil War, the targeting of the urban landscape by explosives shifted from militia and military fire to that of construction, so as to undo the threat that the landscape itself is imagined to pose to the nation. Demolition of the city center began anew and in earnest early in 1992. The demolition continued without reference to any specific plan, much less one established within even the exceptionally fluid legalities of the time.[31] The deliberate use of over-powered explosives on the buildings targeted caused further damage to other nearby structures, necessitating their demolition in turn. At the end of April 1992, a group who called themselves "The Friends of Rights in the City Center" invited the backers of the plan and Eddé by name to a public forum via an announcement in *Annahar*, the renowned Lebanese newspaper. The organization claimed that since they (mainly property owners and tenants) were the ones most immediately affected by any potential plan, they were among those most concerned with the fate of the city center. The meeting held a series of panels on topics ranging from architecture and aesthetics to the social and economic impact on ownership rights. The meeting issued an explicit call to halt any further demolition until a plan had been approved by democratic process.

Even the sanctity of the institution of private property seems to be relative to which political topology that property resides in. The legal concept of eminent domain is usually imagined as being an exception in which the liberal state can only assume control of land in the name of the public interest after compensating its owners at fair market value. In a country where inheritance laws are regulated by patriarchal personal status laws established under the jurisdiction of religious institutions, even this would function to deepen the inequalities of gendered citizenship.[32] In the case of Solidere, private property was technically seized by the state on behalf of a private company it charged with its management and development, a move whose constitutional basis was frequently disputed.[33] Solidere's articles of incorporation were approved in July 1992, with a Board of Founders primarily composed of Hariri's personal associates. This all transpired within the context of what can only be described as a private takeover of the state itself, orchestrated by Hariri. The purchase of the standing government happened so openly that the exact sums paid to specific politicians and MPs at times became the subject of public discussion.[34] Rather than privatizing state assets—the move frequently equated with neoliberalism—the state itself was captured. The existing Beiruti elite was initially skeptical of Hariri as an outsider and member of a newly wealthy class who made their fortunes in the Gulf. The billionaire gradually shored up his place with the lubricating effect of money and the promise of its continued future flow.[35]

Less than a year after Hariri's election to the position of prime minister in 1992 and just a few months after the outgoing Parliament approved a new master plan for the city (not publicly released for a few months), some of the greatest destruction of the city on record took place—far more than the physical toll of the Civil War. Yet it would be a mistake to conceive of the project as only coterminous with the war at the level of the economic productivity of destruction. The political form of the project as whole built fragmentation, legal exception, and economic exclusion into the urban landscape.[36] This principle would eventually become a more diffuse practice, taking the shape of informal and exceptional allowances made for high-end and high-rise projects throughout the city.[37]

Hariri commissioned a new plan from Dar Al Handasah later in 1993 developed by the urbanist Angus Gavin, who would continue to work at Solidere in various capacities for many years. The Gavin plan differed from the Eddé plan in a few key ways, but especially in terms of the economic strategy it embodied. Contrary to the Eddé plan, it went to great lengths to perform a certain version of local and historical sensitivity, and made architectural and archaeological preservation hallmarks of the plan. Doing so created an alibi for the destruction that it entailed, including of archaeological sites and finds.[38] While the plans differed on many points, they both sought to effect a break with the war, aiming to erase its traces and remedy its causes. The Gavin plan slated some three hundred buildings for detailed renovation as a matter of top priority, and designated a more even mix of residential, commercial, and office space. Unlike the Eddé plan, which dealt with the Normandy landfill by creating a detached island off the coast, the Gavin plan created a peninsula out of over sixty hectares of reclaimed land, in part using debris created by demolition. According to the first Solidere annual report in 1994, the reclaimed area accounts for a third of the area's 1.8 million square meters, zoned to allow for 4.5 million square meters of built-up space. Echoing the religious exception that manifested in the Mandate period, another eighty thousand square meters belonging to the various religious endowments in the area were designated as exempt from seizure, as were government offices. Approximately half of the total space was designated as Solidere's private property. The rest was designated as land in the public domain that Solidere was to develop and maintain on behalf of the state (mostly roads, sidewalks, and a few open spaces). This of course implied the destruction of many existing public and semi-public spaces, such as the historic cemetery in nearby Minet El Hosn, whose contents were added to the reclaimed land at the Normandy landfill.

The nature of projects like Solidere is that their activity and profitability are geared more toward property management than new construction. Solidere's efforts are directed primarily to the sale or lease of property to developers, and then closely managing the forms their projects can take in accordance with a master plan. The company has restored far more buildings than it has built, the majority of which are located in the area near the Place de l'Etoile, reimagined as the Foch-Allenby sector.[39] On the one hand, the demolition that occurred in anticipation of an eventual master plan arguably opened up sufficient tabula rasa space. On the other hand, the costly process of detailed restoration could both address concerns about "local" and "historical" sensitivity, and accommodate the need for higher budgets and therefore larger scales of investment, and eventually the claim of much higher property value as a whole. The Gavin plan stressed site-specificity and historical sensitivity, a depoliticizing discourse that tends to cast the project's contingencies as inevitabilities. The economic form of the project is rendered as both a given and the most desirable, which therefore necessitates exactly and only the plan put forward. The company's promotional literature would later exceed this logic, describing the plan as a natural outcome of physical geography, casting Beirut's timeless historical importance as a result of its geostrategic position (never mind the reclaimed land, or the relatively minor historical importance of Beirut prior to the mid-nineteenth century). As will be examined in the section on images and the citizen-investor below, the supposedly essential Lebanese qualities of entrepreneurial spirit and bon-vivant tastes became a chicken-*and*-egg rationale—both the reason for general economic recovery that would make the company a safe investment, and why the company would itself generate that recovery.

To return to the discourse of architectural salvage, the Gavin plan meant that older structures and nostalgia could be plugged into new visual and financial circuitries. For buildings deemed salvageable, original property owners were given the option to do independent restoration. To be eligible, they were required to submit a proposal that met the requirements of Solidere's highly detailed restoration brief. Owners were required to guarantee financing and completion of the project within a two-year time period, and pay the company a charge of 12 percent of the property's estimated market value. The company's primary achievement was fostering a real estate market, clearly in evidence in the valuation of property deemed unsalvageable. Solidere would often close a settlement to purchase land from its owners at one "market valued" price, and then flip it for a vastly higher sum soon after. Sometimes the turnaround time on such deals was less than a day.[40] The addition of the property to company holdings seemed to communicate the security of its future—the powerful work of financial devices made clear. The invisible hand truly is magic, especially when it can enable trust in a promised future return in profitability.[41]

The restoration project abhorred inconsistency, which would presumably detract from the effect of a complete neighborhood transplanted from the colonial era. Instructions went so far as to specify the exact type of stone to be used in building façades—of a particular yellowish color native to a quarry near the town of Mansouriyeh, just outside Beirut. This level of detailed attention was part of a process of regular visual inspection. Mounir Douaidy, the financial director and general manager of the company, once stressed to me the importance of the effect of aesthetic harmony of the restored buildings. He explained that investor money was directly connected to the form of the space, so much so that he would personally take regular walks through the areas under restoration to make sure that shareholder interests were looked after.[42] The visual economy of Solidere is quite directly premised on a vigilant financialized gaze.

The justifications surrounding the master plan and the early years of Solidere's self-reporting are perhaps never more problematic and symptomatic of this conjuncture than when they mention the types of people and subjectivities meant to inhabit or be ushered in by the creation of these spaces. The space attracting the right kind of people or the space creating the subjectivities that fit it—the two are readily conflated in the company's materials, but also the popular discourses about the spaces that resulted. The imposition of proper class and gender comportment on the space became a necessity. The cosmopolitan ethic and business-savvy of "the people" apparently did not apply to the thousands of war-displaced who moved in during the war, finding precarious habitation in the abandoned area. Living bodies and rubble became biopolitical problems for the project, in that their presence embodied the social outcomes of the war and potentially obstructed the social space promised and demanded by the project. Solidere's annual report claims that as of the end of 1996, 1,284 original tenants and owners and 20,962 displaced families had been relocated, at a total reported cost to the company of $263 million.[43] In the clinical grammar of the annual report, clearing buildings and clearing people both fall under a section titled "Land Preparation." Population management became corporate imperative, underwritten by special tax-exempt status granted by the state. Compensating the war-displaced, many of whom were Shi'ites from South Lebanon, had more to do with the goals of the Amal and Hizbullah leadership solidifying a clientelist system and sharing in the institutionalized graft created by the Hariri government than it did with any genuine attempt at restitution.[44]

None of this should authorize romanticizing the material condition of the city, or the dangers associated with living in proximity to a toxic garbage dump or in crumbling buildings, whose collapse could kill yet more of the war-displaced living inside them. Moving from concrete to paper, complicated inheritance laws made it so individual properties often had large numbers of claimants.[45] These issues alone would warrant a collective and coordinated effort. Yet projects like this redraw the relationship between the categories of "the social," "the psychological," and "the material." Like the contradictions internal to liberalism, they also redraw the lines between the state and society, the public and the private, legitimate and illegitimate manipulations of property rights, and in turn making certain kinds of violence legible and necessary, or illegible.[46] Thus the decision to order a construction crew to collapse a building on a family that refused to leave on February 16, 1996, can be described as a sad inevitability or murder, depending on one's ontological and political commitments. On the other side of this coin are the new financial circuitries enabled by such violence, and those who would applaud the company's "achievements."

The forms of inclusion and exclusion that conditioned Solidere's emergence and functioning, and the emergence of Hizbullah as a provider of social services, express the logic of the structural inequalities and political cantonization of the postwar consensus and its facilitation of global capital. Both organizations were and are fully compatible with IMF and World Bank recommendations on structural adjustment, business-oriented reforms, and market economy policies. Applauding the institutional framework wherein state might and the interests of capital combine, Gavin and Maluf (1996) commented that the Solidere plan was "empowered by law to unite existing property owners with new investors" (16). A more fundamental question could have been asked about the type of community that the plan might have supported, and the conditions of equality that it might have fostered. As the visions for the future of the space examined here demonstrate, there were forms of life— and imagined possibilities for the space—that were deemed to not add value.

This carving of the social conditioned the emergence of a new way of seeing the city and its futures, centered around the figure of the citizen-investor. Images of before/after presumed this kind of viewer, who was also an economic actor to whom images and experiences of the city would be geared. Rather than being the domain of "the real,"[47] economic activity and the financialization of postwar construction is itself thoroughly defined by the creation and circulation of images of before/after, meant to be viewed in the manner of a citizen-investor. Before shifting focus from the emergence of Solidere to the visual phenomena that animated the economy of postwar construction, one last point about the financial structure of the company should be made. The forms that investment took are key to understanding the nature of the Solidere system, and the usefulness found for images within it.

As a corporate entity, Solidere has enjoyed a curious relationship to the government, which was particularly affected by the Civil War that preceded the 1990s but also by the continued Syrian presence, and the new ways these elements were brought together by the rise of the Hariri regime. The project that Solidere sought to manage illuminates the workings of a much broader system that transformed rubble into money by selling the notion that war-torn cityscapes are an opportunity for global investors. Solidere issued two types of stock. Type A shares were initially issued as one form of compensation to property holders in the area, and Type B shares were issued to investors, who initially were required to be Lebanese citizens, companies, state agencies, or Arab firms. Property holders applied to the Ministry of Justice, which organized an appraisal process to determine the value of the property, which would then determine the number of shares allocated.[48]

This process had the effect of simultaneously creating a market and converting the majority of the property into tradable financial instruments. It also made it so that "payment" to property holders took the form of a promised future increase in value that the creation of Solidere would precipitate, even as it awarded shares based on valuations at current and not projected market value, a necessary component of ensuring that value could be realized for the system. Type B shares carried a stipulation that foreign investment could only be into property managed by the company or put on the market, and not directly into Solidere itself. This requirement was later waived. Type A shares were initially valued at a total of $1.17 billion, and the 6.5 million Type B shares were valued at $100 each. Type B shares were oversubscribed by 142 percent in the first few weeks, or at $926 million across 20,000 subscribers. These shares were traded in US dollars, not Lebanese lira, and initially, on the London rather than the Lebanese stock exchange. In 1996 the company offered Global Deposit Receipts (GDRs), creating a different form of direct foreign investment.[49] Solidere also issued a 1:10 stock split that year to encourage a more fluid trading market, taking both A and B shares from $100 to $10 per share. They have tended to trade near that price ever since.

The other side to the Solidere financial gambit was the avenue to globalization it offered to local elites. An example of this can be found in the catering of the design of retail space to local commercial conglomerates, particularly in the newly built Beirut Souks. Although designed in the mid-1990s, the so-called Beirut Souks didn't open until late in 2009. This project was particularly useful to the company because it offered the opportunity to hold an international and internationally juried design competition. Although not the only space zoned for commercial use, the Souks are a vital part of the Solidere plan. As these things go, a team led by Jad Tabet—one of the fiercest critics of the Eddé plan—was selected to be part of the Souks planning team. Tabet sought to make the Souks appeal to a broader section of the Lebanese middle class, and the kinds of middle-class merchants previously found in the area, by designing significant portions of the Souks to be small shop fronts whose rents would be subsidized by nearby "anchor" department stores.[50] This effort was eventually defeated in favor of a strategy that would almost without exception cater to global and luxury brands. As it turns out, a significant portion of the stores that would open were for brands owned by a handful of Lebanese retail conglomerates.[51] This selective linkage between local elites and global consumer capital is in turn mirrored by the type of consumer who could afford to shop or even be in the space.

Where regimes of colonial rule and state development had been stymied by vested interests in previous decades, state-supported neoliberal market urbanism succeeded in implementing urban plans and financial schemes. These transformations were underpinned by the mobilization of a very particular way of seeing the space.

The Before/After Image and the Citizen-Investor

The before/after image is one of contrasts—a shot of severely damaged buildings or urban scenes followed by or sometimes adjacent to an image of the same space after construction. It takes many different visual forms—cinematic, photographic, computer generated—and often these in various combinations. The before/after image comes in two main variations, which can be differentiated in terms of the kind of contrast they create. The first type creates a contrast between damaged buildings or streets and architectural illustrations or 3D computer renderings (a future to come). Depending on the nature of the imaginary present, the future to come may also be imagined as a return to the past. The second type achieves the contrast via visual evidence of the same space after the completion of work (a future achieved). There is a variation of this second type that textually consists solely of an after shot of work completed or to be completed, but that refers to a heavily implied "before." Although images indexing actually completed work have historically increased as the presence of damaged buildings and their images have decreased, all variations of the before/after image have and continue to historically overlap in terms of their actual circulation. Not all work in the area commenced or has been completed at the same time, and some buildings have either never been restored or never been completed—famously, the former movie theater known as "The Egg" and the monolith-like skyscraper Burj El Murr.

Solidere is not the sole creator of the before/after image, but the company's monumental operationalization of it exemplifies the contradictions of this image. It is quite common to find before/after images in the promotional material of other, smaller local real estate projects, or in the Elissar project designated to resolve postwar issues in South Beirut. Following the 2006 war with Israel, which devastated significant portions of South Beirut, the Hizbullah-led Wa'ad project (which can be translated as "the promise," referring to the promise made by the party to make damaged neighborhoods "exactly as they were, only better") also heavily depended on the before/after image, although the two projects do not parallel each other in their organizational structure or economic form.[52] Beyond the Wa'ad project, the before/after image was put

Figure 2.3 Car traffic was frequently rerouted during the years of construction. The image featured on this billboard was from the first plan for the city center. Photo courtesy of Kirsten Scheid (ca. 1993).

to new work in this later period, albeit reformulated for a new context and conflict.

Many who lived or moved through the space in the first years after the formal commencement of the Solidere project were quick to comment that few contrasts were greater than that between the clean spaces promised by before/after images, and the active work site in the middle of Beirut. As anyone who ever sat in the frequent traffic jams on ever-changing routes through the area could report, the images that often appeared on signs and temporary structures on location created a stark sensory contrast. The din and dust produced by excavation, demolition, and construction is by definition absent from the before/after image, which skips past the interstitial period and the labor of construction. The before/after image represents a sense of the past as a fixed entity, and promises historical progress without contingency. The stasis of the present—much like being stuck in traffic caused by construction work—is projected backward in time. In truth, it is the future that is foreclosed in the before/after image, as is the means by which it is delivered.

In one sense, the before/after image is specific to the conditions in Beirut, and those in other attempts to attract financial investment in the particular formation of globalization in early 1990s. However there are many instructive

Figure 2.4 Ongoing restoration work in the background, images of archaeological finds in the foreground. Photo courtesy of Kirsten Scheid (ca. 1993).

similarities that one might find in other cities, other cultural forms, and at other points in time. Much has been said about post–World War II Germany and the cinema, literature, and architecture that grappled with it to its afterlife. Vidler, in his reflection on W. G. Sebald's observation that postwar German literature and architecture (and images of before and after reconstruction) instantiated a mode of "looking and looking away at the same time,"[53] finds a similar dynamic in many postwar countries, and in urban planning itself. Vidler shows how the desire to clear rubble and build things bigger and

Figure 2.5 Construction work in the foreground, an after image and helicopter in the background. Photo courtesy of Kirsten Scheid (ca. 1993).

better than before is one of the effects of air war on postwar architecture and planning, and finds expression in the fetishization of the process of redesigning and rebuilding the World Trade Center in New York City after 9/11.[54] Solidere and its before/after images are in a sense heir to this tradition, although the nature of the destruction in its area was primarily caused by militia combat and continued by its own activities, and only secondarily by aerial bombardment.

There is a temptation to characterize the before/after image as one that is primarily cinematic in nature, or to characterize the urban spaces they are tied to as having cinematic qualities. Cinema and ruins have long been linked both at the level of the historical subject of cinema, and in the sense that both express a particularly modern way of organizing a relationship with the past and temporal change.[55] One might find certain basic similarities with "rubble films" set in postwar Berlin, in the sense that both emphasize a focus on forward historical movement after a war, and a fixation on rubble that gradually ebbs as an overt textual reference. As the robust literature on the relationship between cinema and cities indicates, there is a clear basis for the claim that the before/after image are candidates for consideration as a cinematic visual.[56] However, there are two points that limit the usefulness of considering the before/after image as an inherently cinematic image. Following Brunsdon's (2012) critique of the interdisciplinary "cinema/city" literature, there are fundamental, perhaps even insurmountable epistemological and methodological problems that plague this comparative endeavor. Even while studies investigating a particular cinema or genre in connection to a particular city are often exemplary in their insight, many encounter difficulty when reaching for more general theorization that reaches beyond specific case studies. Having said this, the before/after image is suggestive of this period of globalization, and the cultural forms and contextual factors that condition its appearance in Beirut are not unlike those of other places and histories. There are surely other construction projects and planning discourses in earlier and later historical moments that have depended on a similar aesthetic formation.[57] However, the before/after image obtains a particular velocity and vector when informed by the rise of digital technologies and the process of financialization distinct to the early 1990s.

The second issue is that the before/after image—even when it appears in film—bears the trace of cartographic imaging, especially of the sort made possible by digital mapping such as GIS. While the before/after image often relies on the cinematic convention of the dissolve, it is different from the "morph," in which the process of transformation itself is central.[58] Rather, the before/after image is akin to (and sometimes actually based on) the informatic process of converting space to a series of data points, entering said data into a database, and then using powerful software to analyze and output that information in visual form. One of the key features of GIS-enabled spatial visualization is that it makes it easy for a user to specify a data set as a layer, which can then be selected or deselected in conjunction with other layers—think of similar features in Google Maps or Photoshop.[59] Even though many such information technologies have no inherently "visual" counterpart, with the before/after image, it is how this technique is used to perform visual mastery over space that matters most. Select one layer and you have a current or past state of rubble; select another and you have the clean lines and clear future of the Solidere plan. This is not to suggest that a visual-centric understanding of media can explain the relationship of the media to the city but, rather, that the mobilization of this visualization technique expresses the remaking of the media logic that define cities to begin with.[60]

The before/after image demonstrates a key aspect of the relationship of images to media infrastructure—that the one is used in the production of the other, in something like a stuttering feedback loop. In addition to repeating the cultural form of informatic layering, digital (and automated) mapping and map-making also occasionally appear as a theme or protagonist in before/after images, especially in Solidere's promotional materials. The visual production of urban space both depended on and expressed the digital process underlying its real construction. GIS formed a key infrastructural component in the Solidere project's land management and engineering systems. The prevalence of the trope in this period should be understood as an expression of the centrality of this way of knowing and experiencing space to the financial logic of postwar construction. The work of the before/after image in this institutional context is how it dramatizes the connection between urban planning, information technology, and financial investment to an image of the future of the space, reducing room for critique or political disagreement to nitpicking about the efficiency or speed of implementation. In a country emerging from a period of nearly two decades with a government in or near total collapse, the ability to effect or plausibly promise change quieted many dissenting voices.

Many of the contradictions and paradoxes of the before/after image appear in compressed form in films produced by Solidere.[61] Three films in particular demonstrate the connection between the before/after image and the citizen-investor: *A Project as Grand as Hope* (1992), *Which Beirut Tomorrow?* (1993), and *Lebanon on the Move* (1995).[62] The first two films played primarily in corporate boardrooms and other official spaces, at local movie theatres before feature films, occasionally on politically affiliated television stations such as Future TV (owned by Hariri), and accompanying Solidere's representatives on financial road shows. The third film is more explicitly geared toward the financial and business sector, and at six minutes in length, is a little less than half the length of the other two. These films each demonstrate a different aspect of the work of the before/after image, and give clear expression to the visual relationships that constitute the citizen-investor. The first and third films express ebullient self-confidence while differing in terms of how they create a relationship between the before/after aspects of the image. *Which Beirut Tomorrow?* was produced in the context of heavy public criticism, and spends comparably less time showing off spectacular urban transformation in favor of dwelling in the tension of the "before" portion of the image.

Recent work has shown how industrial film can reveal a great deal about the tensions within organizations by expressing how they have sought to educate or persuade their workers, customers, or the public at large.[63] The films examined here differ from many of the histories examined in this literature, which typically focus on large corporations, foundations, or state educational agencies located in advanced industrialized countries that sought to create what Acland and Wasson (2011b) term "useful cinema."[64] Solidere should therefore be understood as a somewhat unique case, as it was conceived as a private company that would assume the task of producing an urban landscape on behalf of the state, that enjoyed the backing of the state, but whose profits would remain private and untaxed. Furthermore, even at its most popular moments the company never found broad and general support, either with the public at large or with the original owners of the land it assumed control over. As McCarthy (2010) has argued about films that staged race relations in the postwar United States, such texts are best understood for how they articulate and enact a model of citizenship.[65]

The "usefulness" of the films discussed here lay in their ability to address an ideal viewer—a citizen-investor—who is characterized by the capacity to invest in the transformation of the space, either financially or at the very least emotionally.[66] The spatial transformation displayed to citizen-investors depended on a mode of neoliberal subjectivity, as well as sensory reorientation toward the space itself. A good citizen-investor accepts the inevitability of the course of action depicted in the before/after image and feels the clearing of rubble to be progress. This viewer also desires the future that the act of visual circulation is presumed to make more likely. Thus the before/after image reshapes the distribution of sensible ways of thinking and feeling the future of the space. It blames the buildings for never having quite lived up to the promises made on their behalf. The citizen-investor looks at the space so as to certify that it is being optimally configured for investment opportunity, and disdains any other use of the space. The viewing position imagines urban space itself to be subordinate to the needs of developers, and abhors criticism of this goal. The citizen-investor need not hold national citizenship, nor does holding national citizenship necessarily guarantee the ability to actually benefit from or even spend time in the spaces transformed. At the same time, foreign investment is cast in the glow of good citizenship, regardless of the passport held or diasporic status of the actor (unlike onsite Syrian construction workers). The lack of Lebanese citizenship doesn't prevent participation in this way of seeing the space, as before/after images did some of their most important work within transnational circuitries. The citizen-investor presumes a certainty that mastery over space will lead to the maximization of profit equated with the public good—a distinctly masculinist viewing position keyed to the gendered nature of both citizenship and nationalist discourse, particularly as they pertain to narratives of national progress. As is the case with the political project of neoliberalism more generally, the citizen-investor (perhaps unconsciously) presumes a resubordination of women within a global political economic order whose transformations are entangled with existing racial and ethno-religious formations.[67] It is no coincidence that the Taif order reinforced political sectarianism, attacked unions, rolled back the welfare state, and made Solidere possible—as with the new conservatisms of the era, these all depend on women doing the work of social reproduction within a family unit. This unit of course also presumed female migrant labor under the *kafala* system.[68]

Which Beirut Tomorrow? gives the extant damage to the area the most screen time, creating the juxtaposition with an after to come through staged interviews and discussions with people concerned with or directly affected by the condition of the city center. The representational burden of national recovery is placed on figures of youth, giving a generational twist and sense of inclusiveness to the civilizing impulse and presumed solution for the city center. The film is prefaced by a paragraph of text describing a new generation whose only experience of Beirut is of a war-torn city. Comparatively minimal narration—which like the dialogue is in Arabic with English subtitles—links scenes of architects and archaeologists discussing the area's "heritage," interviews with college students in an architectural drawing class, former residents of the site, average "man on the street" interviews, and even an interview with a squatter. The film is interspersed with two vignettes, which engage the space in two different phenomenological registers. The first vignette is of a young man walking through the ruined streets of the city center, in and among badly damaged buildings. His walk through the space is accompanied by an ominous, lower-register staccato piano and occasional cuts to a first-person perspective, and is interrupted from time to time by a wild and disorienting vertical spinning of the camera. The second vignette is of a small group of middle-aged men sitting at a drafting table and talking about the architectural history of and possibilities for the city center. They pore over drawings and old photos, calmly discussing the rich architectural history of the city center and how to achieve a balance between modern and traditional styles.

These two vignettes contrast visual disorientation and being in the space with visual mastery over the space and its surfaces at a distance from it. The key function of the second vignette is to restabilize the disruption of the first, anchoring the narrative in a forward-moving historical trajectory. One of the characters in the second vignette—the architect Ousama Kabbani, who was associated with the project—asserts that of the three original souks in the area,

Figure 2.6 Young man walking amid the rubble and ruined buildings of the city center, *Which Beirut Tomorrow?* (1993).

Souk Ayass was the one that had the most character, referring to a photo with an arcade (see figure 2.8). This idea—that the French colonial influence is the one with the greatest architectural and economic value, and therefore the type worth preserving—is a problematic byline whose 1990s globalization-era colonial nostalgia is echoed in much of the discourse promoted by Solidere. These two vignettes also underscore the rest of the film in a heavy-handed way, emphasizing the imperative to reconstruct by alternately moving the viewer through the space and revisiting it through the measured and expert tone of the older generation assessing how to deal with it. The only squatter depicted in the film with any voice is a former shop-owner, who says he is on the side of a solution. The "good" subject becomes a citizen-investor, contrasted with those who would use the space in ways not conducive to investment—such as occupation out of necessity, or as a form of disobedience toward a nascent and unequal civic order. The citizen-investor need not invest financially, as compliance with the social and affective normativity of the new space was how it was made to increase in value. Reasonable individuals are those who comply with the spatial order, and who orient themselves toward an enforced futurity of the space.

Of the three films examined here, the enigmatic scenes of the young man walking through the broken and desolate cityscape most directly address the specter of trauma and its relationship to place that the before shot always has the potential to evoke. The character first emerges from the darkness deep inside of a ruined building. He moves in a kind of daze, as though not totally present to himself or his surroundings. He walks over to a foxhole window sur-

Figure 2.7 Older men discussing architectural history and reconstruction, *Which Beirut Tomorrow?*

rounded by sandbags, which comes to frame first his vision of the outside, and then that of the camera. Suddenly, the camera spins into a first-person perspective whirl, and the viewer hears the jarring ratatat of automatic gunfire. He can be read as an instance of the trope of the young militiaman commonly found in Lebanese film, caught in and perpetrating unending destruction.[69] A similar character appears in another film produced by *Which Beirut Tomorrow?* director Bahij Hojeij, titled *Beyrouth: Le Dialogue des Ruines* (1993).[70] His relationship to the space contrasts with the scene that follows, in which students sit in an open-air architectural drafting class on a balcony overlooking the area (figure 2.9). We first see these students engrossed in their training in Western fine arts under the watchful eye of their teacher, participating in the future by becoming literate in the skills the new nation needs to move forward. They then share their opinions with the viewer as to what the space should become, mainly echoing a familiar rhetoric of wanting to balance tradition and modernity. This contrast between properly liberal subjects (equated here with Westernized sensibilities demonstrated by academic discipline and appreciation of the fine arts) and the trope of the militiaman is one that marks many Lebanese films that deal with the Civil War.[71] In this instance, the geopolitical dimensions of war and postwar construction are collapsed into psychological atavism, creating a dichotomy between those who move the nation forward and those men who are trapped in its back-eddy, threatening to drag the whole of society back into unresolvable ethno-religious violence.

The young man can also be read as an anthropomorphized embodiment of postwar traumatic memory, like a ghost haunting the decimated cityscape and

There you had arches, arcades, narrow streets, etc.

Figure 2.8 Photo of an arcaded street in Souk Ayass, *Which Beirut Tomorrow?*

the technologies of construction.[72] Ghosts, vampires, and other undead figures also populate postwar Lebanese cinema more generally, as do ruins.[73] The spectrality of the character is marked by his bodily displacement, which manifests as time and space out of joint, created by the ruins.[74] It is this pierced or doubled temporality that the before/after shot skips but, in so doing, repeats the spatiotemporal bifurcation of traumatic memory.[75] In this reading, the haunted can only be laid to rest by replacing the unhomely, disruptive presence of the ruin with the clean geometries of the new urban plan. The dead buildings and mangled architecture are therefore framed as requiring erasure through perfect restoration or new construction. Of course, this erasure is a project that is never actually completed either in the imaginary or in the city. There are numerous buildings in Solidere's area and around its perimeter that remained more or less as they were at the end of the war up to the time of writing. The spectrality of the young man represents the presence of a phantasmal or fantastic temporality indigestible by the regime of time imposed by postwar construction and the before/after image—a temporal doubling commonly found in postcolonial film and visual culture.[76]

The film closes on a shot of a van driving down a debilitated road, which then switches into an identical view in archival footage of the same street from an idealized prewar past. In this permutation of the before/after image, the future becomes a return to a pre-traumatic golden era that the young people in the film would have never experienced.[77] Acknowledging the melancholy and nostalgia of the space, which in its current form is haunted by its past, is allowed insofar as this affective register enables a conversation about the

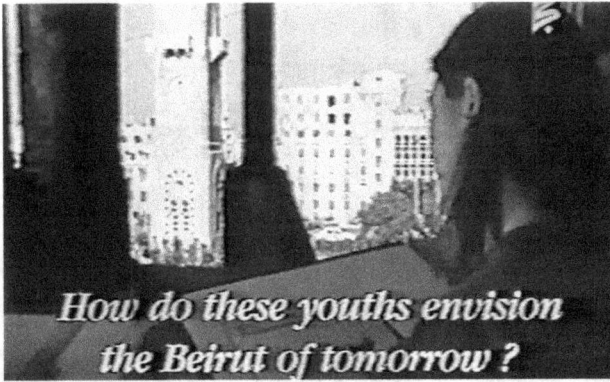

How do these youths envision
the Beirut of tomorrow ?

Figure 2.9 Students in an architectural drawing class,
Which Beirut Tomorrow?

future of the space. Rubble is sorted from ruins, and illustrations of a future-to-be reassure the worrying experience of being in the space.

A Project as Grand as Hope exemplifies a different temporal accentuation that can characterize the before/after image, and is far less reticent in its use of the before/after image than *Which Beirut Tomorrow?* The film initially focuses on the condition of the city center before the application of the Solidere solution, justifying the latter in terms of its dramatic contrast with the former. The film guides the viewer through the whys and hows of the transformation of damaged buildings into a prosperous future, and relies more heavily on voice-over (in English and Arabic versions) and the voice of expertise. After opening with a brief montage narrating the "Golden Age" of leisure and tourism in prewar Lebanon, the film shifts to footage of damaged and ruined buildings, which in turn makes quick cuts to the iconic and bullet-ridden statue in Martyrs' Square. This image is then superimposed with a depiction of a flat-lining EKG. The narrator then informs the viewer that since the war began in the heart of the city, reconstruction would have to begin there to bring back life to the entire body (actually using the phrase "open-heart surgery") (see figure 2.10). Images of damaged transportation infrastructure, tangled power lines, and leaking pipes are followed by moldering binders (symbolizing the land registry system), squatters, and the Normandy coastal garbage dump. Relief for these symptoms of the postwar ailment finally comes in digital form, and the first after shot of the film is of a computer-generated map, which quickly and precisely renders individual plots of land. Although it would seem to be a GIS map, and Solidere was one of the first entities in Lebanon to possess the technology,

Figure 2.10 The heart of Beirut with an EKG, *A Project as Grand as Hope* (1992).

the company wouldn't officially come into existence until almost two years after this film was released. Soon after the map finishes rendering, the image cuts to a top-down view of an architectural model of the area positioned to line up exactly with the street plan of the digital map. The camera then pans across the clean, blank white cityscape of the model dotted with green trees, followed closely by the Solidere logo. The application of a technological fix to the "problem" of space and powered by investment capital is quite literally depicted as the solution for Beirut.

The rest of the film repeats this basic formulation—seemingly insurmountable problems solved by ambitious thinking and futuristic technology, all brought to you by the company. This is the obvious and vanilla version of the before/after image. Damaged buildings are followed by illustrations of restored buildings in the areas that were eventually slated for close restoration by the company (around Foch, Allenby, and Ma'arad streets). Hollowed-out shells of buildings and empty streets become promontories and hubs of commercial life. The Normandy dump becomes a corniche with lush gardens and broad highways. In one scene, a mechanical printer fills in the details of a map of the city center, while illustrations of the space-to-be flash by in a panel in the corner of the screen (see figure 2.11). The film goes on to make even bigger claims. As a result of the project, industry and finance would be stimulated and local and global investment opportunities would be created, all of which

Figure 2.11 A map is printed via automated process as artist visualizations of the city center flash by, *A Project as Grand as Hope.*

would trigger an economic boom that would bring more money to state coffers and stabilize inflation.[78] Whether the emphasis of the film is global finance, local infrastructure, or coastal land reclamation, the equation is that without Solidere there is a devastated city center, but with Solidere there is a prosperous future. The performance of efficient implementation of a plan thus works to deflect criticism about the *type* of future it brings into being, replacing it with a discussion of how quickly and profitably that future would arrive. The present becomes uninhabitable.

Lebanon on the Move aligns with the clichés commonly found in the booster rhetoric of 1990s globalization—that professional management and clever maneuvering in the free market would erase the messy and unproductive particularities that would otherwise keep the city and its people from a date with global capital, or even worse, slipping back into the causes and aftermath of the Civil War. The film echoes the rhetoric of bringing local landowners and global investors together through the institutional structure of Solidere. It opens with a moving aerial shot, seemingly from a helicopter, that travels from an idyllic mountain scene to the bay north of Beirut, and then over the open construction site as it would have existed in late 1994. This shot is accompanied by the voice of a male narrator (like *A Project as Grand as Hope*, a crisp and British-tinged accent in English), who confidently discusses economic indicators and on-screen graphics that suggest an ongoing and accelerating economic boom in the country and the investment opportunity presented by the real estate sector. The mobile aerial gaze that constitutes this opening sequence is a shift away from the fixed and detached perspective of the bird's-eye view associated with urban maps and illustration (or the panorama, for that matter), to a visual form that enacts intervention in the space. Much like the conventions of architectural visualization it borrows from, imaging becomes immanent to the process of construction. Images become imaging.[79] The citizen-investor is given a visual and financial overview of the site, notably detailing the total potential built-up area allowed by the project, and that Solidere's business strategy involves no assumption of debt by the company. This opening sequence also manifests a key contradiction in Solidere's rhetoric. At times, national economic recovery is framed as an outcome of the company's activities, and at other times this contextual and epochal shift is presented as a given that points (positively) toward the project's success. This inevitability is imagined here to be the outcome of the supposedly inherent national/ethnic qualities of cleverness and entrepreneurial ingenuity of the Lebanese.

With the aerial journey to the site complete, the on-screen work site switches to an aerial photograph of the northern part of Beirut. A graphic line then traces a border around the targeted area, followed by the main punchline of the film. As images of damaged buildings and infrastructure flash by, the narrator asks the citizen-investor "Why is this a sound investment? A safe investment? Would you like to live here? Work here? Shop here? Enjoy yourself here? Of course you wouldn't. But how about here?" The stream of images becomes a stream of after shots, in the form of meticulous illustrations of what the space was promised to look like after construction. This tension/release structure—where the before/after contrast is temporally delayed in the image—frequently features in cinematic variations of the image. Presumably, the gratification that follows in the second part of the image is one that citizen-investors can actualize though affirmation of the play of the image, much as financial investment was secured through the circulation of these images. *A Project as Grand as Hope* and *Lebanon on the Move* exemplify different variations on the relationship between before and after—the latter primarily emphasizing a short delay of gratification. The visual culture of before/after more broadly would typically come to present both images at once, and in many cases, would simply cut the "before" part. Why have before/after when you can train the gaze on just the after?

The English-language voice-over and general tenor of *Lebanon on the Move* suggests the film's primary intended use would have been to circulate beyond just Lebanon, and especially alongside the architectural mock-up of the project that was taken on the Solidere traveling financial road show. The film quite explicitly articulates the citizen-investor as a viewing position that forges a connection between local spaces and global capital. Near the end of the film, the voice-over confidently proclaims that "The difference in value between this . . ." (image looking down a devastated street) ". . . and this" (image of the same street made whole again, viewed from an identical perspective) "should be self-evident." The sequence continues, highlighting the opportunity for shareholders to own marketable securities tied to Lebanon's recovery. This sequence equates the desirability of a collective solution with the needs of investors. Investors also get the added benefit of a warm feeling that they are contributing to the betterment of the urban future. The Civil War itself was anything but disconnected from global and regional economies, and the lines between state and non-state actors became increasingly blurred in the 1990s.[80] Rather than erasing the Civil War—the frequent lament about Solidere's legacy—the company is one part of the rearticulation of that conflict's territorial and political fragmentation within a new political topology.

The before/after image finds somewhat different expression in books published by Solidere meant to showcase the thinking behind and results of their work. *Beirut Reborn: The Restoration and Development of the Central District* (1996), authored in part by Angus Gavin, combines an outline of the historical claims anchoring the master plan with the conventions of a coffee table book. *Beirut City Center Recovery: The Foch-Allenby and Étoile Conservation Area* (2004), authored by Robert Saliba, is an architectural survey of the neighborhoods that had been slated for detailed restoration. Although titled similarly, *Beirut City Center* (2006) is a photographic survey of the entirety of completed work in the area at the time of its publication. These three books each exemplify variations of the before/after image, matched to the kind of investigation of the space they highlight. They also circulate quite differently, and reach readers in a very different modality from that experienced by viewers of the films mentioned above. They tend to be priced like architectural publications or corporate gifts, well out of the range of affordability for most Lebanese. Images of before/after take the form of photographic and architectural drawings, sometimes as direct side-by-side comparison.

Beirut Reborn was published in the first years of construction. While debates and accusations had continued apace despite the project already being underway, the promised results were not yet in evidence. Quite to the contrary, the experience of the space for most people was driving through a construction site, which alternated between being loud and dusty, and desolate. Between 1992 and at least 1997, it was quite common for even those on short visits to Lebanon to remark that there was a big difference between the life promised by these visualizations and the reality of the massive hole in the urban landscape created by demolition. *Beirut Reborn* set out to explain the rationale behind the master plan in a tone that wouldn't shy away from its grandiose claims. The book situates the project within a 5,000-year history, commenting on the then-live archaeological digs. The corporate slogan "Beirut: Ancient City of the Future" (and the Latinate *Berytus Delenda Est*, for added effect) was pushed quite heavily at the time. The book is replete with images of ancient ruins and artifacts from periods ranging from the Phoenician to the Roman to the Ottoman. It also features artist visualizations of the hoped-for outcomes of restoration and construction.

Beirut City Center Recovery, however, is an architectural assessment of the completed restoration work. The book discusses the history of the French colonial aesthetic, and inventories the anatomy of each building individually. The book also explicitly and favorably links Solidere's institutional and political framework to what it sees as the success of its restoration activities, justifying the former in terms of the latter. The book's introduction argues that Solidere's critics have only to see for themselves what the results have been. Entire chapters are devoted to documenting and detailing balconies, windows, and stone restoration techniques. Most tellingly, the book's author Robert Saliba, an architect and urbanist, argues that Solidere's rationale extended an approach to heritage and preservation ordinarily found in archaeology to the whole of the Foch-Allenby and Étoile area, which he fairly assesses as being composed of structures from the early post-industrial era and more recent historical evolution of the city:

> In recovering Foch-Allenby and Étoile, Solidere extended this notion to encompass the area's early twentieth century architectural heritage, giving considerable attention to the early modern office building and incorporating the French Mandate legacy within its patrimony. Thus, Beirut is the first city in the Middle East that has come to terms with its colonial heritage and, by extension, with its modern heritage. (Saliba 2004, 13)

This argument seems incapable of acknowledging the fundamental continuity between the social and aesthetic ideals that the area embodies with colonial and capitalist exploitation, or the structural relationship of those systems to the destruction that brought about the Civil War that damaged the buildings in the first place. Yet it is precisely these continuities, these relationships to past violence, that are frequently overlooked and erased, and that legitimate the postwar political economic order.[81]

In the book's conclusion, the author extols the virtues of emergency-driven and private sector–led urban planning and design, arguing that Solidere marked "a turning point breaking half a century of modernist dogma and idealistic discourse" (Saliba 2004, 200). This break is presumably with the weak and ineffective state agencies that he sees as having fumbled the urban planning of Beirut through the course of the twentieth century. While Solidere does mark a certain kind of political intensification, this argument weakens the ability to critically assess the effect of the creation of Solidere *on* those same agencies in the postwar period, or more importantly, the role of the project as a whole in closing down other possible approaches to the postwar predicament. Like the "neoliberal realism" that characterizes many proponents of the Solidere plan, social considerations and aesthetic forms are cast as less real than the demands of the market, even if they are thought to be pleasing and desirable.[82] Like many celebrations of the after image, the book applauds the beneficence of the company in taking extra care in preserving these buildings and excels at describing the play at the surface of buildings. Scant attention is paid to the forces shaping the usefulness of those surfaces, or the political imperatives defining what buildings survived to be restored. Critical questions about what shape the social could or should take are left aside in favor of cataloguing how well the company accomplished the goals it set for itself. This reduces architectural critique to a kind of detailed certification that the buildings and neighborhood match the after image. Like much popular discussion of the area, debate about other possible desires or visions for the space are silenced by appealing to a feel-good response to the surfaces that result from restoration.

Beirut City Center (2006) is closer in genre to a standard coffee table book, and consists largely of photographs of work completed. At a textual level, it consists almost entirely of the after part of the before/after image but is laden with the implied reference to what was before. The photographs invoke a space whose physical construction is largely complete, but which retains a sense that the buildings and streets have yet to fully come to life. Most structures are photographed in a frontal manner, and the light progresses through the book from morning to night. Very few images of construction or restoration in progress are present, and none at all of rubble or damaged buildings. There are also very few people or cars, and when they do appear in its pages, they seem deliberately included. The foreword to the book, written by Solidere's chairman Nasser Chamaa, remarks that the spaces and buildings depicted in the book seem "caught in a limbo of transition between the past and the future—startlingly individual in character and somewhat devoid of the kinship shaped by time and the formative imprint of human habitation" (Saliba 2004, 7). The foreword concludes with a forecast, that by the close of the Solidere project in fifteen years' time, the buildings would be interwoven with life and the project would have transformed Beirut "into a truly united city [blessing] its people with revitalized spirit. One can say that this, in its essence, was the ultimate dream that fired the vision of Rafiq Hariri and inspired the Solidere team" (Saliba 2004, 7). Indeed, the spaces do not bear any direct visual reference to the depredations of war. The book as a whole seems at pains to reassert the promise of the before/after image, and this last comment seems to be directed at the protests that at that point were ongoing in the city center. Much like the period that follows, the political project of neoliberalism appears here particularly thin and sterile, fractious and unconvincing even on the face of it, its telos the veneration of supposedly great men.

Conclusion: Consensus Is a Lenticular Image

If the postwar settlement was a form of consensus marked by the watchful presence of the Syrian regime and Rafiq Hariri's rise to power, the stability of that consensus was brought to an end by his public assassination by car bomb in February 2005. The public killing of the intermediary who helped put together the Taif Agreement was a message that all political bets on the country were off. The killing kicked off a series of massive protests for and against the Syrian regime's continued direct involvement in Lebanon, whom some accused of orchestrating the plot alongside Hizbullah operatives. Those protests would coalesce a new and highly polarized political factionalism, with groups named for the dates of their biggest rallies—Hizbullah and its allies thanking the Syrian regime for its postwar role (March 8) and the Future Movement and its allies organizing a counter-demonstration calling for Syria's immediate withdrawal (March 14).[83] Martyrs' Square was the epicenter of these demonstrations, as it was for later protests in Beirut. The UN special tribunal convened to investigate the matter became a touchstone for domestic politics for years afterward. Public assassinations became a defining feature of the urban landscape in the years that followed. The March 14 coalition was led by Sa'ad Hariri, the second of his father's sons, who had no prior political experience. The movement was soon dubbed the "Cedar Revolution" by a member of the US State Department, replacing the term "Independence Intifada" that it had originally given to itself.[84] Within a month, Syrian military and intelligence forces had formally withdrawn from the country. This new political polarization, tied to what has been called a regional cold war between the United States and its proxies and their opponents, only became more complex after the 2011 advent of the Syrian Civil War.[85] The post-2005 period was also premised on the reorganization of political sentiment in line with this new binary in the domestic political landscape, in which the politics of memory played a constitutive role.[86]

Hariri memorialization embodied many of the contradictions of the postwar period, and took many forms other than the brief mention in the coffee table book discussed above. The Future television channels owned by the Hariri family interrupted regular programming to give continuous coverage of the events following the assassination. Many other television stations echoed this sentiment, including Hizbullah, who referred to Hariri as a martyr to the nation. Just as telling is the memorialization that wrote on the spaces of the city, of which there were two primary forms: that which took place in fixed and relatively permanent locations, and that which took place in a dispersed and temporary manner. The former established a space of its own, while the latter became a part of everyday spaces. The primary fixed locations were the shrine opened on Martyrs' Square, and a statue of Hariri near the site of the bomb blast and the nearby sculpture evoking an explosion at the precise location (at the edge of the Solidere project and in front of the Saint-George Hotel). The owner of the Saint-George has never renovated its primary structure since, and maintains that the Solidere plans remade the coastline in such a way that the hotel's view, territorial integrity, and viability were compromised. The Hariri statue stands next to damaged buildings, and rubble remains meaningful even and especially within sight of the project.[87] Both of these pieces were placed in a traffic median flanked by often fast-moving cars.

The Hariri shrine was located next to the massive Al Amin Mosque that he had built, and is more amenable to visitors. The shrine was for many years housed in a semi-permanent tent, and included memorials dedicated to the bodyguards slain along with Hariri. The construction of a more permanent structure began in 2015, the decision seemingly being to no longer wait until the resolution of the investigation. The original structure was a relatively subdued affair, with the addition of artificial turf having been one of the only features that kept it from feeling like an extension of an adjacent parking lot. Prerecorded Qu'ranic recitation was piped in via loudspeaker. Fresh flowers, a few plaques, security guards, and large format photos were all that would greet visitors and keep the grave company when none were there.

Figure 2.12 One of the primary variations of Hariri Jr. and Sr. as they appeared in campaign materials. Note the deterioration at the edges (2010).

The shrine established a central reference point for the political organization of grief, which otherwise primarily took place in dispersed form. The tools of contemporary advertising were quickly deployed by both March 8 and March 14. The local Saatchi and Saatchi affiliate produced for March 14 what would be the first of many branded political campaigns. Its billboards placed slogans such as "The Truth" in white block letters on a solid black background. One billboard was placed at a prominent intersection of the ring road of the Solidere project (where it connects to Hamra Street). It featured a profile shot of Hariri with an electronic ticker counting the days since his death, and thus also days without "the truth."[88] Even though the billboard remains there at the time of writing, the days enumerated have long been inaccurate, possibly the result of glitches caused by long-term exposure to the power surges of Beirut's volatile electrical supply.

Hariri memorialization was quickly embedded within the political campaigning of the Future party, backed by the United States and led by his son Sa'ad. Posters of Hariri Sr. proliferated throughout many parts of Beirut (and other cities), supported by a larger budget than that of most other campaign advertising that would eventually clutter the urban landscape. Images of Hariri Jr. would soon follow, resulting in four basic combinations. The first was a photo of Hariri Sr. alone. The second was of Hariri Jr., sometimes accompanied by a cadre of prominent members of the Future party. The third variation would occur upon placing a photo of the father and a photo of the son next to each other (see figure 2.12). The fourth is a single photograph, featuring the son smiling in the foreground, and an unmistakable photo of the father in the blurred background. This photo within a photo echoes the mediation of spatial experiences that would take place within the reality of urban space. Yet posters have a materiality of their own. They become damaged by rain, fade in the sun, and peel over time before eventually joining the detritus of the city. They are also more easily modifiable than official shrines by whoever wishes to do so. Rather than tying a national public together around a common space or figure, the posters demonstrate how deepened social fragmentation and ruination are the truer outcome of the before/after image.

A string of public assassinations of prominent public figures followed Hariri's, as did respective public memorials. Many of those killed had taken outspoken anti-Syrian positions, including the journalists Jibran Tueni and Samir Kassir, Phalange party leader Pierre Gemayel, and former leader of the Lebanese communist party George Hawi. As surviving politicians became more and more fearful, private security zones popped up near their residences and offices across the city. In May 2008 tensions between these two factions escalated into a two-day-long gun battle across the city, with Hizbullah taking decisive control of the city before turning things over to the Lebanese Army. Secure Plus, the private security company that Hariri Jr. had built up in lieu of a militia,[89] quickly folded in the face of the more committed and better funded and trained forces of Amal and Hizbullah. Like during the Civil War, checkpoints, limited-access roads, and bunkers proliferated throughout the city, as did new radical groups.[90] Vision also became heavily policed. No-photography zones popped up, and unauthorized or "suspicious" photography could lead to detention by Lebanese internal security forces. A new urban geography of

Figure 2.13 Lenticulating print in Beirut Airport (2013).

overlapping sovereignties emerged on top of the disjuncture and exclusions created by postwar construction.[91] These sovereignties, which corresponded to geopolitical spheres of American and Iranian influence that the two polarized coalitions are under the influence of, became reflected in the fiefdoms of the fractured postwar consensus. Memorial photos generally followed the territorial logic of neighborhoods that had become more and not less defined by sectarian homogeneity since the end of the Civil War.

The Beirut airport, connected to Downtown by a highway built to bypass the poorer districts of South Beirut, was renamed for the "martyred" former prime minister in June 2005. Until the end of 2015, a series of transforming lenticular prints taken from the photo series published by Ayman Trawi in the book *Beirut's Memory* (2002)[92] hung in the west wing of the airport departures hall. This photo series, originally commissioned by Hariri, comprises the quintessential before/after images. The departures hall thus bids tourist mobilities goodbye with images of a space designed for a parallel form of circulation. Transforming lenticular images of this kind are produced by combining multiple photos shot with a specially designed lens into a single digital image, and then print-ing them on a plastic surface such that only one image is visible from any one angle. The result is that when a viewer moves past an image (or vice versa) it appears to change, a technique sometimes used in movie posters. Lenticular images (such as the ones on Cracker Jack prizes or movie posters) are often confused with holographic images. The basic true lenticular effect, in which an images changes when viewed from a different angle, predates lenticular photography or nineteenth-century experiments with stereography, and was actually achieved in painting as early as the end of the seventeenth century. As travelers leaving the country would walk or ride past the approximately three-by-four-foot prints on the moving sidewalk, the image would transform from one of ruined buildings and desolate streets to warmly lit cafés at night and impeccably polished buildings with children riding past on bicycles (see figure 2.13).[93]

The thing about lenticular images is that the visual change reverses when movement occurs in the other direction. The uncanny effect achieved by the posters is that when a viewer would move past them in the opposite direc-tion—in this case, from right to left and back away from the direction of the departure gates—the transformation appears to happen in reverse. The build-ings revert to their damaged state, and streets become scenes of ruin. Restora-tion never speaks more clearly of the contradictions of the postwar city and its images than it does here. These lenticular images highlight the foundational instability of the relationship between the before/after image and the spaces they helped make possible. The postwar transformation of the city center was always bound up with a way of seeing space, distinctly expressing the contra-dictions of postwar capital accumulation. The clichéd contrasts of the before/after image depend on an orderly visual mobility, which in the case of the im-ages in the airport is also true of the place of the viewer in relation to the image.

This unresolvable quality lends the before/after image to a dystopic and morbid reading: that the war will not remain just a memory or in the past, that the erasure of rubble leads to its ultimate return, and that a return to the war-time cityscape is inevitable. Capitalist realism's repetitions are made to seem inevitable, radical critique to appear anachronistic, and decolonization an im-possible horizon. These lenticular images show how in the imaginary distilled in the before/after image, destruction becomes a center of gravity in the same moment it is disavowed, in hopes of displaying the city as a foregone conclu-sion. For those who live in and near the many buildings that bear the marks of the war, this incompleteness is all the more concrete. Even in the images generated to secure financing for the neoliberal city, and the citizen-investor that they hearken to, the war continuously asserts itself. Yet the before/after shot image also ultimately and unwittingly signals the malleability of space—demonstrating that there have always been other possibilities for what has become of the city since postwar construction began.

3

Concealment, Liveness,
and Al Manar TV

> How a people reads the sky tells you a great
> deal about who they are.
>
> —John Durham Peters (2015, 170)

Critical approaches to infrastructure often move to historicize and contextualize what has been built into an existing system. The aim is to find the social, ethical, and political designed into the everyday or not so everyday, uncovering the decisions and path dependencies that shape the conditions of possibility of life and communication. Sociotechnical systems, like state and corporate power, are also often thought to function smoothly until a moment of dramatic breakdown reveals that which had been naturalized. Infrastructure is thought to be one with itself, often spanning the whole of a political territory or the entirety of the globe, or even what makes those wholes hang together. A more recent trend in the study of infrastructure imparts a different perspective, particularly as seen from parts of the world where the incompleteness internal to all infrastructure is more readily apparent. State projects are found alongside their double in semi-legitimate, paralegal, or pirate infrastructures.[1] The territory and the infrastructure are less than unified, the polity is plural and political authority multiple, and the system in a condition that lies somewhere between constant repair and partial breakdown. Infrastructure and urbanity may indeed be signal experiences of modernity,[2] but it is both an uneven and incompletable project which the state doesn't always monopolize. The virtues of access and connectivity are found alongside ways of doing things that routinize evasion, fakery, and knowing whom to bribe.

If it is true, as Peters (2015) argues, that ontology may often be a matter of forgotten infrastructure, then Hizbullah's mobilization of modalities of concealment in the war and demonstrations of 2006 dramatize the eventfulness that is infrastructural functioning. What of the truth of infrastructure that is discovered when seen from the dialectical vantage point of the decolonizing world, largely absent from Peters' generative account?[3] It may be true that infrastructure generally tends to recede from our awareness when it works well, or that its functioning may constitute a spectacular presence. However, there are also ways of being with infrastructure that aim to avoid detection, where not being seen or recognized is the principal objective. Concealment is easily missed in places where infrastructure functions smoothly, but in Lebanon the mediated everyday is punctuated by power outages as a matter of course. The extraordinary everydayness of Al Manar's live broadcasts is one component in these two events in 2006, which are marked by a swirl of visual vectors that move alongside the televisual, such as those of concealment and militarized targeting. There are antagonisms that overlap with attempts to maintain sovereignty over infrastructure. Rather than continuity and stability, media infrastructure appears as an open negotiation. In the 2006 war and at demonstrations staged by Hizbullah later that year, televisual liveness interlocked with actions that sought to employ and thwart modalities of concealment. This chapter explores the nature of concealment by examining how Al Manar's broadcasts were intertwined with this visual modality. I argue that, as a media-oriented practice,[4] concealment can be grasped as immunization technique, an active but only selectively communicative relation. Concealment and live broadcasting are the two central phenomena, both of which end up participating in the gendered categories of military action, technical expertise, and spectatorship.

The 2006 War in Context

The proximate triggering event that led to the 2006 war was Hizbullah's abduction of two Israeli soldiers in a cross-border raid, an effort aimed at securing leverage in future prisoner exchanges. The raid can be understood against a background of general hostilities—relatively continuous violations of Lebanese air space, public threats, espionage, and cross-border jockeying by both parties in the six years since the official end of the eighteen-year Israeli occupation of Lebanese territory in May 2000. The scale and intensity of the Israeli response seems to have caught Hizbullah by surprise,[5] and makes calling it the Israel-Hizbullah war misleading. The overwhelming majority of destruction wrought on either side of the border was to civilian life, most of which was inflicted on Lebanon by Israeli air power. Most of the arsenal Hizbullah fired at Israel were rockets that were not capable of precision targeting, making the sky in the north of the country an uncertain hazard. Aside from a momentary dip two weeks in, Hizbullah fired as many or more rockets on the last day of the conflict as the first.[6] The war lasted from the initial abduction on the morning of July 12 through the UN-brokered ceasefire on August 14. It has been called the 33- or 34-Day War, the July War in the Lebanese press (to distinguish it from other military conflicts with Israel), and the Summer War, the Lebanon War, and the Second Lebanon War in the Israeli press.

UN estimates put the death toll resulting directly from military action during the period of active hostilities at 931 Lebanese and 44 Israeli civilians killed, with 4,409 and 1,384 wounded, respectively. Military losses were far less, at 250 losses claimed by Hizbullah, and 121 by the Israel Defense Force (IDF). Body counts and bodily injury by definition do not quantify traumatic experience and the social effects of displacement, and the figure of close to a million Lebanese displaced means approximately one in five people. A very different picture of these supposedly less tangible outcomes—and of the social as a whole—emerges if we learn from the insight that social and aid workers have into the construction of the category of trauma and the gendering of care.[7] This is not to say that simply watching war on TV does not carry its own kind of toll, particularly given the diasporic nature of Lebanese society.[8] These numbers also exclude the loss of life, limb, and livelihood that occurred in the years after the ceasefire, such as from the IDF's use of banned weaponry such as cluster bombs.

In Lebanon the affective intensification that make these events intelligible as events takes place in a context where war and its aftermath come to be mundane. This ambiguity requires an expanded understanding of what it means to live before, after, or in anticipation of wartime—an ambiguity inherent to the categories of the event and the ordinary, or the nature of interruption.[9] Like in other episodes, the location of violence was marked by geographic disparities, where the meaning of place was significantly transformed by what was deemed targetable by the IDF. For example, while points of infrastructural importance were bombed throughout Lebanon, the majority and most intense bombardment took place in the south of the country. The bombing of Beirut was specifically focalized on its southern suburbs. This made it so that it was possible for some to watch what was happening on TV within earshot of the bombing, but have some degree of certainty that the bombing would not extend to their location. Ethno-religious identity collapses into political affiliation, which collapses into a widened scope of what constitutes a legitimate target. The toll of uneven exposure to violence—like the environmental damage and toxicity caused by damaged infrastructure—is marked by a range of attitudes toward how deserving those targeted are of the violence, often depending on one's political relation to Hizbullah.[10]

The war became the subject of a range of film and video works, some of which began filming during the war itself, blending fact and fiction. For example, *Under the Bombs* (dir. Aractingi 2008) principally tells a fictional story of a mother who returns to the country from the Gulf and journeys to the south in search of her son, and includes footage of bombardment shot on location both during and after the conflict had ended. *Posthumous* (dir. Salhab 2007) is documentary in its aims, but eschews narrative and realist conventions so as to reflect on the act of witnessing. It does so via the possibilities of a palimpsest-like image, superimposing scenes onto one another without completing the cinematic and temporal dissolve between them.[11] *33 Days* (dir. Masri 2007) gives more straightforward documentary treatment to how people adapted to the war, spending time with those displaced to Beirut from the south, and even with a TV news team. Short film and video work, whose format and production needs were a good fit for rapid-response filmmaking and exhibition, also spread in this period.[12] Other feature-length films also explored the line between documentary and fiction; for example, Joana Hadjithomas and Khalil Joreige's *Je Veux Voir* [I want to see] (2008) follows actress Catherine Deneuve and Lebanese artist Rabih Mroué on a trip through the south, pushing back against both common news portrayals and political appropriations of the destruction there.[13] As was the case with literary output in this period, the 2006 war was both unevenly experienced and sometimes prefigured by the ever-present memory of the Civil War, creating multiple planes along which public memory and the ordinary are interrogated.[14] A great deal of this output turns from a reflection on the unresolved nature of past conflict to the lived experience of witnessing the event unfold—and given the combination of general infrastructural bombardment and more specific targeting of South Beirut, made it so many watched bombs fall both on TV and with the naked eye.[15] The war also left its mark on Israeli cinema, particularly in works that explored the reactivation of memories of previous wars, and exploring the ambiguities of perpetrator trauma.[16] The lived experience of war (outside of immediate danger) can have its own kind everyday life, which can in turn end up suffusing a sense of the ordinary in the time that comes after war.[17]

The 2006 war has been the subject of intense study by military practitioners and defense experts—those who seek to make warfare more "effective." It attracted this kind of attention because of two aspects: it involved the first sustained air campaign by a state other than the United States since World War II; and it did not achieve the stated objectives of eliminating or significantly degrading Hizbullah's military capability. There is some disagreement in this literature as to why the IDF was unable to achieve these objectives. Some studies argue that the years of militarized response to the Second Intifada degraded IDF readiness for combat operations against an adversary who was significantly better armed, trained, funded, and prepared. In these accounts, counterinsurgency operations in Palestine are described as having dulled the ability to fight a conventional ground war. Policing the Second Intifada is said to have left ground forces without the kind of training, equipment, and intelligence network needed to effectively engage with Hizbullah, much less in a terrain that the party had been preparing in relative secrecy for years.[18] Other studies go to some length to argue in defense of the Israeli Air Force (IAF)'s performance record against a popular perception (within Israel and in military circles) that an overreliance on air power was to blame. This kind of response pushed back against seeing the war as evidence of a failure of air power in contemporary military doctrine more broadly.[19] Daniel Halutz, the chief of staff of the IDF from 2005 to 2007, was the first person in the senior post to come from an air force background, and would later resign in the wake of negative commentary about the war by former IDF leadership. However, it would appear that the "lessons" of the 2006 war were learned (or compensated for) in the comparatively less restrained 2009 assault on Gaza. Ever since this second war, the two have often been studied in tandem or in comparison by theorists of air power in particular. This pairing is a good indication of the extent to which the genealogy of IDF practices in Palestine and Lebanon are unevenly interwoven, one serving as the testing ground for the other.[20] The two end up being hypervisible within the arena of military study, made into the proving ground for Israeli martial valor.

The context for such practices to even be thinkable is a broader historical shift in which air power has transformed the location of the battlefront and the designation of legitimate targets. Echoing the sentiment that the 2003 invasion of Iraq was the latest in a series of episodes in which Western superpowers conduct weapons testing in Arab countries,[21] Derek Gregory (2006) argues that this indistinction between the terms *civilian* and *combatant* is part of the legal history governing the spatial expansion of the wartime frontline across society as a whole. This shift is in no small part tied to the advent of aerial bombardment earlier in the twentieth century. Gregory also argues that the war in 2006 in particular "worked to both widen the scope of a permissible target and to displace the concept of the civilian in ways that disclose the biopolitical project that has become central to late modern war and, most of all, to the 'war on terror'" (2006, 35). The verticality of aerial warfare had long been a crucial part of the management of the social, well before the 2006 war or the intensifications of drone warfare in the years that followed.[22] As discussed in chapter 1, the production and management of space and society in the British and French Mandates was fundamentally bound up with aerial reconnaissance and civilian bombardment.[23] The circulation of techniques of rule and those who claim expertise in its enforcement move through "horizontal circuits" with places like Palestine and Lebanon serving as important nodes or reference points.[24]

When the entirety of the social is framed as mere support for a military adversary, it is often the case that military objectives widen to the debilitation the social as a whole.[25] The 2006 war is a key moment in the deepening severity of responses to unconventional aerial attacks by the United States and its allies like Israel.[26] Even in the early stages of the war, IDF targets included major roads and bridges that it claimed could be used to move the captured soldiers out of the south. This soon expanded to key parts of the infrastructure throughout Lebanon, including the airport, major roads and highways throughout the country and to Syria, and fuel storage facilities; IDF also imposed a naval blockade. Significant evidence exists that medical personnel and first responders were routinely targeted, as well as buildings associated with people involved in non-military parts of Hizbullah.[27] In other cases, civilian and residential areas deemed to be sources of support were redubbed "Hizbullah strongholds," and entire buildings and blocks partially or totally destroyed, particularly large sections of Haret Hreik and other neighborhoods in South Beirut. What the so-called Dahiyeh doctrine demonstrates is the close pairing of killing and urban destruction with what can be described as power's productive capacity to not-let-die.[28] Civilian loss of life in South Beirut and the south of the country would have been significantly higher had vast sections of the population not correctly deduced that their choices were to flee or be targeted.[29] Beyond just a refusal of any social nuance, the phrase "Hizbullah stronghold" describes military architecture and not neighborhoods, and conflates political sentiment with a racialized military targetability.[30] The term also implies a model Lebanese liberalism that should already be opposed to a conflation of civilian and combatant imagined to be forged not by the biopolitics of targeting and civilian bombardment, but by Hizbullah's mere existence. This distinction between a liberal and illiberal Lebanese-ness was an Israeli state talking point at the time. The contorted logic underpinning this racialized distinction found a kind of culmination at the special meeting of the UN Security Council on July 14, where the Israeli ambassador argued that Lebanese liberal sentiment recognized that Hizbullah's presence was the true source of the conflict. Remarkably, he then made a direct appeal to his Lebanese counterpart, saying that in his heart he too agreed that Hizbullah was at fault, and that if he could, he would publicly agree that Lebanon stood to benefit from Israel stepping in to do the job of "cutting out the cancer" of Hizbullah.[31]

In the modernizing logic of War on Terror discourse such as this, aerial bombardment becomes the midwife of the future return of Lebanese liberalism, essentially through a plan for urban improvement. This hearkens back to the brutal roots of civilizational training for self-rule in the era of the French Mandate. In this biopolitical logic, to be capable of self-government was to demonstrate the capacity to recognize self-interest, as evidenced by recognition of the cultural and military superiority of the West. The 2006 war echoes the Mandate in at least three aspects found in this earlier period. First, as in the Mandate era, when the deployment of air power against civilian areas was first introduced, armed insurrection against a world power with air superiority was seen as primary evidence of the irrational and illiberal nature of a group, a racialization that both justifies and produces uneven exposure to violence. Second, as in the Mandate, when the bombed began to see the killing of non-combatants such as children as deliberate, the rhetorical claim to justice was often made through recourse to emergent international humanitarian frameworks.[32] This resonance can be seen in the use of cluster bombs by the IDF, who dropped massive amounts of the banned munition in the final days of the war, particularly expired and defective bombs that would remain scattered and waiting to detonate for years to come. Third, again as in the Mandate, there were attempts to hide from and even poke out eyes in the sky.[33]

There is a curious contradiction between two key points that recur in both popular and military commentary on the 2006 war, irrespective of which party is thought to be most at fault. The first point is that entire buildings or city blocks should (or should not) be completely or partially levelled because of actionable intelligence that Hizbullah was using civilian shields, who were (or were not) to blame for placing military targets in civilian areas. The second point—less discussed in popular discourse but confirmed in ballistics studies conducted by both Human Rights Watch and US investigators—is that Hizbullah fired the vast majority of its rockets in locations that were far from any inhabited areas.[34] This pattern of fire by Hizbullah is also confirmed by the fact that the majority of targets bombed by the IDF were actually locations in uninhabited areas such as valleys, mountainsides, and fields. Unlike NATO in Kosovo, the IDF did not release any operational details or records of how it determined targets, so the best evidence is probably what it actually bombed. While towns in the south sustained the heaviest bombardment, many of these were also towns in which Hizbullah fighters had confronted the IDF's ground offensive to prevent their occupation. The south of the country bore the brunt of the aerial and all of the ground assault. The IDF sometimes engaged in the practice of dropping pamphlets demanding people immediately leave areas where a more total approach to bombing would ensue, a practice that was coupled with sending text messages to the populace with similar warnings. Anything that moved in the south effectively became a legitimate target, because continuing to exist or move about in entire areas of the region was presumed to be giving support to Hizbullah activities.

Yet according to the IAF's public statements, it had bombed most installations of known military value within the first four days of the conflict. Air power's primary role thereafter, other than a general assault on Lebanon's infrastructure, shifted to armed patrolling, surveillance, support for ground operations, and rapid response to newly identified targets—often guerrilla hit-and-run missions that remained nearly impossible to anticipate.[35] The conflation of civilian and military targets is not plausibly a result of the spatial mingling of the latter with the former, and is more obviously the product of the process whereby militaries grant themselves the authority to determine the conditions under which all are and can be targetable. Yet even this intensification had little effect on Hizbullah's ability to continue to fire back. The contradiction here is that while anything could and potentially did become a target, the targets were nowhere to be found, or at least not until it was too late. In the politically stultifying grammar of defense expertise, the primary issue was the inability to locate targets of significant value in a timely way to begin with.

What is continuously suggested, sotto voce, is that the doublespeak of collateral damage and Hizbullah strongholds is not the only factor at play. The 2006 war, like the visual culture of the event, is suffused with modalities of concealment. Critiquing problematic news discourse is important, but there are also those media phenomena that do not appear publicly, by design. At the intersection of the infrastructures of satellite TV broadcasting, military surveillance and targeting, advanced information systems, and guerrilla tactics, there was an antagonistic set of relationalities whose primary aim was to *not* be seen.

The Mediation of Concealment

In the visual culture of war and protest, concealment is a crucial modality whose significance is easily misunderstood. Concealment is a heterogeneous set of practices and tactics that aim to keep people, places, and things out of sight, undetected, or unnoticed. If visualization brings people and spaces into the light, acts of concealment and the sociotechnical systems that enable them keep them in the dark. Concealment is formed in relation to media infrastructures and systems of surveillance. To the extent that infrastructure creates conditions of possibility for mobility and circulation, concealment is a visual modality that remains undetected while in motion (or not). The temporal nature of concealment is often defined by the unstable dynamic between spectacle and surveillance, but rather than their inverse, it is better understood to be in an open relationship with them. For example, a sensor or camera can be placed so as to remain concealed and optimally capture sound or images for broadcast audiences. The modality of concealment can fold into itself, or be folded into media forms like live broadcasts. Much as the techniques of war have served as the grist for media theorization[36] (say, from early optics to cybernetics), so too can concealment.

Concealment can also become a crucial part of the functioning of media infrastructure, or even extend to its physical presence. Consider how the placement of cellphone towers and internet cables in everyday spaces are sometimes designed to be unremarkable—that overlooked part of the everyday that might be termed "infrastructural concealment."[37] Concealment itself is not how infrastructure fades into the background, but a modality of deliberate non-appearance, which in some crucial moments can require the concealment of the infrastructure's material form or informatic signature. To make sense of the kind of mediation that occurs when concealment takes place requires a different understanding of the tensions of seeing and being seen. Peters succinctly encapsulates the intellectual ambit of what he terms "infrastructuralism" as "[sharing] a classic concern of media theory: the call to make environments visible" (2015, 38). To extend this insight, one might ask what concealment itself substantively is, particularly given the violent fractures that constitute visual culture. It is true that some kinds of infrastructure are built to hide their physical form, and in some parts of the world, also function smoothly enough to fade into the background textures and rhythms of the everyday. However, the events of 2006 demand that we consider concealment itself as a distinct modality, one that requires a reckoning with the nature of mediation adequate to the constitutive unevenness of infrastructural modernity. Concealment is not the unnoticed part of our habits and habitats, even if it might exploit them. It is better understood as a highly selective communicative mode.

The present study's focus on the visual should not be taken as a return to the long-since-corrected equation of mediation with a parched understanding of "the visual." If concealment is a visual modality, it is one that results not exclusively from so-called visual relations—the present focus on visuality is a key analytical limitation. In practical terms, concealment often means masking the heat signatures generated passively by human bodies and equipment or more suddenly by the launching of rockets, clarifying that the visual dimension is decisively intermingled with nonvisual elements. Techniques such as sonic masking and soundproofing—while clearly important for a fuller elaboration of concealment as such—are not given full treatment here.[38] The present theorization of concealment also gives limited treatment to digital and informatics strategies of anonymity and encryption—as used to secure electronic signal transmission, shield digital activism, enable the dark web, or to evade capture by data mining operations.[39] Much like the kinds of anonymity that a range of social theorists have found to be endemic to modern urban experience,[40] digital anonymity is also always a relative matter, and as locative mobile media demonstrate, is best considered as a part of lived place and space.[41] Like anonymity (often a matter of protecting identities, a chief virtue of journalism), concealment is socially productive precisely in the manner in which it delimits the spatio-temporal dynamics of observability.[42] Anonymity typically refers to the prevention of identification (or the refusal of identity),[43] but a state of concealment is about prevention of detection in a more immediate sense.[44] Hiding and remaining unidentified are both a question of how a range of tactics come together, a management or limiting of social relations. This in part explains why military forces sometimes maintain secure internet infrastructure that are structurally inaccessible from the wider internet, as is likely the case with Hizbullah's fiber optic network.

Concealment depends on social and technical systems of secrecy. While trade secrets and state secrets often depend on concealment, concealment is better understood to be a characteristic of a medial mode. However, the blackboxing of technology and proprietary software, for example, is not the same thing as the concealment that they might underpin. The secrecy that such blackboxing can enable might, for example, be better understood to apply to the algorithmic process of anticipation than to the location and likely movements of people and things.[45] Much like the techniques of control developed to counter them,[46] techniques of concealment typically take the shape of the social and infrastructural context in which they appear—speed limits, network protocols, and signal-to-noise ratios. To circulate is to accept and be acceptable to the terms and conditions that render one detectable and manageable. This difference between the technique(s) and the mode that results can also be seen in practices of obfuscation.[47] If obfuscation refers to a technique that generates enough false positives for a target that is presumably otherwise identifiable or targetable, then the state of obfuscation that applies to the individual emerges from but is not the same as that technique. Additionally, obfuscation refers to a much wider range of techniques than concealment, which in the present discussion is understood as a set of visual relations endemic to an infrastructural condition. As with camouflage,[48] the technique that maintains a relatively uncommunicative relation is not reducible to the modality that results: the mask is not the masked condition.

The achievement of a state of concealment does not arise from purposive acts alone, and cannot be understood to result solely from intentional mobilizations of the techniques of the unobserved. Making concealment systematically reliable means adapting to existing conditions, and so often bears the mark of the technical, political, and social incompleteness of a specific media infrastructure. It is one thing to find the hole in a surveillance system that is presumed to always work, and whose overseers are thought to be as unblinking as they are incorruptible. Yet there are many social conditions where infrastructure seems to begin to crumble before construction is even completed, where things are left not fully built, and where malfunction and repair are the uneventful everyday. Rather than thinking of media infrastructure in terms of a normal functioning and pathological malfunctioning, it is more productive to focus on the negotiations and modifications that define its continuity. This more contingent and eventful understanding of infrastructure is also necessary to grasp how concealment functioned in 2006. One of Hizbullah's strongest domestic political claims is that it emerged from the failure of the Lebanese state to protect its own territory, much less provide a system of redress for its disenfranchised citizens. It is this confluence of geopolitical antagonism and advanced infrastructural incompleteness that makes a focus on Hizbullah's media a fruitful one. All infrastructure is incomplete, but the visual culture of concealment in this case illuminates the general condition.

Much like the dynamics of secrets, there are those who are deliberately included in and excluded from concealment, and in the case of Hizbullah's military operations, not even all field commanders were given detailed knowledge of all the locations of hidden weapons caches, much less the timing and exact movements of other field operatives. At the same time, concealment is also quite historically specific, often transforming alongside weaponry, battle-field strategy, and surveillance techniques. For at least the last century and a half, it has often developed in response to attempts to see from above. The increased centrality of aerial observation in World War I, and aerial bombard-ment thereafter, followed on a transformed place of vertical observation of territory in cartographic practice.[49] As location and movement became in-creasingly knowable and trackable in real time, movement and hiding moved below the surface of the earth. Hizbullah's guerrilla capacity is in no small part due to its extensive network of underground tunnels, bunkers, and weapons caches—an open secret that nonetheless seems to elude even advanced surveil-lance techniques. Concealment can also coexist with those tactics that aim to hide in plain sight, that encourage misidentification by being conspicuous. As with the "narcotecture" of the tactics of the Central American drug trade and the strategy of the "war on drugs," there are architectural forms that announce themselves publicly, those that hide their real function behind a façade, and those that aim to evade detection completely.[50] Concealment, properly un-derstood, is not the misdirected attention of the DEA agent but the quality of hiddenness that obtains in the relation between the person or place hiding and systems of detection.

Concealment should not be naively valorized, as not all oppositional rela-tionalities result from admirable politics.[51] Displaced persons or the undocu-mented may seek concealment, but so might the militias or state agents hunting and disappearing them. Concealment may prevent safe houses from being seen, but it can also make prisons harder to find. Not all demands for transpar-ency are created equal. Much like the infamy of prisons in Syria and US black sites, it is possible to be generally aware that something is concealed without the concealment of the specific location ending. It is also no coincidence that the deliberate limitation of detainees' knowledge of where they are or even of the internal layout of the spaces they are being held through regimes of en-forced numbing, blindness, and silence are crucial to the sensory formation of these kinds of confinement.[52] Knowing that no one can find you can be a relief, or it can be part of the torture. In the case of Hizbullah guerrilla fighters, con-cealment is also premised on a militarized masculinity with roots that extend at least into the social formations of the militias of the Lebanese Civil War.[53]

Concealment has no necessary archive of its aesthetic formation per se, or at least none that even the most enterprising researcher would find after the fact if the modality of concealment remained uncompromised. It is better understood as an anti-inscription practice, or a non-sensory relation that gives nothing into evidence to the other save for a generalized sense of suspicion (in both observer and unobserved) that some other kind of trace may have been left unintentionally. In theory, hermeneutic methods should be of little use in the analysis of concealment, as any record or textuality is at best a secondary outcome. If seeing concealment were a desirable goal, the analytical mode best suited to the job would be military surveillance, or sousveillance, depending on the situation. Yet understanding concealment is crucial to making sense of the stakes of visual culture in the contemporary world. The events of 2006 are suffused with concealment that even made live television coverage of the event possible.

Rather than thinking of the relationship between media and events in terms of how media circulate the event (by focusing on the broadcasting of the event and social media commentary about it as it happens), the present analysis examines how concealment also structures the material possibility of the event as such, through a focus on Al Manar's continued broadcast signal during the war and demonstrations of 2006. Al Manar sits on a geopolitical fault line formed by the intertwining of regional and domestic politics. The post–Civil War allocation of Lebanese domestic broadcast licenses reflected two primary goals—maintaining a balance of sectarian control (no one group granted more licenses than another), and affirming the clout of powerful business interests.[54] Al Manar was one of a number of organizations allied closely to Hizbullah, and included publishing houses, newspapers, and production companies. The leadership and staff of the station has typically been made up of party members, and quite consciously positions its editorial line as one that aims to tell its own side of a story.[55]

It is the category of live television that allows Al Manar to most illuminate the relationship between media infrastructure and concealment. Liveness has long played a role in debates seeking to fix the medium-specificity of broadcasting, to unpack the ideological and economic projects of broadcast institutions, and in phenomenologically informed accounts of the temporal relation between media technologies and the users.[56] The promises of liveness in Arab and Lebanese television have long been bound up with political claims to represent competing realities, even if the genres that it arrives in are understood to be manufactured.[57] If television and liveness have always been globally and historically varied technological, institutional, and industrial formations,[58] then Al Manar's specificities allow for the opportunity to grasp the relationship between infrastructure and concealment.

Al Manar's origins lie in the transformations of the Lebanese broadcasting during the Civil War, a period that saw the vast multiplication of broadcasters, often by militias. Part of the bid for public legitimacy in the televisual sphere took the form of a bid to a closer, more responsive, and more authentic relationship with audiences, which affected the programming styles, production values, and type of Arabic used. This was drawn in contrast with the state and commercial channels that came before, an appeal to closeness with the "modern" sensibilities of the public staged through a renegotiation of gender—principally through the geometry of a female face to a male audience.[59] Al Manar would rework this gendered dynamic within the televisual sphere within its own protocols of modesty. The channel began satellite service in 1997, joining the then-booming and contested field of Arab satellite TV. Al Manar broadcasts often reflect a self-awareness of the channel's simultaneous presence in domestic politics affairs and of its place in a broader regional and global mediascape.

The already fraught relationship between Hizbullah and Western-allied Arab governments took a sharper turn in the first years of the US-led War on Terror. Carrying the satellite channel in the United States was legally deemed to be a form of providing material support to a terrorist organization in 2004. Not long after, Al Manar was also banned in a number of European countries after running afoul of rules regulating anti-Semitic content.[60] In the era before online and in-app livestreaming, the politics of satellite carriage was a question of the geographic contours of a viewing community. During 2006 the Al Manar signal was carried on Arabsat 2b, Badr 3, and NileSat, covering areas that extended beyond just the territories of Arab states.[61] In the two weeks from July 15 to 28, Al Manar saw a massive increase in its ratings, estimated as a jump from the eighty-third to the tenth most-watched channel in the Arab world (Al Arabiya edged out Al Jazeera as most-watched news channel in this same period).[62] At times, other news channels—domestic Lebanese, regional (such as Al Jazeera), and even the likes of CNN—rebroadcast footage taken from the Al Manar signal. Two kinds of footage were at a premium—coverage shot on the front lines in the south, and speeches by Nasrallah, who granted few interviews to channels other than Al Manar during the war.

This sketch of how Al Manar circulated in the period leading up to and during the 2006 war indicates a level of conflict unusual for most discussions of TV broadcasting, typically understood as the more stable and steady endeavor of states and major conglomerates. Al Manar's difficult position—even within the landscape of Arab television[63]—makes for a useful point of entry into considering concealment in the multiple visual vectors comprising the events of 2006. Concealment, military surveillance and targeting, and the technics of live TV simply don't come together the same way in places where watching bombardment on TV rarely if ever coincides with also being the target of that bombing.

Techniques of the Unobserved

The six objects examined here each demonstrate a different dimension of concealment. The first pair consist of concealment captured on camera for disparate purposes—a hidden Hizbullah camera unit that records a fighter's sudden transition out of a state of concealment, and footage taken from a drone cam capturing and guiding the targeting of a similar fighter. This first pair demonstrates how concealment captured is concealment uncovered, with stark differences in outcome. The second pair illustrates the conflict over the Al Manar broadcast signal: a short clip aired on Al Manar dramatizing the momentary disconnection of the signal following repeated bombing of the channel's headquarters, and attempts by the IDF to jam and hack the channel. This second pair exemplify how concealment can become bound up in conflicts around control over media infrastructure, and the cultural imaginaries that result. The third pair exemplifies how concealment can be combined with the staging of televisual liveness: first, in a televised rocket attack on an Israeli naval vessel coordinated with an on-air speech by Nasrallah, and second in the practice of tele-conferencing Nasrallah in to party rallies and protests later in 2006. These examples are not meant as a comprehensive account of all kinds of concealment, but are selected to demonstrate the political stakes and infrastructural dynamics that this visual modality is a part of.

1. Hit-and-Run Video

All this talk of concealment may give the impression that there is precious little concrete material to analyze, lest the discussion of concealment be limited to the imaginaries and decommissioned artifacts that sometimes turn up after the fact. Beginning in the 1980s, Hizbullah have videotaped and documented some militia operations conducted in concealment, and then later circulated those records alongside personal testimonies of fighters in popular media. Like the militant film movements of the 1960s and 1970s who originated this technique, the perceived value is realized by putting such records into circulation and thereby giving voice to a perspective that was originally hidden by necessity, an after-the-fact exploitation of the precarity of the apparatus that aims to extend itself to the viewer.[64] Filming guerrilla operations depends on the concealment of both fighter and camera crew. In a genre that I term "hit-and-run video," viewers are invited to see from within or even in alliance with a state of concealment.[65] Hizbullah has at times documented acts of concealment because of the perceived value in demonstrating martial capacity, but in other cases to provide journalistic evidence for claims about the nature of the facts of an event. After Operation Grapes of Wrath in 1996, Hizbullah reorganized and systematized combat documentation for the purpose of demonstrating the veracity of public claims regarding its military conduct.[66] It is possible to seek recognition as a political goal while also employing the tactics of concealment to make recording possible.

Even in the early years of what was once called Web 2.0, hit-and-run videos could be found on Hizbullah and Al Manar websites, and would unofficially find their way to online video-sharing platforms such as LiveLeak and dailymotion.[67] One such clip, titled *Hezbollah tactics during July War*, embodies this concealment of both fighter and camera crew.[68] The voices of two men remain off-screen while filming an empty hillside with a row of trees at the crest. This establishing shot is soon followed by an abrupt cut in which the camera (now zoomed out but in the same position) shows the launching of a series of rockets, the dust and smoke billowing in the wind and obscuring any discernible figures. The (English) captions then explain to the untrained viewer that the rocket crew successfully completed their mission. The use of the plural "they" in the captions might refer to a common division of labor in such operations, in which assembling a rocket launcher at a chosen site, arming it, and then firing it is divided into three distinct tasks performed separately by different teams. This requires a degree of skill and coordination, but makes it so the entire process can be mobile and completed rapidly. Soon after the launch in the video, the camera zooms in slightly to show a fighter escaping on a motorcycle, which both the camera crew and the captions point out. The video doesn't show where the fighter came from or leaves to.

In 2006 the movements of such fighters often existed in a state of concealment until the moment of the launching of rockets (and particularly the heat they generate) definitively ended it. In the video, the camera unit stays in place, presumably undetected, and records the dust clearing to reveal a rocket launcher. Unlike the fighter, the camera unit also sticks around to film the bombardment of the launch site that soon follows. Soon enough, after another abrupt cut, there is an initial missile strike followed by a series of bombs. The crew's casual banter continues, one person scolding the other for not recognizing the distinctive explosions of cluster munitions. The sound of a fighter jet indicates that a final strike is incoming, which then destroys the rocket launcher. This final sequence is the hit-and-run video genre's cinematic formation of a missile strike. First there is the sound of the jet off-frame, followed first by the sight and then by the sound of the explosion. In this case, the camera then zooms out to a wider angle to capture flying debris. The camera eventually zooms out enough to give away something about their position, as the camera shows a doorway and a darkened interior, and the hillside appearing much further away than suggested by the framing of the initial shots.

This video captures the fighter-motorcycle–weaponry assemblage phasing out of a state of concealment. The framing of the shots and the editing draw the viewer's attention to the performance of the guerrilla operation, but also highlight concealment itself. After the fighter flees the launch site and the camera's frame, it might be said that he (maybe) returns to a state of concealment from both the viewer and military surveillance, which in this case, are different perspectives. The use of "he" pronouns here is deliberately retained to reflect the distinctly masculine gendering of guerrilla fighters in the imaginary that surrounds such clips. This terminology guides the viewer to appreciating the dedicated masculine body, the skill required for the performance of battlefield mastery, and the political and spiritual commitment for such risk-taking. The viewer witnesses daring feats in the face of overwhelming odds, a viewing positionality made possible by the concealment of the camera crew who, by virtue of being privy to the location of the launch beforehand, are able to get footage of the landscape before, during, and after the rocket launch. The duration of each of these stages maps onto the shifting relations of concealment between the guerrilla fighter and the camera unit, and the guerrilla fighter and military targeting apparatus. The concealment of the camera unit is the condition of possibility for after-the-fact video replay. This additional visual circulation is not necessary to—and possibly endangers—the concealment of the fighter. Footage taken from hit-and-run videos circulated widely during and after the war, particularly in music videos on Al Manar, and in user-generated videos online. The online user-generated content typically patches together material taken from Al Manar programming, live news coverage, amateur footage, and weapons demonstration videos. An even cursory search with terms like "July war tactics" or "Hizbullah tactics" will turn some of these up. However, it is important to emphasize that concealment is not the same thing as the secondary recirculation of said material in celebration of military acts. Concealment is a specific modality within the event itself, not primarily a theme or aesthetic found in cultural memorialization or the video cultures that emerge in the wake of the event.

It is important to note some of the aesthetic, technological, and political specificities that define this particular hit-and-run video, and therefore the nature of the discussion of concealment so far. Hit-and-run videos typically involve a camera that stays on or near the ground. The camera is often close enough to the action to capture it, but far enough to keep the mission and camera unit safe. Given that the war is circa 2006, on Hizbullah's side of things the camera is probably not in an internet-enabled smartphone, and so the moment of visual capture and the moment of circulation are distinct. However, there are other situations in which Al Manar broadcasted from concealed locations or by concealed camera units near the battlefront, and as examined below, even staged attacks on Israeli forces for live broadcast. Finally, although the recording of hit-and-run videos does, strictly speaking, compromise the state of concealment, the outcome is limited by the crucial factor that this kind of looking is temporally separate from the moment of its circulation, and is not part of a process of targeting by an opposed force. Concealment need not be total, and is defined by the difference between those who do and do not know (or can and cannot) compromise it. If it is true that one should not automatically equate concealment with "resistance" in anything other than a specific and situational sense, then it is also true that not all attempts to maintain a state of concealment are successful.

2. Targeting Concealment

Concealment is often arrayed against live surveillance connected to weapons systems—those techniques of anticipatory inscription that guide the delivery of force.[69] Concealment needs to be timely, lest it be uncovered by forms of targeting that make it possible for detection to be rapidly converted to destruction, and captured in what might be called guncam images. These imaging techniques have been productively engaged in the literature on drones—an interdisciplinary conversation that has engaged the intertwining of political, technological, and cultural dimensions of warfare.[70] In this literature, the question of drones and visuality are most often theorized in relation to a situation that is both quite specific and almost ubiquitous—powerful governments and military agencies employing drones to watch and/or attack people from above. The ten years between 2005 and 2015 are crucial, in that this period is defined by a rapid escalation in the use of drones to kill—primarily by the United States and its allies in countries such as Afghanistan, Iraq, Pakistan, Somalia, and Yemen. Armed drones are also used elsewhere, and really anywhere that counterterrorism or military operations decide they need to go.

The use of drones in the 2006 war is different in at least two significant respects—both sides in the conflict utilized drones (albeit with very uneven capacities), and both sides were capable of attacking the other's home turf (albeit with significant limitations in distance, scale, and precision by Hizbullah). The IDF routinely utilized drones for reconnaissance purposes, and only more rarely as the method for attack. More specifically, the IDF utilized Hermes 450 and Searcher 2 model drones to transmit targeting data to AH-64 Apache attack helicopters in real time.[71] Hizbullah also deployed drones of their own— most likely the Iranian made Mersad-1.[72] Hizbullah had successfully flown drones into Israeli airspace as early as 2004, and although the Mersad-1 can be configured to carry a weapons payload, in 2006 they were used only for reconnaissance. Concealment can enable circulation under conditions of targeting and surveillance, but can also depend on countervailing surveillance. The visual vectors in the event are multiple. Hizbullah's attempts at concealment included routine monitoring of the sky for the presence of aerial surveillance, the tactical movements of fighters sometimes coordinated to wait for surveillance aircraft to leave before deploying for guerrilla operations. The hidden weapons caches established throughout the south long before in anticipation of a future war remained concealed in fixed points (typically in hillsides far from inhabited areas).

The macabre details of the tools of war should clarify and not obscure the political nature of the broader process in which these imaging techniques are embedded. The majority of surveillance and guncam images of the 2006 war did not circulate beyond the immediate intended operational purpose of targeting.[73] However, in response to international criticism of the scale and intensity of the IDF's response to the Hizbullah abduction, some guncam footage was declassified and released to news agencies to legitimate the claim to be responding to clear and present threats in a precise way. Most of the footage seen on TV news, in this and arguably other situations, are only those parts that seem to demonstrate precision targeting—meaning that a (supposedly) verifiable target is visible in an image, and requires a timely response. Yet the evidentiary meaning of these images is by no means guaranteed, and like the use of satellite imagery in the run up to the 2003 invasion of Iraq, requires a great deal of interpretive scaffolding to ensure that they are read "like a state."[74]

Figure 3.1 is an example of this perhaps all-too-familiar kind of guncam image, but this particular image stages a situation that is the guncam/drone warfare equivalent of the torture/ticking time bomb scenario, as popularized by the TV show 24 and pro-torture apologia. Both scenarios imagine a foe who either poses or has knowledge of an imminent security threat, and that the prevention of this future threat justifies the decisive application of violence to extract information or interrupt a clear and present danger. In the video clip

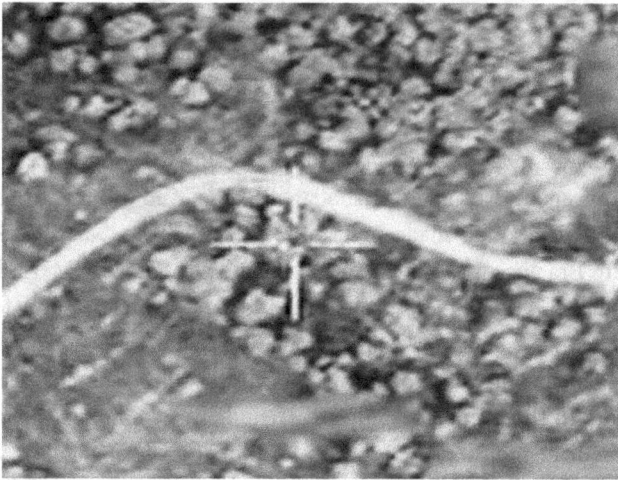

Figure 3.1 Still from *Israeli Strike against Hezballah's Katyusha Rocket Launcher.*

that this image is taken from, the viewer is shown what appears to be a hit-and-run operation, possibly like the one documented by the concealed camera crew in the hit-and-run video discussed above. The slow circling of the camera overhead is coupled with the movements of the fighter, a barely discernible blip whose concealment has been overcome. The missile strike follows soon after, the violent verticality brought to fruition. With guncam images, the line between anticipatory and reactive violence become slippery, the one blending into the other.

There are many similarities between the surveillance drone–aided helicopter strike mentioned above and the armed drone strikes that feature more prominently in contemporary debates. This kind of image demonstrates the degree to which concealment and targeting can become intimately bound together in a self-perpetuating process, or what Chow describes as the self-referentiality of war, which changes from "negative blockade to routine, [becoming] the positive mechanism, momentum, and condition of possibility of society, creating a hegemonic space of global communication through powers of visibility and control" (Chow 2006, 34). The mode of racialization produced through such violence finds its expression in the affective present tense of guncam images. For some, these images are horrific because they are evidence of a violent "them" trying to harm "us," with untold others lurking in concealment, waiting for the opportunity to inflict sudden harm.[75] The logic of preemptive killing is made to seem justifiable. For others, the horror may be found less in the potentially imprecise application of preventive violence (the endlessly repeated and frequently self-discredited claim about precision strikes) than in the inability to complete the fold of a loop demarcating "us" and "them"; the process of elimination becomes defined by its incompletable nature. Drone operations, and the kinds of aerial killing that they are a part of, deliver violence to (and by) people who are already dehumanized, in spaces where killing is already deemed acceptable.[76] There is a different resonance when viewers understand themselves to potentially be categorized as the silent blip on the screen—in seeing oneself made into a silent target. Responses to this moment of recognition have typically been less than silent.[77] These differences are made manifest in wars such as this one, where guncam images have circulated globally, but also in both Lebanon and Israel.

Baudrillard (1995) famously critiqued the first regular appearance of images similar to these during the first US war on Iraq, decrying a war that never took place. Here again, Al Manar proves useful to media theory. The images discussed in Baudrillard's text would presumably have been those released by the US military, typically circulated on CNN with a viewing audience assumed to be very far from where missiles meet targets. How much critical purchase is gained, though, by describing such images as unreal in situations and places where people can both hear and feel the bombs fall around them, while also watching multiple and conflicting news reports of the event they are a part of?[78] There may be something missed in imagining all such images to be like shadows in Plato's cave, especially given the centrality of underground bunkers and infrastructure to Hizbullah's tactics of concealment. As Massumi suggests, via Deleuze and Guattari, there may be conditions where "the resemblance of the simulacrum is a means, not an end. . . . there is a power inherent in the false: the positive power of ruse, the power to gain a strategic advantage by masking one's life force" (Massumi 1987, 67).

It is certainly true that in the biopolitical logic of risk management—which has always had a racializing logic—there is typically first a spatial designation of an area in which circulation and mere presence are presumed to be indicators of threat, and therefore targetable.[79] Since the Obama administration (and after the 2006 war), areas such as the Federally Administered Tribal Areas in Pakistan felt the effects of the increased use of drones by the United States.[80] Racialization also typically involves a conceptual structure in which the other is an unstable presence, or an inability for foundational violence to either stabilize the existence of the other, or to ensure that their continued presence will not be a future threat. For targeting systems in the 2006 war, concealment became a weaponization of this spatial incalculability.[81] For as long as trickery, deceit, and an incapacity to produce truth have been thought to be negative attributes of racialized and gendered others, techniques such as guncam images have been utilized to attempt to fix the truth of their bodies within frames that render them legible and violable. If the recirculation of guncam images in TV news originates in an attempt to justify the outcomes of extensive bombardment, it does so by suggesting that the (dishonorable, cowardly) employment of concealment is the true culprit for the loss of civilian life. It is also as though even the condition of visibility found in guncam images—and other moments in which concealment is uncovered—reaffirms the continued existence of concealment elsewhere.

A significant accomplishment of the critical literature on drones has been to bring witness testimony and phenomenological accounts into public discussion of the consequences of drones.[82] 2006 complicates this strict dichotomy of speaking targeter and silent targeted, given that Al Manar's broadcast continued (almost) without interruption despite heavy bombardment, and given Hizbullah's ability to return the gaze and return fire. This reciprocity should not, of course, distract from the vast imbalance in devastation wrought on civilian life, or from the subsequent militarization of the experiences that resulted.

3. The Faithful TV Signal

The Al Manar broadcast signal, the condition of possibility for the viewing community, depended in an acutely material way on the concealment of broadcast infrastructure. The channel embodied a uniquely positioned perspective within the Lebanese television landscape, and catapulted to a previously unattained popularity at the forefront of regional attention. The fact of continued transmission, much like the journalism it circulated, came to have a symbolic value of its own. As support for Hizbullah or Lebanon grew, the Al Manar signal came under concerted attack by the IDF. The offices of other Lebanese media organizations also came under attack, albeit less severely, as did some of the cell towers of both Alfa and MTC Touch, the two major domestic service providers.[83] Al Manar's main offices were bombed repeatedly from the earliest days of the war, and on July 16 the signal was briefly knocked off the air following an air strike. This was likely the result of the destruction of the channel's primary transponder, connecting it to the main satellite uplink utilized by most terrestrial Lebanese broadcasters, located in Jouret El-Ballout (about twenty kilometers northeast of Beirut). While bombing totally destroyed the station's main archive, the signal only remained off the air for a few minutes, or the time it took to switch over to a concealed secondary transponder. This backup system seems to never have been located.[84] Sometimes the infrastructure facilitates the concealment of people; other times the catastrophic loss of the television signal is a known potential outcome, and the infrastructure is more rigorously concealed.[85] Television forms an important part of the everyday in ordinary circumstances, and can play a similarly comforting role in the everyday of war—perhaps serving as a crucial link to a felt community of viewers, or even becoming a link to ordinariness itself.

The channel remained on air for the remainder of the war, even broadcasting live from the front lines. Soon after the temporary disconnection, Al Manar began to air a clip titled *An Inextinguishable Flame* dramatizing the episode. The Arabic word for flame used here, *sha'la*, bears the connotation of a light by which one may see, and plays to the channel's name (Al Manar can be translated as "the beacon").[86] *An Inextinguishable Flame* exemplifies the importance of the technical functioning of media infrastructure to the form taken by religious belief and political commitment in the context of live television. This is the case not because Al Manar is somehow more religious than other satellite news channels but because of what the clip reveals about the articles of faith found in communal and transnational viewing experiences more generally.

The narrative arc of *An Inextinguishable Flame*, which runs about two minutes in length, begins and ends by highlighting the spatial relationship between the Al Manar newsroom and people watching the channel on TV in their living rooms. The spaces of the newsroom and living rooms are arrayed against two other spaces—an air force control room and the cockpit of a fighter jet. The clip opens on the date of the bombing (July 16) on a black background, and the sound of an Al Manar news presenter describing the devastation of the day. He soon appears on screen and in the station's studio. As he continues to elaborate on the events of the day, the camera pulls back to reveal him to be on a TV in a living room watched by a group of people whose ages make them legible as an extended family. Over the course of the clip, the viewer is also shown two other living rooms, and the headdress worn by one of the men signifies a viewing audience extending to the Gulf. This imagery of the television in the family circle and in a gendered domestic space dates to television's earliest days, and in this case highlights that the audience is multiple.[87] The clip cuts between scenes of a fighter jet taking off and closing in, and the audiences at home and the newsroom unaware. In one moment, a concerned mother covers a child's ears so as to protect her from the description of the details of war. The score, which began slow and with vocal lamentation in a minor key, builds in tempo and symphonic density until the tension culminates in the impact of the strike, initially seen via guncam and then confirmed on the control room's radar. Communicative collapse becomes military and affective catastrophe. To the dismay of the audiences at home, their TV screens turn to static. For a brief period, the viewer is shown the audiences watching static as the score shifts to a low mournfulness, confusion turning into despair.

Total disconnection appears to be an intolerable communicative experience even in melodramatic recreation, equated with unbearable injustice and narrative irresolution. But in *An Inextinguishable Flame*, the viewer already knows that the on-screen audiences need only keep their faith, and the signal will return. Soon enough, the non-diegetic score begins to pick back up even as the on-screen audiences seem to sink. As the music begins to swell, a new character appears—not Nasrallah or a commando, but a man with white hair in a small room full of communications equipment (figure 3.2). The communications technician seems to have already completed his work, and looks upward mouthing words as though in prayer, with his hands cupped as to indicate the performance of *dua'*, or prayer of imploration. Even though the gesture is only shown briefly, it would be quite recognizable in its specificity to viewers familiar with it. Soon after, a beam of white light shoots heavenward from a cityscape seen through guncam. The beam connects with and charges a satellite, which then fires the signal back to Earth and into television screens (figure 3.3), to the relief of the people at home. The signal also returns earthbound weaponized by its communication with astral technology, and the fighter jet is forced to take evasive action to avoid the bombardment of light. With the jubilant audiences watching the returned broadcast at home, and the score triumphant, the clip ends with the Al Manar logo on a white background, with the tagline "An Inextinguishable Flame."

Underpinning the allegory of the properly oriented TV family, then, is the steadfast masculine expertise of a communications technician. The viewer, but not the audiences in the clip, are briefly shown the inside of the heart of the concealment, the source of the return of the signal. God may not be in the TV, but does seem to be forward-compatible with broadcast satellite protocols. Evidence of divine favor in return for steadfastness in the face of adversity is thought and felt to work through the functionality of broadcast infrastructure. The audience completes the circuit of miraculous reconnection of the live feed, reaffirming the justice to be had by those who tune in to the truth, in the face of those who are led astray by the (fake) news of the misguided. God helps those who don't switch the channel at the first sign of technical difficulties. The clip contains a contemporary articulation of political themes

Figure 3.2 The communications engineer, *An Inextinguishable Flame.*

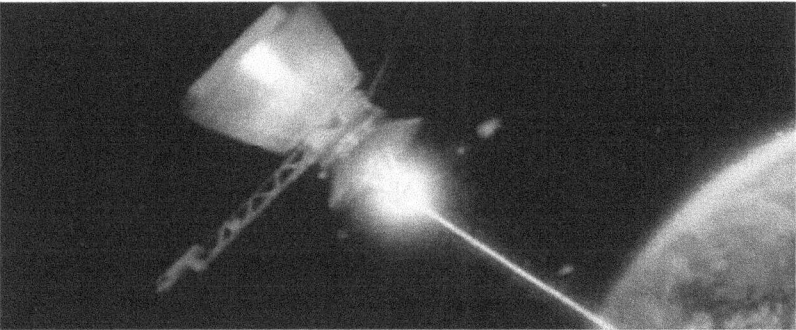

Figure 3.3 The moment of reconnection, *An Inextinguishable Flame.*

that have deeper historical roots, not only in Hizbullah's rhetorical claims to be defenders of the nation[88] but also with religious or theological connotations of the aesthetic formation of the "seen" and the "unseen."[89] However, it is also no accident that media technology figures prominently, both in this clip and to the lived experiences it reimagines. The specific form taken by religious expression, practice, and experience are an adaptation to the media forms present, putting the capacities of the infrastructure to new purpose. To see material culture and aesthetic form as merely incidental carriers of truth would be to commit to an unnecessarily flattened and static view of the history of religious traditions.[90] Matter subordinate to spirit, the paper supplement below the Word—a set of philosophical and theological propositions that would limit our understanding of meaning made both of the technology and of the inner compatibility of broadcasting with modern religious experience.[91] Attacks on infrastructure like the ones dramatized here are attacks on both the social experience and condition of possibility of a viewing community.

The clip has much in common with the structure of feeling found in dedicated or partisan TV viewing habits, secular or religious. The texture of religious and communal experience had long been adapted to the circuitries of live television well before this episode and, despite the intensity of the channel coming under concerted attack, should not be understood to be totally new. The Al Manar broadcast schedule had for decades programmed content that was explicitly religious, including live coverage of religious commemorations and sermons. Viewing Al Manar undoubtedly was one means through which many felt connected to a broader community and its history. Were it to be understood as a ritual form, one would need note that it appears to be one underpinned by the more general formation of mobile privatization, in that it depicts domestic spaces understood to be a private refuge from the world that media or television nevertheless keep it connected to.[92] Official guidance as to how to correctly parse divine will in the earthly events of 2006 was given by Hizbullah later that year—the miracle of 2006 was not said to involve direct divine intervention (into combat or TV broadcasting), but was to be found in the cumulative outcome of individual and collective dedication. *An Inextinguishable Flame* shows the miraculous can emerge from steadfastness in the face of tremendous odds and devastating injustice. The beam of light that signifies the restoration of the signal leaps almost directly from the cupped hands of the communications engineer. In the clip, the cut is from a camera positioned in intimate proximity to and focused on his up-turned face, to a downward-looking gaze from far above the earth's surface, ideally positioned to see the beam shoot upward before it eventually connects with the satellite in orbit. Defeated by the force of the connection's restoration, the fighter jet spirals away in defeat. Staying tuned is equated with military victory, and passing the spiritual test is defined not by the absence of fear but in remaining firm in the faith that the signal would return despite it. The figure of the technician can therefore be understood to be placed in affective terms alongside, or mirroring, the people waiting at home.

An Inextinguishable Flame demonstrates the extent to which an ethics of counter-witnessing is bound up in visual and sensorial subjectivity—a way of being both immersed in and opposed to a global visual culture hostile to the truth of the community. This mode of engagement depends on a near-continuous consumption of images, particularly those that are produced in a nearly simultaneous temporal relation to the event, or where the broadcast *is* the event. In this case at least, the viewing ethic is imagined as a trial of staying tuned in to the truth rather than the drama of turning away from the plurality of the false found elsewhere in the media landscape. The moment of *dua'* affirms holding fast until the return of the signal, a certainty possessed by the viewer but not the characters. In warzones, on-air technical difficulties can include issues of greater severity than a malfunctioning studio microphone or audio delay.

A different facet of the vectors enabled by concealment can be found through a brief counterfactual consideration of *An Inextinguishable Flame*. What if the primary overt reference to a specific religious tradition were removed—if the clip did not feature the very brief *dua'* scene? Other than inferring the identities or political attitudes of the viewers from their dress, or from the confluence of fighter jet contra the Al Manar newsroom depicted, what would make this clip specifically Islamic (or more specifically, Shi'ite) in nature? It could be argued that the opening of the clip on the date of the bombing is a historical reference that bears a relationship to a specific community, but even then the date is reckoned on the Gregorian calendar. Taking a different approach, a case could be made that the structure of feeling dramatized in the clip, and the way it marshals memory, give it an unmistakable stamp. It would not be a huge leap to see the clip's dramatization of an audience distraught by news of Israeli bombardment, the temporary disconnection and then return of the signal, and the reaffirmation of faith rewarded (guided by lamenting vocals and a synthesizer-based score) all invoking the aesthetics of a politically committed stance vis-à-vis Israel that Hizbullah has adopted for some time. This is to read an implied viewer off of the image; ethnographic research could undoubtedly yield rich insights into the resonances with actual audiences. A more detailed study could also be made of both these and other citations of Islamic tradition in Al Manar's programming. Yet the concealment of the backup transponder, and the geography of audience, battlefield, newsroom, mobile camera units, and numerous other actors would seem to be equally important to understanding the specifically live televisual nature of the event dramatized. The continuity of the signal, the fact of its arrival, is both materially and symbolically crucial.

4. Jamming and Hacking the Signal

With the war grinding on, and with Al Manar continuing to broadcast, the IDF turned to two other tactics to disrupt the signal—jamming it and hacking it. Signal jamming refers to attempts to temporarily introduce noise and other kinds of electronic interference into a signal that otherwise continues to function autonomously. Signal hacking, on the other hand, is when one party takes control of another's broadcast—typically playing content of the hacking party's choosing or blocking the broadcast entirely. These two tactics may differ in terms of how they take advantage of a channel's continued broadcasting, but both reflect an infrastructural antagonism that in part resulted from the concealment of the Al Manar transponder. Attempts to jam and hack the channel probably date to the late 1980s. According to Al Manar's public relations office, IDF technicians were able to introduce static and other kinds of interference on at least ten separate occasions during the 2006 war. Beginning in the last weekend of July, the signal was repeatedly hacked and temporarily replaced with a number of short clips, two of which I call "Target Nasrallah" and "Dead Bodies." If signal jamming is akin to an act of vandalism or desecration, then these two examples of signal hacking were tasked with the pedagogical function of discrediting Nasrallah on the party's own channel. Although signal jamming occurred with greater frequency, these cases of signal hacking play out the overarching objective ultimately underlying both tactics—to demonstrate the continued vulnerability of the otherwise concealed signal through a brief performance of technological domination. In both cases, the act of overriding the effect of concealment was to display the vulnerability and targetability of male bodies.

It is no coincidence that both clips aim to discredit public statements made by Nasrallah in ways that emphasize the ongoing violence of war. Both clips aired in Arabic, and drew on snippets of actual statements made by the party leader. "Target Nasrallah" does so by airing a segment from a speech he had made on July 25, in which he commented on the IDF's air superiority.[93] The clip opens and closes with a sketch of Nasrallah (in crosshairs) that flashes to the staccato of gunshots, and with a caption identifying the new broadcaster. The rest of the brief clip shows guncam footage depicting airstrikes, with captions identifying targets as Hizbullah rocket launchers or bases of operation. The clip ends by accusing Nasrallah of dragging the entire country into war, a criticism that had been made both within Lebanon and beyond, and which the original speech responded to. The clip also accuses Nasrallah of "hiding the truth" of the results of his actions from the eyes of his constituency, like a supplement to ensure that the lessons of bombardment would be correctly instilled, clarifying to recalcitrant subjects what their senses may have muddied.

"Dead Bodies" is even grislier, in that it doesn't just threaten Nasrallah, or attempt to equate aerial bombardment with the perspective of a guncam. The clip dwells on photos of recently killed Hizbullah fighters, overlaid with the sound of a helicopter in flight. The sound of helicopters circling overhead is one point where the soundscapes of militarized urban policing and counterinsurgency dovetail.[94] Like "Target Nasrallah," the clip cites a televised speech by Nasrallah (on the subject of inflicting heavy losses on Israel without sustaining much in kind) and accuses him of hiding the truth of dead bodies "all around you" from the viewing public. The evidence of the corpses presents a challenge to the heroic representation of fighters. With the loss of life disproportionality civilian in nature, and given the high rate of internal displacement within the country at this point, the clips are better understood not as public service announcements but as the kind of performance of the capacity for violence that results when said violence stops achieving tactical goals. Like with the practice of dropping leaflets in residential areas warning people to leave before bombing ensues, the outcome of such interventions is not primarily informational. The actual message is in the ability to take control of the signal, or to follow leaflets with bombs. The exercise of sovereign power resides in the communicative gesture itself.

In 2006 the vulnerability of communication signals was also an important part of the cultural imaginary. The Israeli ground offensive was met with fierce opposition, even sustaining heavy losses of Merkava tanks that had previously been a symbol of invulnerability. Unlike previous attempts on Lebanese territory, the push failed to advance very far north of the border. This outcome was primarily due to Hizbullah's years of preparation of a largely underground infrastructure that enabled surprise attacks and entrenched defensive positions, and an information environment that was described (by both adversaries in the conflict) as Hizbullah fighters seeming to appear to know Israeli troop movements in advance. While this impression of advanced knowledge may be readily explainable as the outcome of Hizbullah's detailed understanding and reshaping of the terrain, stories began to circulate that the security of IDF field communications had been compromised. In addition, on more than one occasion, Al Manar reported the names of IDF troop fatalities before Israeli media.[95] Many IDF field units utilized radio frequency skipping to keep lines of communication secure—a technique whereby a signal is not just encrypted, but continuously jumps from one frequency to another in a synchronized and randomized manner. When coupled with Hizbullah's efforts to spread the rumor that it had access to unspecified but sophisticated listening equipment, some IDF officials grew suspicious that IDF signals may not be secure. More careful study would later prove such rumors to not have been true, and more explicable by the interception of other, less secure communication such as cellphones.[96] In truth, the effect of anticipatory guerrilla action is more readily explained through the laying of traps and luring the IDF into pre-planned ambushes.

While Hizbullah may not have been able to listen in on secure military communication, and didn't jam or hack Israeli television channels in the way that the Al Manar signal was, they did manage to pair concealment with continued broadcasting in other crucial ways. As in the imaginary expressed by *An Inextinguishable Flame* and found in the practices of signal jamming and hacking, concealment is an antagonistic spatiotemporal relation between detection and the unobserved. Conversely, concealment can also be paired with live television to stage spectacular events for a live viewing audience.

5. The Word and Deed, Live

The final pair of objects demonstrates how live television can become bound up with concealment in ways that illustrate the stakes and political ambiguity of the modality. The relation between concealment and television coincide with the ideology of televisual liveness—that is, with the coordinated simultaneity of historic event and broadcast camera. Hizbullah's practice of recording field operations historically began with a delay between the moment of recording and the moment of mass circulation. Something different is at work when the concealment of the camera unit and field operatives are joined with the live broadcast—namely, the ability to remain concealed becomes directly equated with the ability to communicate the moment *in* the moment. It also comes with the risk of giving away the location of the camera unit, or appearing to threaten anything shown in the frame.

In the past, taping guerrilla attacks typically involved making a recording in the field, and then replaying the tape on Al Manar at some later time. For example, when Hizbullah filmed their assassination of a high-ranking military officer via roadside bomb in the final years of the Israeli occupation of Lebanon, the film crew was concealed, but the moment of recording came well before the broadcasting of the tape.[97] Something different is at work when the event of recording is coterminous with that of transmission. For example, the liberation of prisoners held in the infamous Khiam prison following the liberation of the south was broadcast live on Al Manar, a moment of great or even overwhelming affective intensity bound up in the sense of witnessing a long-hoped-for moment unfolding before the eyes viewers and participants on the ground.[98] Both bank on television's promise to approximate "being there," or to relive the original simultaneity of the act of witnessing through the possibilities of endless playback (even when the time of viewing comes long after that of the original simulcast).[99] However, the live coverage of the liberation of Khiam's prisoners does not depend on concealment directly, but reveals how the end of the occupation made the need for it no longer as immediate.

The bombing of the INS *Hanit* on live TV, timed with a Nasrallah speech that made reference to the act of bombing as it occurred on screen, represents the union of televisual liveness with multiple types of concealment. This involved the concealment of two camera units who were on standby, of the team firing the rocket, and of Nasrallah. Maybe it goes without saying that the broadcast infrastructure was also concealed. Previously, naval vessels had operated off the Lebanese coast with impunity, and in plain sight of those on land. This first-ever incapacitation of an Israeli ship was integrated into a speech by Nasrallah, and also timed to coincide with and interrupt a press conference of the IDF's chief of staff. The speech begins by discussing the stakes of open warfare, both lamenting its arrival and promising to make good on the threat to deliver unanticipated tactical surprises. Nasrallah then begins to speak in the present tense, referring to the current presence of the ship off the coast, and then directing residents of Beirut to look to the sea to "look at it . . . as it burns." During this part of the original broadcast, the image on screen switched from a still of Nasrallah (a standard visual replacement during speeches), to footage of the vessel recorded earlier that day, to live footage showing the ship, and it then being struck by a missile. Al Manar continued to roll on the spectacle of the ship burning at night, the light of the fire lasting for a few hours as fuel barrels had been ignited. The strike killed four crew members, destroyed the onboard helicopter, and nearly sank the state-of-the-art vessel.

Other than possessing land-to-sea capabilities that the IDF either didn't know about or failed to act on, the strike was premised on the staging and coordination of three key elements. First, the camera crew were instructed to roll on the ship throughout the day, in anticipation of capturing an eventual strike on camera. The time-sensitive component was the coordination of the delivery of the speech with conditions optimal for a successful strike on the ship, but only switching to the live camera unit moments before the strike itself so as not to signal a pending threat or give away their position. The airing of the speech—likely prerecorded—was itself the signal to launch the strike. It is important to note that the promise of liveness—of being present at the unfolding of the event—involves remaking the event to fit the form of a television broadcast. The artifact of liveness was a crucial part of the effect of surprise, as the performance of martial capacity appears to be most fully realized with the publicity of the strike for people who could watch with the naked eye, for domestic audiences, and for transnational audiences that included Israel. The simultaneity found in staged liveness such as this broadcast is a technical artifact, made coterminous with the real-time nature of concealment. It would be a mistake to equate the coordination of such an attack on live television with technological novelty. For example, this coordination of a military operation with a broadcasted statement has led to a popular comparison with Nasser's "Delesseps" code word—spoken during a radio broadcast to cue troop movements. Clearly, much older media forms have the potential for simultaneity as well. This episode should not be thought to lend credence to the paranoid fantasy that imagines that "secret messages" will be unwittingly communicated via broadcast to sleeper cells, as some once argued may happen should Bin Laden tapes be played on Al Jazeera. The non-equivalence between Al Qaeda and Hizbullah aside, the live coverage of the strike on the *Hanit* exemplifies an antagonistic kind of visual relation enabled by concealment—to create a reciprocity of force, to show the act to a broad audience as it transpires, and then replay it within the (uneven) landscape of global television. The footage of the attack soon found its way onto other news channels as well. The attack on the ship gave tangible fulfillment to a desire commonly felt in many coastal towns to strike out against Israeli naval vessels deliberately positioned as visible but untouchable threats. The broadcast makes the ability to act equivalent to an intervention into the realm of televisual images.

The specific positionalities and conscious beliefs of individual viewers aside, the structure of this live broadcast greatly resembles the structure of the performance of miracles—those acts or events which are meant to give into evidence the presence of or active intervention by forces from the beyond. A precise definition of the term *miraculous* is needed here: "a marvelous event or an event that causes wonder, an extraordinary event that remains inexplicable in terms of ordinary natural forces, an event that violates natural law and so is usually attributed to some super-human or divine cause or else is used as evidence for the superhumanity or divinity of that cause" (Naas 2012, 97). Although all broadcasting is premised on some degree of hope that the tech will work, this is not a claim about the beliefs of actual viewers. Far from it—the structure of belief or disbelief that the live broadcast creates is not premised on the viewer's political sympathy or adherence to a specific religious doctrine. The visual circulation of the event of the strike is not the kind of sacred experience reserved for the initiated, or which requires protection from a contaminating outside. The truth of this image is to be found in how it is directed both at those within the communal experiences created by Al Manar but also to those outside it.

Beyond the communications technician praying for hardware to function in *An Inextinguishable Flame*, this performance of the "miraculous" for all to see is an illuminating allegory for the "miracle" of live television's promise to see a simultaneous elsewhere. Watching historic acts performed on live TV directed by a vocal leader who responds to a structure of feeling—the important part is not a presumably irrational belief or excessive religiosity specific to Al Manar and its viewership. Rather, this example suggests the extent to which those experiences often described as religious can be deeply compatible with seemingly banal things like television talk shows. The performance of the miraculous is premised on concealment in the face of targeting, but like with other acts performed for a modern public, the message is communicable to an audience that includes party members, the ambivalent, and the definitively opposed.

6. Public Concealment, or Nasrallah Has Left the Building

The articulation of concealment with broadcasting was expressed in a different form in the live broadcasts of political rallies later that year. The exceptional conditions presented by war dramatize the dynamic relation of concealment to the never-complete process that is infrastructural continuity. Modern attitudes toward public protests, however, alter the stakes found in war—what comes to matter is not that the guerrilla fighters, weapons caches, and underground bunkers remain concealed, but that a large number of protesters come together in the same place at the same time to make their voices or demands heard. Of course, protests that are not sponsored by major parties often abruptly compel participants to a newfound understanding of the value of concealment when the police intervene. Nasrallah's increased symbolic value during and after the 2006 war made him into an even higher-value target than he was before. In the rallies and demonstrations that Hizbullah held in the year that followed, the secretary general would increasingly be present only via a live feed from a concealed location. This decrease in public appearances should not be any more surprising than the fact that Al Manar anticipated the bombing of their main office and had built a backup system. During the 2006 war, the IAF succeeded in bombing Nasrallah's offices, but not in penetrating the bunker underneath. One RAND study contrasted his resilience under fire favorably to Stalin's reported brief nervous collapse following the Wehrmacht's surprise attack in 1941—a comparison that perhaps inadvertently equates the German and Israeli air forces.[100] Relatively unfazed, Nasrallah would go on Al Jazeera soon after, his first direct appearance on a channel other than Al Manar since the start of the war, to promise a shift to open war. Nasrallah's appearance via live feed in the postwar period encapsulates the dovetailing of concealment with the symbolic power of public protests.

The bombing of the naval vessel and the Hizbullah-led demonstrations both involved the coordination of televisual liveness, but in the latter, the stakes of the visibility of party members are reversed. Rather than concealed rocket teams, protesters loudly claimed public presence and made political demands. While both place an implied political or spiritual weight on watching live television, the two events involve a very different set of relations to modalities of concealment. The rallies in December of that year illustrate the blueprint for the relations between liveness and concealment in Hizbullah rallies and protests in the years that would follow. At these rallies, there was a temporary alignment between four spatially dispersed elements—viewers at home, the protesters or rally attendees at the place of the protest, a screen displaying Nasrallah (near to but not among the protesters), and the speaker in his secure location. The relationship forged between these spaces is deeply informed by the geography of difference in the city, even serving to recalibrate its parameters. There are two events that usefully illustrate the infrastructural conditioning of sectarian difference—the in-person appearance of Nasrallah at the "Divine Victory" rally in September 2006, and a speech delivered about a week into the sit-in demonstration in December.

Since the 2006 war, Nasrallah has only rarely appeared in public, but broadcasts of his speeches had long been central components of party communication, and even historical events unto themselves.[101] Speeches from this period also aimed to negotiate Al Manar's place in local, regional, and global media landscapes. After the end of the war, Hizbullah branded memories of the event with the slogan "Divine Victory" (in Arabic, the slogan *nasr min Allah* is also wordplay on the party leader's last name). One billboard created as part of this media campaign depicted Nasrallah's hand extended upward past the frame of the signage, highlighting the hand that delivered victory. The Divine Victory rally, which took place in an empty lot in the southern suburbs of Beirut, was Nasrallah's first public appearance since the war that July. It was carried live on other channels and highlighted in replay afterward. The speech (less than an hour long) begins by referencing the towns and regions in Lebanon that the attendees came from, and referring to the regional and global geography of those in the television audience. The victory Nasrallah proclaimed was not just Hizbullah's military success, but also the unwavering nature of the party's supporters. While he attributed the source of the victory to God (as is common in Islamic gestures of gratitude for good fortune), he also credited the people's collective goodness, firm belief, and courageousness in the face of adversity. The speech contrasts the geography of morally righteous supporters with that of the injustice of their enemies, against whom Hizbullah fighters "stood fast for 33 days in a land exposed to the skies against the strongest air force in the Middle East, that had an air bridge carrying smart bombs from America to Britain to Israel."[102] Personal and psychological steadfastness, and recognition of the truth of oppression are recurrent themes in this and other speeches, and are used to rhetorically connect Hizbullah's struggle to the Shi'ite tradition, but also to that of the Palestinians, and to a universal humanity.

Nasrallah goes on to declare the rally itself a victory against the other Arab nations, who "refuse to fight, resist, use the oil weapon and allow people to come into the streets." Nasrallah's speeches from this period frequently featured references to a global audience watching the party's supporters, whom he characterized as capable of recognizing a fight for basic human dignity and freedom when they see it. He frequently returns to the refrain that the party's true supporters cultivate a relationship to the self whose correctness is evidenced by their determination and presence at the rally. In this speech, Nasrallah articulates that this bearing witness to the truth was the crucial source of the victory being celebrated. Bearing witness to the truth of the victory—in person at the rally or on television at home—becomes a sort of theology of media, but one that thoroughly embraces the textures of the televisual apparatus of public appearance and at-home viewing, increasingly well-adapted to the everyday.

While being present at the rally in person means to participate in the center of the event, the event itself is defined by its televisual staging, and openness to a broader audience who may or may not attend to it in the manner that it invites. Part of what distinguishes the staging of this event from later ones is the location of Nasrallah within it. The camera cuts from a direct view of the speaker at the podium to swooping pans across the audience to capture their reaction. At times the viewer at home is given a split-screen view of the speaker and the audience at the same time. Although individual audience members are occasionally identifiable, the primary device is that of wide angle shots of the group as a whole, dotted with Hizbullah and Lebanese flags, and banners with the official "Divine Victory" branding. This camerawork doesn't invoke the deindividuation of the crowd abhorred by modernist sensibilities as much as it creates an affirmation of the party's cause for the participant (at home or at the rally) by the sheer number of like-minded people. Nasrallah's last-minute in-person attendance—despite obvious security concerns—adds a special weight to the claim of defying physical threats to bear witness to the just cause. Like many of Hizbullah's televised rallies, the speech claims the language of championing the dignity and interests of the oppressed. What is new in this assemblage of cameras, God, banners, people, and celebratory affects, is the direction it gives to the party in the historical narrative of the Lebanese state or even world history. Like the sit-in demonstration later that year, it is best understood not only for what it claims to negate, but like other regimes of power, for what it affirms.

The sit-in began on December 1, following a televised call for protests by Nasrallah the evening before to protest the Siniora-led government that he held was complicit with American interests.[103] Thousands of people occupied the public spaces near the Grand Serail (the prime minister's office) and Martyrs' Square. A permanent tent city was set up nearby and in major thoroughfares, as was an official Hizbullah public relations desk, and booths staffed by allied political parties (such as supporters of formerly exiled war criminal and general Michel Aoun, who would later become president). The demonstration fostered a festive atmosphere well into the end of month, and when I visited, evenings seemed to be the most festive time to go. Musical performances were often staged at night, when many people smoked hookahs alongside coffee and balloon sellers. Stands selling memorabilia could be found at strategic street corners, and heated political discussions emerged between people of disparate party affiliations in view of easily spotted intelligence operatives, undoubtedly a mix of state agents and those of the party who intended to maintain a visibly low-key presence. Despite the concerns expressed by many, relatively few fights broke out at the sit-in.[104] The demonstration effectively shut down most commercial activity in the ordinarily tightly policed Downtown district. The closure of several major thoroughfares also meant that traffic had to be rerouted.

After about a week of increasingly heated public criticism of the sit-in, Nasrallah delivered an official televised response. The speech was carried live on both Al Manar and NBN, the station affiliated with Nabih Berri, speaker of parliament (and head of the Amal movement, primarily allied with Hizbullah at that point). Projection screens were set up at both Martyrs' and Riad El Solh squares. Occasionally, the screens in Downtown showed TV coverage of the protest at the protest, presenting Beirut in televisual *mise-en-abyme*. The use of split-screen made it so that at key moments in the speech, viewers at home were shown audience reactions to the speech shown on the projection screen at the protest, and at a few key points, could see the protesters both in the crowd and on the screen. In this way, it is formally similar to contemporaneous broadcasting techniques found at sporting events. It is important to note that this media geometry of an appeal to "the people" is one that is particularly fraught given the deeply divided political formation of the country at the time. Despite the demonstration's stated aim of bringing down the current government, the speech actually centers around a call for a national unity government—a demand that the March 8 bloc parliamentarians had made when facing the gap between the increased political capital of the war but a fixed number of MPs.[105] In the speech, Nasrallah directly accused the Siniora government of having colluded with American interests during the war earlier that year, and called for an independent investigation into the matter. He specifically did not mention UN involvement in such an independent investigation, as calls for the implementation of UN resolutions 1559, 1701, and the special tribunal investigating the Hariri assassination (which would later implicate a number of Hizbullah members) had become very contentious.[106] Nasrallah would go on to argue in favor of deferring an official inquiry into responsibility for the war, citing the resolution of the matter as being too divisive in the current climate. He also thanked the protesters for being "ethical, forgiving, and tolerant" of their fellow countrymen in this matter.

This event is significant for at least two reasons—the manner in which the speech embodies the connection between concealment and live television, and the way this connection also enables a tenuous rhetorical claim to the nation. The speech makes numerous appeals to cross-sectarian solidarity, demonstrated through gestures of openness to nonaligned political institutions. For example, Nasrallah argued that the party enjoyed wide popularity across sects, evidenced in public opinion polling. This claim should be understood to be an appeal to a non-sectarian neutrality via one of the key technologies of procedural democracy, deflecting claims that the party wanted to install a theocracy. Even more explicitly, he argues that the purpose of the demonstration is not to install a "Shiʿite government," and that he would be the first to abide by a government that represented "Sunni interests" by truly representing the national interest and recognizing the need for defense. Nasrallah continues this line of argument by repeating that the wish that all attendees share is to create a government capable of representing all Lebanese, to which the audience repeatedly exclaims in unison "al muwatineen" (the patriots). In moments such as these, the camera cuts away from Nasrallah on the live feed to show reaction shots of the crowd at the protest watching Nasrallah on the public screen, demonstrating the importance of the live performance.

It should be expected that this ethno-religious tension, formed at an intersection with class, arose during a protest in Downtown Beirut. What is notable is that the contestation of the meaning of the protest and future of the nation was, at the same time, about a violation of the norms of the space. By organizing and even paying for protesters to leave their jobs to stay in the "center" of the city, Hizbullah temporarily combined the cultural technology and disciplinary apparatus of Solidere with its own. Much of the public commentary deployed openly sectarian and classist slurs about the protesters, imagined in civilizational terms—"dirty protesters" described as matter out of place in urban space. The sit-in gradually became a symbol of a political stalemate that lasted a year and half, culminating in street battles in May 2008. After being accused by the government of infiltrating Beirut airport security so as to spy, and of possessing an illegal telecommunications network (a secure but open secret), Nasrallah publicly declared that any action taken against Hizbullah's communications infrastructure would be treated as an attempt to disarm the group by force, and tantamount to a declaration of war. Hizbullah then quickly took military control of most of Beirut, and battles between those supportive of and opposed to the party soon spread to other parts of the country in the days that followed. One of the Future TV buildings in Ras Beirut was vandalized, shot up, and partially burned, the ruin remaining as a reminder in the embittered years that followed.[107] When the Lebanese army deployed a week later to prevent continued violence, Hizbullah returned control of the streets to the state with a much weaker ability to claim that it would never use its arms domestically. Soon after, the Qatari government organized a summit of the Lebanese political leadership. The Doha Accords that resulted ended the Siniora government, and increased the proportion of Shi'ite members of parliament. Sectarianism was given new legs, just ones that awarded Hizbullah greater official say in national affairs. Much like the demonstrations in 2005 that led to the Syrian departure, there was no real discussion of abolishing the sectarian system, much less of bringing the Civil War's criminals to justice. Grand claims to the nation were cashed in for a rearranged pile of domestic bargaining chips, minted in the currency of the ongoing regional conflict.

Conclusion

The nature of concealment can be found not in its aesthetic qualities alone but in what future it is used to open up or close down. In the face of the racialization produced through violence inflicted within, to, and through media infrastructure, there needs to be an anti-racist politics that is adequate to the task of a feminist de-escalation of the militarization of concealment's geopolitics and its theological potentialities. When regional conflict is made to appear to be a foregone local conclusion, there needs to be a media history of its eventfulness. This chapter has wrestled with the problem that concealment presents for critical investigation, albeit in ways limited by this particular context, and by an analytical focus on the visual register. Although much of what is concretely discussed here are images generated as part of the dynamics that result from concealment, concealment itself is a separate modality at work in the events analyzed here. It would be fundamentally in error to equate this modality in visual culture—or more broadly, this kind of mediation—with only the spectacles that are often made of it after the fact. For example, although bunkers can contain communication systems and provide the infrastructure for unauthorized circulation, their primary visual modality is concealment. The second conclusion is that, although concealment typically indicates a power relation in which some entity has greater capacity to target another, it would be a mistake to equate concealment with resistance by virtue of its media form. Not all oppositional dynamics involve laudable political formations. Geopolitical conflicts are bound up in the generation and maintenance of global inequalities on local scales, but even further, Hizbullah suggest that there are additional complexities that need to be addressed when resistance becomes "the Resistance." The capitalization of resistance is not simply a manner of writing, but also a visual, gendered, and political economic formation that finds its culmination in the Party's Museum of the Resistance. In the chapter that follows, the militarized antagonism that animates Hizbullah's history of concealment—bound up with underground spaces—is repackaged and remembered in museum form. Although concealment is a temporally specific visual modality, the museum repurposes a decommissioned underground bunker as part of a commodified recirculation of past events and formerly hidden secrets.

4

The Open Secret of Concealment
at the Mleeta Museum

We are heirs to religions that are
designed precisely to cooperate with
science and technology.

—Jacques Derrida (2001, 62)

The Hizbullah "Museum of the Resistance" at Mleeta opened in
May 2010, on the tenth anniversary of the Israeli withdrawal from
most of Lebanon. I visited it soon after, and have been back many
times in the years since. The museum is set on a mountaintop in
the south that was used by Hizbullah in the fight with the IDF and
its Lebanese proxies, and features a visit to an underground bunker
that was used in combat but never discovered. Mleeta restages the
tactics, infrastructure, and theology of guerrilla warfare—which is to
say, the site puts the materiality of concealment on show for a global
audience. Concealment is typically only graspable by those on the
outside when it is also recorded for later circulation, like the online
videos surreptitiously recorded during the 2006 war discussed in
the previous chapter. Unlike those videos, the museum invites viewers into a restaged experience of concealment in the same location
where fighters once concealed themselves. The museum is designed
around the experience of being on and inside the mountain. As such,
an analysis that is adequate to the Mleeta museum and its relationship to official memory must take this experiential dimension into

Figure 4.1 Under the tree canopy of the Path at the Mleeta museum. Photo courtesy of Belal Hibri (2016).

account. Doing so also allows for a clearer understanding of imaginaries of concealment, and the visual forms that define the contemporary geopolitical landscape. If the previous chapters have remained centered on Beirut, this chapter steps outside its immediate border. Our understanding of this urban center would necessarily be clouded if we never moved to the peripheries it creates.

Mleeta raises two points for media theory. First, the museum's architecture embodies and anticipates critical strategies of suspicion that seek to "go below the surface." Some forms of critique can miss the mark when only directed at official ideology that is proudly stated, when presence and gesture is of equal importance to the content of the statement. As Mleeta is designed to foster an appreciation for the experience of concealment from the aerial gaze, it is crucial to attend to the embodied and sensory pedagogy of the site. The museum stages a series of inversions of the surveillant aerial gaze, inviting visitors into secret underground spaces and guerrilla camouflage. This necessitates an analytical shift that can grapple with the pairing of concealment with spectacle. If the previous chapter gave an account of the vectors of mediation within an event and the intertwining of concealment and infrastructure, this chapter's turn to Mleeta's memorialization of concealment focuses on the manner in which the experience of the place becomes central—particularly how it centers and structures a deeply gendered way of feeling with and through the masculinized guerrilla fighter's body.

Second, Mleeta demonstrates how Hizbullah is best understood not as an expression of dissensus in Rancière's sense of the term—not an alternative or radical other *to*, but a different geopolitical camp *within* contemporary capitalism and consumer practice. Perhaps because of their self-stylization as the Islamic Resistance and their involvement in geopolitical conflict, there is a temptation to consider Hizbullah and the Museum as being somehow opposed to neoliberal economic policy or inherently inimical to its cultural forms. However, Mleeta shows how it is possible for a group to be a counterweight to Israeli incursions and the US and Saudi regional geopolitical bloc, but also be crucial to the maintenance of a status quo, and the mechanism by which South Lebanon is more deeply integrated into contemporary capitalism. The gift shop and restaurant at the site are designed to accommodate large tour groups, and are integral to the museum's purpose in a new regional tourist economy. By building on an underemphasized dimension of Rancière's understanding of the distribution of the sensible, Mleeta demonstrates that not all who claim to speak in the name of the part who have no part present a radical critique of or departure from the political order.[1] Mleeta may take an oppositional stance vis-à-vis Israel and even regional and global visual culture, but with what outcome? In Ghassan Hage's (2015) felicitous formulation, what kind of critical engagement is needed to imagine an anticolonial future that is also significantly different from the present—an alter-politics that promises something other than just a vestigial national sovereignty?

Mleeta offers a productive place from which to consider how facsimiles of concealment be folded into something quite different. The museum's articulation of institutional memory practices within an anti-vertical resistance idiom attests to the paradox of the open secret, the re-vulgarization of hidden truths introduced by the *pharmakon* of media. As has been suggested by Derrida and others, that which goes by the name of religion bears a historical and structural relationship with media technologies and communicative forms. Religions create a condition of ongoing instability of cultural and social boundaries that Derrida calls a condition of "auto-immunity." Rather than telling us something primarily about religion or resistance, Mleeta actually tells us something about the role of media and performance in the political formation of communal memory. Mleeta demonstrates the stakes of Hizbullah's fraught relation to global visual culture in its participatory staging of martial prowess, and reforms concealment as a museum display. If the motivation for sharing the experience of concealment is to encourage a visitor's identification with the experience of the guerrilla fighter, then the museum as a whole can be understood as an attempt to safeguard against the loss of memory. However, the way the museum shares the experience of secretive guerrilla combat and then selling memorabilia should not be construed as a set of ironic juxtapositions. Rather, it is better understood as an expression of the unstable relationship between global media and concealment as they intersect with the geopolitical fault lines and circuitries of capital that define both Hizbullah and media infrastructure more generally.

Media, Faithful Secrets, Disbelief

While Mleeta is not solely or even primarily a matter of religious experience in the conventional and reified meaning of the term, the site's relationship to media is illuminated by considering the internal relationship between media and religion. In "Faith and Knowledge: Two Sources of 'Religion' at the Limits of Reason Alone," Derrida demonstrates how the two eponymous sources of what in the Western tradition is called religion are bound up with media.[2] Derrida has many concerns in this essay, including elaborating how it is that some forms of belief or faith are present in many social situations beyond the religious, perhaps even being at the basis of all social bonds. Yet it is media (what he sometimes dubs "tele-technoscience") that the essay returns to. These two sources are the categories and experience of the sacred (or the holy) and belief (or faith). In this conception, media are formatively bound up with the boundaries between these two aspects of religion, and their outside. Naas concisely describes this as follows:

> While one source would thus be turned toward a presence that must be restored or restituted, toward a protection or indemnification of the self or the community [the sacred, the holy], toward an immunization of these from outside aggression or contamination, the other [belief, faith] would be turned precisely *toward* this outside, or toward this outside within, toward all the resources that, as we will see, threaten the self or the community but also make these possible in the first place. (Naas 2012, 68)

On the one hand, religion comes from a turning to the experience of the sacred, the safe, the holy.[3] On the other hand, religion comes from the minimum amount of good faith required for communication with the other. The first source is the experience of that which must save and must be saved; the second source is the communication of the truth or the implicit good-faith treatment of the other with whom one would communicate. In the first case, media define both the experience of the sacred and the cultural experiences that one presumably turns away from that are profane, impure, or impermanent. In the second case, religion is an embrace of the communication technologies that define that outside so as to constitute the community, or maybe to proselytize to those outside it.

The Mleeta museum embodies the condition of auto-immunity that results from protecting the sacred by putting it on display for the world to see. According to the museum and Hizbullah's self-description more broadly, it is the party's rootedness in the land and the people's will, its armed struggle and guerrilla practices, and the commitment of its members and fighters that has enabled it to be victorious—to keep safe the community of believers, and the people and spatial integrity of the nation. At minimum, the Mleeta museum should be understood as an attempt by the party to give institutional form to the memory of the past of a struggle that is ongoing. Mleeta embodies the tension of concealment when some aspect of it circulates in global visual culture more broadly, rather than the tension of concealment with attempts to uncover it.

Mleeta is more interesting for what it demonstrates about the politics of media and sensuous memory than what it communicates about party doctrine, religious or otherwise. Yet giving an account of Mleeta benefits from recent (interdisciplinary) debates about religion, media, and material culture. First, we should be careful not to conflate different kinds of mediation with one another, as doing so potentially equates different kinds of mediation—social, cultural, theological—with one another.[4] It also potentially turns the critique of people's beliefs into a process of debunking the "special effects" that define religious experience—an iconoclastic move indebted to a Protestant lineage of critiquing false belief. As with the video clip *An Inextinguishable Flame* and Nasrallah's speeches I analyze in the previous chapter, the sociality affirmed by the simultaneities of media infrastructure can be as important for the social togetherness that they allow as for the images they circulate. Images might pierce us, but they do so differently when the fact of a shared viewing experience affirms a political community.

Second, at Mleeta, the medium is not the message (McLuhan's classic formulation, and a distinctly Catholic conception of mediation as transubstantiation),[5] so much as it is the staging of the miracles of the resistance. Mleeta is not a case of new conditions of mediation or new technologies transforming religion—a term whose internal consistency requires a great deal of faith that there exists a timeless essence to be changed, as well as a great deal of faith in the transformative power of technology, especially the kind that feels shiny and new. Rather, Mleeta is a contemporary manifestation of a much longer history of the internal relationship between capitalist development, social transformation, and techniques of communal belonging, of which media are an important aspect.[6] Furthermore, Mleeta says much less about that which is beyond this world than it does about how this world should be arranged—arrangements of language, gesture, attention, affective attunement, and communication and weapons systems.[7] We gain much more insight into Mleeta if we also consider how it is part of a particular group grappling with the import of their historical moment—a moment when finding one's political bearings in the media landscape is crucial. The aesthetic contradiction of Mleeta is that it makes past acts of concealment legible—both revealing the secrets of the military struggle but also assuming that its visitors will include ardent supporters, distant admirers, skeptics and opponents of various stripes, and those without any particularly strong sentiments at all. Put differently, Mleeta aestheticizes committed action to demonstrate the legitimacy of the cause to the politically committed, but in a manner that is open to the comportment of the skeptic or the uncommitted.[8]

Visiting Mleeta

The entry fee at Mleeta is nominal, suggesting that profits from ticket sales are not as important as their affordability to the general public. Even when I have taken out-of-town guests to Mleeta, I have encountered it as a visitor unaffiliated with the party. More specifically, I encounter it as a diasporic Sunni Beiruti who did not live the reality of the occupation of the south either directly, or indirectly through family the way that many others might have. Which is to say, my experience of the site is already inflected by a set of expectations quite different from those whose experiences are mediated through the lifeworld of South Lebanon or with a more pro-Hizbullah orientation. My encounters with the all-male staff are fundamentally shaped by being a cis-gender man, even if I have gone in groups with women. I have also usually encountered it as a person who can get there in a private car. The drive south from Beirut typically follows the coastal highway before turning off to go up the winding and scenic mountain roads that lead to the site. Visitors are guided to Mleeta by the white text on brown background signs that are the hallmark of the Lebanese Ministry of Tourism, which indicate more than just the correct route. They bear the imprint of the government, but steer people to a site built, funded, run, and mainly about a particular political party. This contrasts with other historical sites with official signs, such as Roman ruins or other landmarks from a more distant past. This overlap between the functions of the state and the activities of a political party repeats the manner and geography in which welfare and

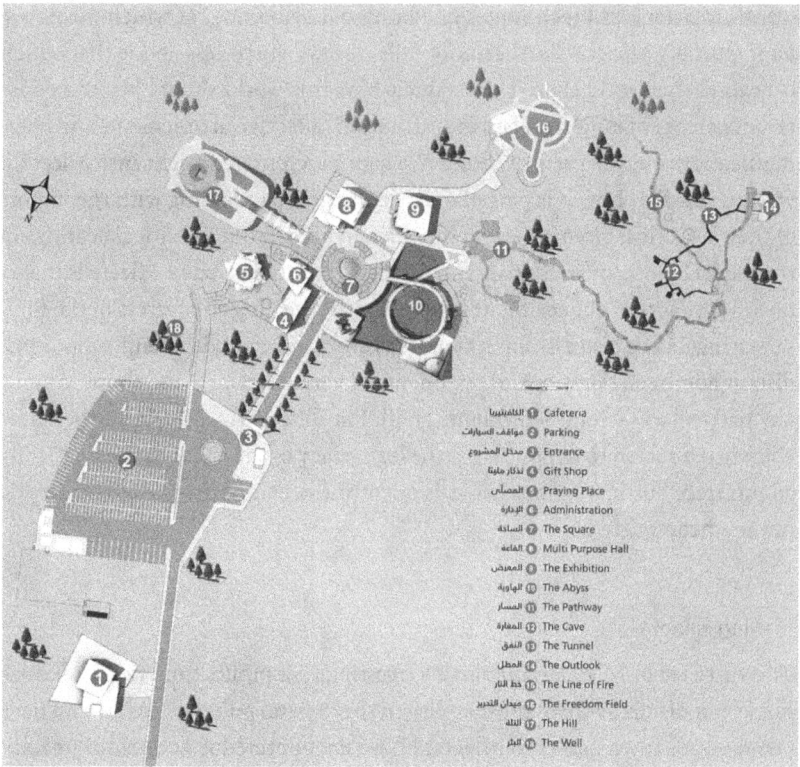

Figure 4.2 Site map of Mleeta museum, ca. 2016.

الكافيتيريا ①	Cafeteria
مواقف السيارات ②	Parking
مدخل المشروع ③	Entrance
نذار هدايا ④	Gift Shop
المصلى ⑤	Praying Place
الإدارة ⑥	Administration
الساحة ⑦	The Square
قاعة ⑧	Multi Purpose Hall
المعرض ⑨	The Exhibition
الهاوية ⑩	The Abyss
المسار ⑪	The Pathway
المغارة ⑫	The Cave
النفق ⑬	The Tunnel
المطل ⑭	The Outlook
خط النار ⑮	The Line of Fire
ميدان التحرير ⑯	The Freedom Field
التلة ⑰	The Hill
الجدار ⑱	The Wall

memorialization are managed in Lebanon, in which the government can often be largely absent.[9] As is the case in many places in Lebanon and particularly in the south, the road is also dotted with Hizbullah and Amal signage.

The tension between telling the particular history of Hizbullah and the national or even universal claim that Mleeta aims for is a key aspect of the site. The museum both wants to claim that the party is the Resistance and the champion of the oppressed, but also that their extraordinary military successes are for the whole of the nation or even oppressed people everywhere—a vindication of past injustice and possibly even evidence of divine favor. Perhaps claims to the nation are always troubled, but this trouble plays out in a noticeable way at a pavilion at Mleeta called "the Outlook." Visitors are afforded unobstructed south-facing views of the countryside below, above which fly the Lebanese and Hizbullah flags side by side (see figure 4.3). The presence of both flags was typical during my first visits, before the party officially confirmed its military

Figure 4.3 Lebanese and Hizbullah flags fly at the Overlook. Photo courtesy of Belal Hibri (2016).

involvement in the Syrian Civil War in May 2013. From that time until 2016, the presence of the Hizbullah flag there was intermittent, more or less following the domestic contentiousness of the party's discourse. Whether or not this reflects a conscious attempt to soften a potentially vexing claim to the nation, it does illustrate the complicated registers in which such a visible claim could be read by visitors less comfortable with the party's pro-Assad stance.

The museum was established as part of a broader set of cultural and economic policies geared toward creating new forms of tourism outside of Beirut's immediate vicinity. Officially titled the Mleeta Tourist Landmark, it is perched on a mountaintop that affords views of a number of nearby summits that, as the guides point out, were once Israeli sniper and artillery positions. The site also looks down at the nearby countryside at the bottom of the steep incline, and toward the coast. There are plans to open a number of other tourist sites in the area, including a re-creation of the infamous prison at Khiam—once known for the horrific torture that took place there when it was in the hands of the South Lebanon Army and IDF, but destroyed by aerial bombardment by the IDF in the 2006 war. There is even a nearby water park, and rumors of plans for a hotel and shopping complex. The plans for the creation of a "resistance tourism" geography in the south, if not what can be described as an "Islamic milieu," seem well underway.[10]

This trend is one of the ways that Hizbullah can be thought to embody what Atia (2012) calls pious neoliberalism, a term that theorizes faith-based organizations that aim at development projects as evidence of the ways that "actually existing neoliberalism"[11] demonstrates compatibility between religiosity and market ideology. The complex relationships between political movements, the state, and ideological formations belie the idea that there is a coherent and transcendent neoliberal project. Having said this, Hizbullah should be distinguished from the Cairo-based organizations that Atia analyzes, in that it emerges out of a history of Shi'ite disenfranchisement and activism particular to Lebanon, and the different ways that neoliberal policies have worked with the Lebanese state.[12] One of the founding principles of Hizbullah was armed liberation struggle against Israel, formed within the political economy of the support of Iran and portions of the Lebanese diaspora. Hizbullah also emerged from a geographic dynamic that is distinct from that in Cairo, particularly with regard to the history of rural-urban migration and slummification and their relationship to South Lebanon.[13] If the south hadn't been historically marginalized by the concentration of political and economic power in Beirut, there wouldn't have been the need for policies meant to address it.

Mleeta's committed leisure is part of a participatory, experiential, and location-based turn in war museums both in Lebanon and globally.[14] Mleeta is also a product of the emergence of new spaces for fun and leisure that are meant to be compatible with contemporary practices of Shi'ite piety.[15] However, the museum seeks to impart a much more explicit historical-political message than many of these spaces, albeit in a way that seeks to accommodate an audience that may or may not profess political or religious affinity for that message.[16] While Mleeta is not primarily a martyr memorial or a memorial museum like Qana, it is like Qana in the sense that sectarian identity is not always antagonistic, or resolved into a national framework.[17] Institutions like these are premised on site-specificity but reframe the significance of violent conflict for a transnational and post–Cold War public.[18] The importance of the link between location and memory, of remembering on and with the site, is one feature that is shared between Mleeta and memorial museums, albeit in very different registers. For example, Mleeta avoids the personal testimonials that are frequently a part of such memorials, and the primary reference to individual and civilian sacrifice is a plaque emblazoned with a past Nasrallah speech that does so.

This attempt to impart the origins and values of the Resistance so as to evince attachments to it are not unlike similar anxieties within post-2009 Iran, where many pro-regime filmmakers began to work to find ways to reach a younger generation that had grown more ambivalent about or averse to content perceived to be overtly propagandistic.[19] Mleeta also has some similarities with the Sacred Defense Garden and Museum in Tehran. Both are museums that focus on the recent past, both are set on hilltops, and both differentiate themselves from martyr memorials by minimizing references to sacrificed fighters in favor of valorizing the military achievement of reclaiming and defending the land against a foreign aggressor.[20] The primary focus shifts from the religious to the nationalist, although of course the two remain intertwined.

I have gotten slightly different versions of the guided tour depending on how the guides have placed me, or how they have placed the people I was with. When I have gone alone, I have usually been read as an expat Lebanese sympathetic to the cause, meaning that our conversations were in Arabic, with varying levels of religious references left in. The one time I visited with someone who identified himself to the guides as a party member, we received more details about two features of the site otherwise given briefer treatment: the locations subtly marked as the places where fighters had died, and the weapons garden. The guides have all been men and more or less middle-aged, and are invariably welcoming, friendly, and on-script. I have heard the tour in Arabic and English,[21] but I have also overheard tour guides speaking French, German, Persian, Spanish, Swahili, and Urdu. This indicates that accommodations have been made for a range of visitors, and that it is likely that there are guides who can offer the tour in other languages as well.

The guides alternate between giving formal descriptions of the site and the history that its features represent, and more informal and personal conversations.[22] Typically when I have visited with people who have been read as Westerners, the group would be treated like outsiders who are presumed to have an understanding of the party's history filtered through a discourse about terrorism in need of correction. Conversations would be in English. Anticipating common liberal political critiques, many of the stories they tell incorporate or end with statements like "see, we aren't terrorists, we just fought for our land and want to live free and with dignity"; "our faith gives us comfort and inspiration, but we aren't fanatics"; or "our problem isn't with Jews or Judaism, it is with the Israeli government." The guides' training clearly reflects a keen understanding of the potential to address the liberal aversion to the figure of the fanatic, and a way to help manage the wariness that might be created by the museum's overt statements of party rhetoric and celebration of armed struggle.[23] Comments like this would commonly emerge later in the tour, after a rapport between guide and guided had been developed. On occasions when visitors brought them up earlier, the questions were given warm welcome. I've found the guides to be invariably patient and open when discussing matters of such a potentially charged nature, and they would typically act as though they were happy to have the opportunity to clear up a friendly misunderstanding.

Most of my interactions with personnel at the site were with guides, and almost all interactions remained within these parameters. The conversational parameters have been very consistent across the years and different guides I have interacted with, indicating a high degree of consistency in their training. The exception is one visit with a white female American visitor, whom the guide was pleased to hear was a professor. On that occasion, the guide was much more impassioned in his conversation than any other encounter, and recounted a story that I hadn't heard on any trip prior to this. The story we were told was of a man who fought with the resistance at the Mleeta site for many years. This fighter was said to have developed a preternatural familiarity with and understanding of the terrain, and had dug a trench in which he hoped to be buried. The man was later injured and blinded, and upon being told he did not have much longer to live, said his final wish was to be buried in that trench and demanded that he be taken back to the then-wilderness near Mleeta. The culmination of the story was that despite his weakened state and lack of vision, the man made his way up the mountain and back to the spot, which the guide then pointed out. The story ends with the man returning to medical care, recovering, and continuing to serve the community at large.

Part of what is intriguing about this story is how it exemplifies a phenomenon common to the unofficial lore of the 2006 war and of Mleeta. Evidence of exceptional abilities (as in the case of the trench man), of a close bond between the land or nature and military activity (especially at Mleeta), and even angelic intercession or divine involvement—all are presented within an evidentiary framework where the listener is invited to consider a series of statements presented as fact, and asked to come to their own conclusion as to their significance. As with stories that circulate in both popular and semi-official accounts of the 2006 war, it is never the testimony of believers or party members that is given as evidence but natural phenomena or the testimony of outsiders. Upon visiting Mleeta a few months later, I found that the trench man story had been placed on a sign immediately next to the trench, and the fighter's name was revealed to be Jawad. As the site is updated, a selected oral history is written down and given an institutional role, incorporated as one of many ongoing embellishments. Any account of the site, including this one, is by definition at least a little out of date.

On-site and On-screen

Regardless of how I or the people I am with have been read, the guides always first steer people to the cinema hall, skipping "the Abyss," an eye-grabbing installation featuring tanks and other military vehicles located nearby.[24] More recently, visitors are directed to the cinema hall by green arrows painted on the ground. The film that plays in the hall—which is large enough to accommodate a few hundred people at a time—is presented in Arabic, and has versions with English or French subtitles. It runs at about thirteen minutes in length, and has been revised between my first visit at the end of May 2010 and the time of my last research visit in 2017. It is also available on DVD for a few dollars at the gift shop. The film consists primarily of archival, battlefield, and news footage with a synthesizer-driven orchestral score common to films produced by the party. It narrates a fairly standard story of the emergence of the movement, its gradual reclamation of the south from Israel, and continues up to relatively recent political events and Nasrallah speeches.

The film opens and closes with a telling computer-generated scene. A downward-facing camera descends from on high through white clouds to the Mleeta museum and circles the Abyss, instantly recognizable from the advertising for the site, and even more immediately by visitors on their way in to the hall. After circling around the Abyss, the camera somewhat unexpectedly flies over to, and then into the cinema hall where the on-site audience would be seated. The screen on-screen then dissolves to a welcoming address given by Nasrallah, which expands to take up the entirety of the screen in the hall where visitors are seated. Even within a film, Nasrallah is a screen entity. This airborne framing device, which repeats in reverse at the end of the film, is the first indication that a play on location is important to its message. The film is essentially divided into two roughly equal segments. In the first half, Nasrallah introduces viewers to the site and the experiences of the fighters who established it, situating its military role in the broader context of the fight with Israel. The second half places the story of the site into a much broader context, writing the party into a history beginning with the establishment of Israel in 1948, through the Israeli invasions of 1978 and 1982, and up through the withdrawal in 2000 and the war of 2006. The primary mechanism by which a sense of historical authenticity is established is the inclusion of archival footage. The scenes that want to be read as archival establish their past-ness by the graininess and discoloration characteristic of celluloid and video, depicting scenes ranging from British troops in Jerusalem and dramatic gunfights with fighters wearing Hizbullah paraphernalia to aerial bombardment by aircraft of both

World War II and late twentieth-century vintage. It is undoubtedly true that many of the action-film style scenes were actually filmed in battle, or at least performed for the camera during combat. Some of the other scenes appear more noticeably staged, such as slow-motion shots of soldiers streaming past the camera in line formation in an open grassy field.

The first half of the film introduces the viewer to the museum's site as it existed during the conflict, with great emphasis placed on the personal struggles of the fighters that sanctify the land. This half primarily alternates between long takes of the landscape near to and as seen from the Mleeta site, and shots taken in close proximity to the fighters. These shots alternate between the intimacies and affective charge of toiling bodies in exertion and sweeping views affording a chance to reflect on a bigger perspective. The military band/synthesizer score of the introduction is followed by a notable shift in musical tone to a slower and minor-scale piano accompaniment to tales of physical hardship at the site. One of the major lessons of the Mleeta museum is how to feel with the masculinized body of the struggling fighter, and the film leads with the example of the difficult physical labor of digging tunnels into rock. As the viewer is shown scenes of young men digging into the mountainside and carrying supplies, Nasrallah's voice narrates that "these youth came to these hilltops; they carved tunnels with their own hands." There are very few shots of faces, effecting a focus on the body in labor, the body struggling to maintain concealment with minimal infrastructural support, a masculine body doing logistical work and serving as the vital connective tissue of armed struggle. If political leaders and political relations in Lebanon have frequently been figured in the familial grammar of patriarchy, then Nasrallah (appearing primarily as the voice of the narrator) both models and guides viewers to the correct relationship to the site and the bodies that made it important—speaking as though very moved and with great admiration. This kind of appeal to the audience is another instance of how the personalization of politics in the form of direct address to a media audience by a party leader is premised on a broader social and cultural ground defined by what might be termed patriarchal connectivity.[25] Nasrallah's feeling for the fighting sons of the nation links the affectively charged viewing experience to the documentary (and staged) footage of suffering, defiant, and triumphant masculinized bodies.[26] This resonance with traditional Shi'ite themes of sacrifice in the face of oppression would be apparent to many viewers, but is presented within a nationalist frame throughout the film.

Soon after these scenes, Nasrallah informs viewers that they too will soon explore this very terrain, and that although the grounds have been improved, most will still find some parts to be difficult. This foreshadowing of the embodied experience of the site is essential to one of the missions of the film, which is to anchor potential ambiguities of meaning. Nasrallah plays the part of the spiritual tour guide here, giving admiring testimony to the heroism, sacrifice, and martyrdom of the fighters who constructed, lived in, and launched military operations from the site. It is in the final moments of this first section when Nasrallah explains Mleeta's tagline, as he claims: "Here, on the very land you stand on . . . under airstrikes and under artillery fire . . . Here, their spirits became a link between the land and the Heavens." The connection between the experience of airpower from below, affective resoluteness, and a reversal back into the sky is made very explicit.

The second half of the film shifts gears to tell the official story of the emergence of Hizbullah as a necessary response to Israeli incursion. The sound of Nasrallah's voiceover is replaced by the clickety-clack of captions that appear on screen as though from a typewriter. The story tellingly begins with the creation of Israel in 1948, describing Jerusalem as the first Arab capital to fall, followed by Beirut in 1982. The dates in the timeline are primarily those of military significance, and the assassinations of major figures associated with Hizbullah such as Sheikh Ragheb Harb and Sayyed Abbas Al Musawi. Although there is mention made of a "concessions era" between 1988 and 1992 (culminating in the iconic footage of the Rabin-Arafat handshake), no mention is made of the other potentially important events, such as the Iranian revolution, the rise and expulsion of the PLO, the beginning or end of the Lebanese Civil War, or even Hizbullah's official founding in 1985.

The film narrates a history that consists almost solely of foreign invasion, and struggle and eventual triumph against it. Because it presents an unapologetically bombastic take that errs on the side of the less-than-subtle, the film lends itself to a dismissive reading by those who might see it as blatant propaganda. Yet it is undeniable that the subject it engages and structure of feeling that it speaks to are palpable and lived realities for many. Almost every audience that I have been a part of has sat and watched solemnly, or at least the kind of quiet that people become when being polite in an official space. Groups with children would sometimes filter out when interest would fade. On one occasion the audience was much more visibly and vocally emotive; at climactic moments the audience would cheer and clap, or tut-tut in disapproval of villainous actions taken against the cause. Also at that screening was a woman who sat in the front row who quietly cried to herself, from the first moments of the film to the very end. As I watched her walk out (without trying to seem like I'd noticed), I realized that I had never heard a man express grief at the site.

It would not be a stretch to imagine that many who visit Mleeta would have lost someone in the conflict whose memory the museum mobilizes into service of the cause. It is crucial to see how the film, like the museum, taps directly into just how vivid, recent, and omnipresent this struggle is, without either discounting the power of the framework within which it is made meaningful to people or how real the affective charge can be.

The conclusion of the film draws an explicit connection between the history that the party writes about its military efforts in relation to this site, and a contemporary historical moment in which viewers/visitors encounter it. This contemporary moment is essentially defined by two interrelated factors: the politics of the party's bid to be the primary embodiment of anti-Israeli resistance; and the "balance of forces" announced by Hasan Nasrallah in a televised speech, an excerpt of which closes the second half of the film. In this 2011 speech, Nasrallah promises that the party intends to exact reciprocal damage for all future attacks on Lebanon. Perhaps unsurprisingly, the targets named are primarily infrastructural in nature.[27] The film reflects how the temporalities of live and archivable television are a key part of what it means to be contemporary with the party. These two factors come together in the person of Nasrallah, who typically appeared on screen rather than in person at rallies in this period, typically "live" from a concealed location. The periodizing echo of live televisual address, and this speech in particular, can also be found in another part of the site—the exhibition hall, which is the part of the site most frequently updated, and which I discuss at greater length below.

The final sequence of the film is an almost exact mirror reversal of the opening CG sequence—the camera flies backward out of the cinema hall, around and through "the Abyss" installation before vanishing back up into the sky, and dissolving from white clouds to a blank white background with the museum's logo. The relationship of the sky to infrastructure is quite different here from that in An Inextinguishable Flame. Rather than an older male communications technician laboring to get the television signal back to the satellite and into the domestic space of the home, it is the labor of guerrilla fighters with the land that creates a spiritual testimony the museum then brings to its visitors. To return to the museum's tagline "Where the Land Speaks to the Heavens," the work of faith is bound up not just in the act of narration, but also in laboring on and functioning of infrastructure. In the film Nasrallah uses the Arabic term hablin, a strong rope, to specify the means by which land and heavens become linked—not a dematerialization of the sacrificial body, but a rematerialization of the connective testament it gives.[28] This sacralization is framed as the condition of possibility for a secure line of communication with the future—an appeal made directly to the audience.

The bracketing of the film by the framing device of the mobile and aerial gaze positions the viewer quite specifically inside a cinema hall—but more importantly, on the location of a site whose historical significance is refracted through the effect of on-site viewing. The site's key cinematic component suggests that much can be gained by examining the space itself—by considering how modalities of concealment are restaged within the spatial experience of Mleeta. By engaging with the museum at this experiential and sensorial level, it also becomes possible to more closely apprehend what happens when concealment is decommissioned, only to be redrafted in consumable form.

Verticality, Under Tree Cover, Underground

The attraction that appears in most of the advertising for Mleeta is an installation called the Abyss, a large open space encircled by elevated walkways with captured Israeli military vehicles placed as though sinking into the concrete. It is also decorated with captured helmets that are strewn across the ground. If the film points to a history of Arab military defeat that Hizbullah then reverses, then the Abyss posits that deadly serious levity is one answer to post-1967 cultural malaise.[29] The most prominent feature is a captured Merkava tank whose gun barrel tip has been twisted into a cartoonish knot. The guides (and the signs) make a point of explaining that this tank was generally considered to be indestructible prior to the 2006 war, and perhaps second only to the air force as an emblem of the invincibility of the IDF. A second Merkava tank is placed as though it crashed into a wall painted in a burnt orange color, bearing the signature of Imad Mughniyah, whom Hizbullah commemorate as one of their most venerated and cunning military strategists.[30] The guides are usually quite eager to ensure that visitors catch all of the symbolism intended by the installation, some of which may not be obvious. Twisted tank barrels aside, some features presume a degree of familiarity with the party's rhetoric or with the details of the military conflict. For example, the circular shape of the installation and leaning pillars that surround the center are meant to evoke the swirl of a vortex or whirlwind that has knocked over the IDF's special forces, a reference to one way Hizbullah has described the outcome of the occupation of the south and the 2006 war. Strewn at the base of each pillar are the Hebrew initials naming each special forces unit.

In addition to captured military hardware, the Abyss also features ruined writing in the form of Hebrew letters placed flat on the ground specifically

Figure 4.4 Captured tanks and Hebrew letters positioned for the aerial gaze at the Abyss. Photo courtesy of Belal Hibri (2016).

meant to be seen from the sky. When seen from above, the message reads "welcome to the Abyss." Mleeta is a place of reversals, and in the case of the Abyss, the reversal does not return the gaze from above so much as taunts it. This visual reversal is also one in which awareness of the aerial gaze—a very palpable experience for many—is overcoded by the exuberance that comes from performing the absence of fear. The museum visitor might look down at the exhibit from the elevated walkway which circles around the installation, but this lettering offers an open challenge to the view from above. It ensures that both visitors and the aerial gaze are aware that the museum can be seen by surveillance. Sometimes the joke is best enjoyed by those in on it when those at whose expense the humor is had are presumed to be within earshot. The Abyss takes advantage of the contingencies of vertical mediation so as to publicly mock it.[31]

The vertical taunting of the Abyss implies that the specter of impending ruination stands over Mleeta as well. When asked, the guides smilingly explain that the Hebrew letters are indeed there for the aerial gaze. I have heard a guide say that if the museum were to be bombed—which he anticipated as a real likelihood should there ever be another war—it would just be rebuilt. I have even heard a guide give a local history of surveillance aircraft as beginning with high-altitude planes, followed by routinized and continuous satellite surveillance and the regular air force sorties that continue to occur, with the more recent addition of surveillance drones. Chamayou argues that the biopolitics

Figure 4.5 View of top of the hill as seen from the far side of the Abyss. Photo courtesy of Belal Hibri (2016).

of drone warfare consists of a relationship between hunter and prey, wherein "... the primary task is no longer to immobilize the enemy, but to identify and locate it" (Chamayou 2015, 34). One might texture this with the more specific vector that Weizman (2007) describes as a politics of verticality. The reversal of the politics of verticality at Mleeta in general and dramatized by this installation in particular should therefore be understood as a reversal of the politics of concealment, which would aim to avoid detection. In this case, the experience of the deliberately exposed exhibit contrasts with that of concealment. The stakes of this contrast are clarified by a sculpture near the Abyss made of charred old barrels. The placard (and guides) says that these barrels were originally dropped full of burning oil to deforest the wooded mountaintop, so as to aid in finding the bunker and exposing fighters' movements. The story that is told is that the natural qualities of the trees and damp fog of the region themselves conspired against the invading force's efforts to undo concealment. The significance of such a miraculous occurrence is left to the visitor.

The humor of the Abyss is counterbalanced by "the Path," which takes visitors on a walk of a little more than half a kilometer each way down and then back up the mountainside. The climax of the walk, and a key part of any trip to Mleeta, is the visit to the formerly secret bunker. The Path invites visitors to learn of the experiences of the fighters who built and eventually were stationed at this site through empathic identification. The physical difficulty of the hike is as important to understanding what it was to be a fighter as the

Figure 4.6 A dummy fighter sits down to take rest under tree cover. Photo courtesy of Belal Hibri (2016).

experience of being under a canopy of trees. Apart from the Outlook pavilion located at the bottom of the climb (after the underground journey), the entirety of the walk is under tree cover, shielding one from direct sunlight. The foliage also makes a quieter space—muffling the sounds of people, and reducing the wind to an occasional rustling of the leaves. The guides and signage inform visitors that the tree cover made it so fighters could more easily remain hidden from detection. This encouragement to identify with the experience of concealed fighters is augmented by a number of scenes of guerrilla activity staged with full-size dummies. Many of the dummies are posed in ways that adopt postures that very closely resemble human body language and gesture—so much so that I have heard some visitors say that they feel eerie. Some of the scenes staged are of everyday activities such as a fighter standing guard, seated in prayer, or sitting down to take a break (see figure 4.6). The fighter on break leans all the way back, as though stretching from hips to head. The fighter who is praying places his left foot onto the ball of the right foot, a detail that signals a common repositioning during the seated portion of the conclusion of prayer that relieves pressure on the ankle and knee. The inclusion of these small gestures is suggestive of the kinds of minor bodily adjustments that can bring a measure of relief—both humanizing the fighter/dummy, and indicating the rigors of the battlefield.

These quiet moments aside, most of the dummies are staged as though in movement and in the heat of battle, such as two dummies carrying rockets

Figure 4.7 A dummy commando stalks through the trees, challenging visitors to spot him. Photo courtesy of Belal Hibri (2016).

to a launcher. Another scene shows the motorcycle/mobile rocket launcher combination (without a dummy) that was central to many operations, like the one captured in the hit-and-run video genre I analyze in chapter 3. The weight of the supplies and munitions that the dummies carry all suggest the difficult work of soldiering at this site, inviting empathy. There is even a scene of a field medic tending to an injured fighter who lays prostrate while being cared for, medical supplies and equipment all around.

The embodied experience of concealment—walking the mountainside under tree shade (albeit on an improved foot path)—finds an uncanny doubling in these dummies, posed in the dappled light of what was once a battlefield. At one part of the Path, a number of commandos stalk almost unnoticed through the trees, inviting the visitor to appreciate the martial capacities of concealment by adopting the position of an adversary attempting to see past camouflage. The work of the camoufleur has been an important component of the development of military techniques that conceal bodies, vehicles, buildings, and infrastructure in the field, leading to a hostile hermeneutic between combatants.[32] Camouflage is highly situation-specific—affected by the relative positions of the viewer and the unseen, light and weather conditions, the observing apparatus, and the direction, speed, and manner of movement. The Path restages these conditions on site, encouraging the visitor to experience for themselves the relational nature of concealment. In one of the many reversals at

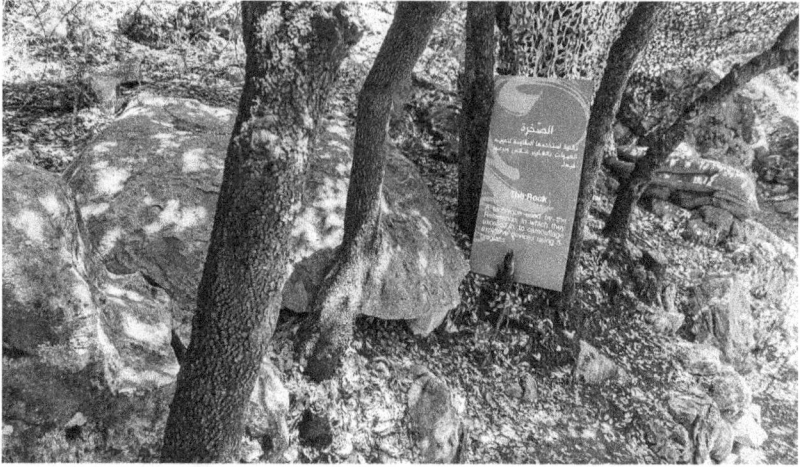

Figure 4.8 An explosive camouflaged as a rock made from fiberglass, celebrating the skill of combat engineers. Photo courtesy of Belal Hibri (2016).

Mleeta, visitors are asked to appreciate the prowess of elite soldiers by adopting the hostile perspective of an enemy.[33] This also gives visitors room to imagine how good they would be at remaining hidden as well.

After walking a little way down the Path, one's eyes adjust to the relative shade. Visitors are then invited to descend further, underground, into "the Bunker." The experience of being in the close spaces of the Bunker is key to understanding the aesthetic formation of Mleeta. It is inside the Bunker that the envelopment of concealment is most directly experienced by visitors imagining themselves to be concealed how and where the fighters themselves once were. Always a few degrees cooler than it is above ground, the Bunker consists of a dimly lit tunnel with two different entrances that connects a number of rooms staged as they would have been when originally in use.[34] The sparsely furnished rooms include a kitchen, a bunk with sleeping pads on the floor, a prayer room, weapons caches, and a communications and logistics center (see figure 4.9).

This last room is outfitted with a computer terminal and radio setup from the mid-1980s, and a copy of a Lebanese military topographical map of the region spread on a table in the middle of the room. In the first years of the museum, the retro feel of the technology was complemented by a poster of a young Hassan Nasrallah from the late 1980s on the wall; the poster hasn't appeared there in some time.[35] More recently, a small radio has been added that plays the sound of military chatter on loop, which echoes for a short distance

CHAPTER FOUR

Figure 4.9 The communications room inside the Bunker, staged with vintage technology. Photo courtesy of Belal Hibri (2016).

down the tight corridor in either direction. It is no secret that hundreds, if not thousands, of underground bunkers, depots, and tunnels were and continue to be a vital part of Hizbullah's military infrastructure. Avoiding surveillance in this case often means going underground, much as it did during the French inauguration of routinized aerial reconnaissance in the Mandate period. Verticality implies depth as well as height, and at Mleeta one goes to the top of a mountain to gain tactical and visual advantage, but then also goes underground so as to remain hidden.[36]

The Bunker clarifies that Mleeta is no distant cousin to the melodramatic mode. Visiting the spaces necessary for rest, food preparation, and daily life while deployed to the front line serves to heroize the fighters by humanizing them. The vulnerability of the fighters, and their capacity to suffer and persist despite overwhelming odds underlines their implied heroism and dedication. Almost every other part of Mleeta shows fighters in light of the work of guerrilla soldiering. Seeing their limited living conditions underscores their toughness (the intense cold and inhospitable weather is emphasized in both the video and the placards), but the contrast of the spare domestic space also allows a glimpse into the details of everyday life. The possibilities of identification or alignment with the fighters—wanting to be like, wanting to be with or physically near to, wanting to care for, among many others—are of course stratified by the positionalities of gender and sexuality that orient visitors. Nevertheless, the opportunity to enter into and observe the close quarters of the formerly all-male space suggests a potential opening up of desire within the enclosed space.

The exposure of the secret of the Bunker is compounded by the heavily freighted imaginary that accompanies its location underground. In thematic terms, the underground has been equated with many things—death, the infernal, malevolent forces and fetid entities, the location of secret truths and treasures, a site of colonial extraction, of worldly and narrative crisis, and with social inversions and political dystopias of various kinds.[37] Although it might seem curious that a space of concealment would be remade into an exhibit and therefore also a venue for selfies, that transformation can also be placed within a longer historical relationship between photography and underground infrastructure. There has been underground photography ever since the first major modern infrastructure projects reworked the existing spaces below cities. Félix Nadar famously began photographing the dense network of tunnels, sewers, and catacombs beneath Paris at the height of Haussmannization, a project that he likened to a journey into the heart of the photographability of Paris.[38] Underground spaces have fascinated the imaginations that dwell above ground ever since the nineteenth century, and find contemporary expression in activities such as urban exploration.[39] Metaphors of excavation have a less-than-innocent past, even as they continue to structure many existing aesthetic, technological, and spatial divisions between the surface and the submerged, form and function. In colonized and formerly colonized spaces, the underground has contained the possibility of anticolonial action and survival.[40] The Bunker is not underground Beirut, but suggests a much wider underground in South Lebanon. Visiting the Bunker does not foster a close encounter with a threat, but as with tours of underground tunnel networks in memorials in Vietnam, it is a visit to a space of valor derived from cunning and necessity.[41] Like with the "tunneling media" such as VPNs that borrow their name from underground and cross-border movement, most bunkers are presumed to be potentially discoverable, as the circulation they permit often conflicts with projects of sovereignty, making uncovering them a function of policing.[42] The Bunker might present how fighters originally used the place, but real and concealed bunkers exist in a suspenseful temporality in which it may or may not be clear if they have been discovered.

In giving visitors the opportunity to see the underground space for themselves, the museum stages the undoing of concealment ad infinitum.[43] When it originally served as a component of Hizbullah's military infrastructure, the Bunker enabled a modality of concealment within the perceptual field and assemblage it was a part of. Underground bunkers such as the decommissioned one at Mleeta weaponize the porosity of the surface of the earth, suggesting that the ground and the underground can conceal even while simultaneously serving as the condition of possibility for communication. In the original iteration, signals unfolded from concealment, but in the afterlife of the site, ex-concealment is folded into an exhibit. If we take the task of critique to only be that of delving below the surface to reveal secret meanings (a conservative definition of hermeneutic interpretation) then critique should take care to not be untimely and outflanked. The Bunker replays a demonstration of unmasking, inviting smartphone photography and social media engagement.[44] The verticality of airpower and aerial reconnaissance in the twentieth century produced new stakes around forms of hiding and concealment, as well as new forms of expertise in deciphering the images and data that exponentially increased in quantity.[45] The Bunker makes it clear that, in addition to interpreting images, it is imperative to understand how modalities of concealment and their undoing are mobilized in service of broader epistemic and political projects.

The history of airpower, insurgency, and counterinsurgency in the Middle East runs through spaces like the Bunker, which in turn end up informing military doctrine and critical theory, even if the latter has sometimes been better at apprehending spectacle than concealment. On one hand, some IDF officials claim to have drawn some kind of inspiration from the Deleuzian/ Guattarian concepts of smooth and striated space in their management of territory.[46] On the other hand, the official discourse of the Mleeta museum claims that Hizbullah learned from the experiences of insurgencies in Vietnam and Latin America.[47] Making sense of the ungrounding embodied by the Bunker suggests the necessity of a different Deleuzian register, that of a geophilosophy adequate to the porosity and expressivity of the earth's surface. Trying to map concealment in Apollonian fashion delivers diminishing returns for our understanding of the stakes of our media condition. We might instead deal with holes in our knowledge as endemic to the nonrepresentability of infrastructure more generally. The surface of the earth is always already worked over by people, made into infrastructure, or even remade by security and military logics. These all include communication-averse stances, conditions of non-resonance, and the deliberately ambiguous relationalities of concealment. Rather than aiming to develop specific knowledge of closely held military secrets, it is more important in this case to develop an understanding of the possibilities and limitations of infrastructure and concealment.

Figure 4.10 Drones at the weapons garden. Photo courtesy of Belal Hibri (2016).

Mleeta narrates the real strength of "the Resistance" as something that exists in the domain of affect and disposition—the political or even spiritual commitment of its members, as well as organizational discipline and a broad social and popular support. Of course, substantial financial, political, and military support by Iran and Syria go a long way in giving tangible fruition to such aspirations. At every turn, Mleeta enlists visitors into participating in a distinctly masculinist and militaristic sensibility. One way in which this happens is in the potentially challenging and ableist experience of walking down and then back up the mountainside, making the visitor's body the means through which one is to imagine and identify with the bodily experiences of the fighters. Those visitors unable to make the walk are treated with some degree of deference, and are instead encouraged to imagine the hardships of traversing and living in the terrain.[48] This process is fostered in the different encounters and experiences throughout the site, particularly in the Bunker.

Another way this attunement occurs is through the presentation of arms—both those used by Hizbullah fighters and those captured from the IDF. In both instances, the visitor is encouraged to imagine the martial potency of those who wielded the weaponry. This potency is always played in a masculine key, demonstrated in the capacity to achieve primacy on the battlefield, and to either dominate the adversary or to stoically face death. The primary place for viewing the weapons of the Resistance is a carefully manicured flower garden, whose foliage has grown increasingly lush over the years (figure 4.10).

If a visitor were to follow the planned sequence of the museum, they would encounter most of the weapons after the Bunker, or toward the latter portion of the Path. This sequence, marked by a return above ground and back into the tree-filtered light, is suggestive of a shift to a more spectatorial role. At first, encountering an arsenal of mobile rocket launchers, sniper positions, anti-tank guns, and other assorted weaponry amid azaleas and rose bushes upon moving fully back into the sunlight can seem jarring, or at the very least a curious contrast. The guides (if they are still with the group) point out that this contrast at the weapons garden is meant to suggest hope for a future state of peace, where the instruments of war that are on display will no longer be necessary. The garden also implies an arsenal that is not yet declassified, whose capabilities have yet to be revealed.

Gazing at the captured Israeli arms, on the other hand, is presented in the kind of humorous tone that results from a big reveal that the big bad other was just a whimpering child all along. Other than the tanks and vehicles presented at the Abyss, there is an exhibition hall that invites visitors to experience victory vicariously, though evidence of Israeli military defeat. The exhibition hall prominently features images of limping IDF soldiers with anguished expressions on their face, many of whom are visibly injured or bleeding. One display presents captured military supplies—Israeli military maps, radio equipment, night vision goggles and field gear, as well as a customized gun that presumably belonged to a top commander. Evidence of Hizbullah's battlefield prowess is also presented in the form of images of and quotes by prominent members of the Israeli government and the IDF, which fill the wall space above and between the exhibits (in Arabic and English). Many of these are taken from the press, or military hearings attesting to the singular threat that Hizbullah poses, its cunning, or damage it has caused. Particularly featured are quotations that reference the 2006 war.

When I have heard guides speak about the images of wounded IDF soldiers (which have come to feature less prominently in more recent years), they have always stressed that these images are not shown to celebrate harm, but to show that the enemy should be regarded as merely human, and neither invincible nor less capable of suffering. These statements of proof of the woundability of Israeli soldiers can also be read against the history of the Arab-Israeli conflict since 1967, in which the IDF was long imagined as impervious to attack. The official script of the exhibition is almost like a bid for recognition of the mutual precarity of life. Yet the triumphant reversal of vulnerability and its equation with humiliation is made so central as to belie this meaning. The ability to finally fix the image of the other within a frame is crucial, and not incidental, to the intimate reciprocities of pain that are presented.[49] As the sexual and gendered dimensions of the military term "impregnable" suggests, martial success is imagined as an at least potentially reversible position of humiliation, cast as a loss of masculinity or feminization (as in the crying soldiers). There are many potential slippages in meaning and viewing position—a vicarious and sadistic enjoyment with those who inflicted the pain evidenced in the faces and bodies in the photos, a masochistic empathy with the suffering bodies as a way to imagine the potency of those who inflicted the pain, or a more blanket refusal to imagine or register the suffering of Israeli soldiers at all.[50] The discourse of violent and terrorist Muslim others who threaten the (liberal) social order is frequently or even paradigmatically applied to groups like Hizbullah, framing them as justifiably killable. The message at the exhibition hall seems to flip this script, but primarily reassigns the roles rather than fundamentally changing it. The soldiers who would have done the wounding, who feature so prominently throughout the rest of the site, do not appear in these photos.

While different from the fantasy of guerrilla participation at the rest of the site, the series of ads that aired on Al Manar in the years after Mleeta's opening are also remarkable for their gendered dynamic. Most of them feature a little girl discovering the Resistance, typically guided by an older man. In one ad, the little girl plays inside of the "Abyss" installation, cheerfully skipping between ruined tanks and IDF-issue helmets strewn on the floor. In another, she runs through a field of tall grass with a bunch of balloons streaming behind her to a man who could be her grandfather. The two then walk to the entrance of Mleeta. At the time of writing, these were all viewable at the Mleeta YouTube channel.[51] These ads encapsulate Mleeta's project of passing the memory of Hizbullah's origins within the context of Israeli incursion and the Civil War.

Mleeta does not just attempt to redress the uneven national experience of Israeli occupation, or the uneven application of violence to South Beirut and South Lebanon. Rather, the museum (and the ads) channel the memory of the fight against Israel into a national narrative in a manner that embodies a generational shift. For a generation of younger people, the common expression "the war"—often taken to refer primarily to the Civil War (1975–1990)—might seem to more directly reference 2006, particularly among those from areas most directly affected by it.

The exhibition hall makes an explicit connection between the history of the fight against Israeli occupation and the contemporary moment. On one wall is a fairly detailed graphic giving a more or less complete and up-to-date overview of the IDF's chain of command and organizational structure. It seems to be updated fairly regularly. Another part of the hall was at one point dedicated to illustrating the Nasrallah speech excerpted in the museum's film, in which the Secretary General promised to respond to any post-2006 attacks on Lebanese assets in kind—airport for airport and factories for factories. A snippet of the speech was presented as text above a series of satellite images of various Israeli military installations, Ben Gurion Airport in Tel Aviv, and so on. In what should be no surprise, the museum's alignment with the experience of being watched from above dovetails with embracing the use of satellite images for military purposes.

To present an impression of concealment is to highlight the vectors and potential frailties of the infrastructures that enable it. Doing so also makes it clear that concealment is not inherently "resistant," especially if resistance is understood as the simple overturning of a specific ruling regime. As with blasphemy, or with taunting the eye in the sky as at the Abyss, this overturning can indicate a potential destabilization of a topology of power or mark another moment in power's intensification. The surveillance drones found at the exit of the weapons garden conclusively show that one should not find the use of arms by a group also targeted by them to be a contradiction in terms. The drones of the Resistance are a reminder that the Mleeta museum and Hizbullah are better understood as a different armed faction in a regional geopolitical conflict to control the circulation of money, people, and affect as they congeal in Lebanon. Hizbullah's creation of a parallel welfare state within a territorial nation-state that historically marginalized its poorest Shi'ites and southern region in general is at least an attempt to create the capacity for social reproduction, but it also constitutes a different way that political horizons can be foreclosed. Examined from a different angle and put in the idiom of corporate mantras, however, being locally attuned and transnationally minded is also just good business sense.

The Resistance at the Gift Shop

The gift shop is the place where one can most clearly see how the distinction between categories that are presumably clashing are forged and negotiated—war and tourism, religion and capitalism, conflict and kitsch. Read more carefully, these categories are better recognized as the sacred and the profane, defined by cultural forms that underpin these contours but also make them unstable. In much of the popular reporting about Hizbullah, the fact that the party maintains a friendly PR desk is played for laughs—cast as an ironic contrast with the clichéd fascination with bearded militiamen ready to die. Such gallows humor has a long lineage in Orientalist discourse, up through more contemporary writing about the "unexpected" contrasts found in the encounter with social and cultural realities deemed exotic and dangerous, but also capable of being domesticated.[52] These expectations are what make the presence of a gift shop at Mleeta seem like a contradiction in terms. Truthfully, I have found myself grinning when coming across Nasrallah coffee mugs or the party logo emblazoned on the kinds of memorabilia found at other tourist traps. In the case of Nasrallah kitsch, the humor stems from the same source that makes all larger-than-life macho public personas seem (more) ridiculous upon being rendered safely commodified. Nasrallah's public persona—like all of the leaders of the establishment political parties, who are all men—is indebted to the tradition of playing the role of the patriarch of the extended political family.[53] Putting his grinning face onto a key chain, fridge magnet, or car mirror ornament is simply an informal way of putting the public figure into domestic spaces, signaling the more general manner in which both spheres reproduce patriarchal relations.[54] One might contrast these with the formality of placing portraits of leaders in storefronts or those of presidents in institutional spaces.

Mleeta is an official attempt to sacralize communal memory, to ensure the continuity of the past within the present so as to secure the future. It is a key node in a broader effort to modulate orientations toward history and lived memory, complete with the aspiration to be recognized as a chapter in a universal human story of suffering and triumph, and the desire for freedom and self-determination.[55] The museum's project of cultivating a "resistance" sensibility takes the affects and practices that mark one set of cultural and media experiences, designated as the shape of the sacred, and transforms them into something more easily purchased and experienced by a range of people, including those who may not (or not yet) have the correct disposition to apprehend its true meaning. As Derrida argues, Abraham is told to not bring anyone to the mountain, but also to share the divine word. The mediation of the word always already creates a condition whereby each new media technology deployed to spread it recreates the internal tension that marks the religious and demands its vulgarization.[56] Which is to say, commodification, spectacle, and anxieties about authenticity must be considered to be internal to the formation of communal and religious experiences and of systems of belief, lest we miss what is political about how those traditions have authorized ways of speaking and feeling about their own history. There is something religious about the production of differential value at scale, but also something religious about the way consumer life makes demands of certain loyalties, attention spans, and even political commitments at greater rates than others.[57]

Figure 4.11 Branded snow globe, one of many keepsakes on sale at the museum gift shop.

In the case of Mleeta, this duality of commodification can be found in the way the architecture of the site restages the experience and outcomes of concealment for its visitors. The project of ensuring that future generations will hold the "correct" relationship to history, of making the embodied experiences and political commitments of the fighters culturally legible, in bringing the many to the mountain, already remakes the past for new circuitries. This is why snow globes of the Merkava tank at the Abyss are the logical culmination of the nature of the Resistance.

The inherent instability of meaning-making processes at the site and the mementos one takes home deepen and proliferate the anxiety that visitors will nevertheless misinterpret things. This anxiety manifests throughout Mleeta's paratexts—from the introductions made at the cinema hall, to the site-specific signage, to the conversational labor and civility of the tour guides. It is only fitting that none other than Nasrallah himself is enlisted in the task of welcoming and guiding visitors, arguably one of the oldest forms of spiritual instruction. In this case, visitors walk past the gift shop on their way in to the site and again on their way out. The gift shop and the branded experience that Mleeta provide are not antithetical to but of a piece with how authenticity is experienced in contemporary culture. The blurring of the boundary between the authentic self and commodity self is a key aspect of contemporary brand culture, in which "authenticity" defines personal relationships to brands themselves.[58] Rather than the appropriation or fostering of counterculture by guerrilla marketing firms, or deploying advertising techniques against a guerrilla force by their opponents,[59] Mleeta is better seen as the mobilization of branding practices by a Lebanese Shi'ite political party with a proficient guerrilla fighting force.[60]

Overt references to religion are at a minimum at Mleeta when compared to much of Hizbullah's cultural output, at least if we take the term "religious" in the conventional meaning as pertaining to texts, rituals, and persons that participate in a sacred tradition. One of the few openly religious components of the site is at the beginning of the Path. Visitors first hear an audio recording of Sayyed Abbas Al Musawi reciting the Qu'ran, and then see a small alcove containing a number of his personal effects (see figure 4.12). Al Musawi was Hizbullah's first secretary general, until his assassination by Israel in 1992, and was known to pray with fighters prior to their deployments. The graininess of the recording is suggestive of the authenticity of an original analog recording. This technical-historical marker signifies the proximity of the original to the speaking body, not its unsuitability for the task of Islamic recitation.[61] By contrast, the martyr shrines that appear on the Path thereafter are anonymous

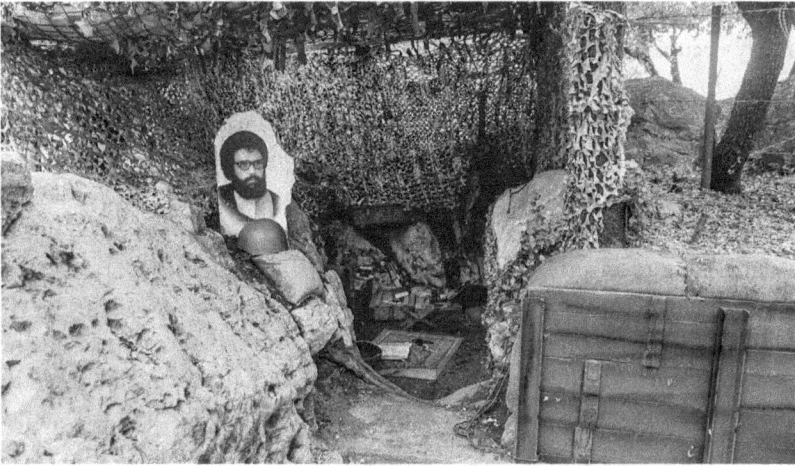

Figure 4.12 Visitors first hear Abbas Al Musawi reciting from the Qu'ran before seeing some of his personal effects at the entrance to the Path. Photo courtesy of Belal Hibri (2016).

and silent roped-off affairs, presented almost without commentary. When asked, I have heard many people who have visited the site say they didn't even notice they were there. Yet the mementos and DVDs on sale at the gift shop, the staging of Al Musawi's alcove, and the subdued markers of fallen fighters are far more similar than they are different. The mementos are designed to be easily taken home or gifted, and one takes home the memorials in the form of being affected by having witnessed their site-specificity, but the two are of a piece with one another.

Conclusion

This chapter has examined how concealment, memory, religion, and commodification coalesce in Mleeta. The restaging of concealment is quite unlike the visual modality itself, but at the site it becomes part of a broader cultural and pedagogical project. I have argued that the museum's experiential and site-specific form of public engagement makes the performance of the masculine embodiment of the fighter central to this project. Mleeta is designed as a space of affective intensification, and the primary means to this end are the many instances where visitors are asked to feel with a fighter's body. This gendered subject position is one premised on military potency but also physical suffering, the capacity for mastery in the face of overwhelming odds, and transcendence while being rooted in the soil. The space stages a series of reversals—the formerly occupied achieving dominance, open-air exhibits that extend vertical taunts to aerial surveillance, and of the open secret sold as commodified experience and mementos. These reversals are not a deviation from but closely follow the internal logic of Hizbullah and their broader political, economic, and cultural project. The gendered identifications at Mleeta enshrine a militarized ordering of the social world, an expression of how Hizbullah's deep commitment to an anti-US and anti-Israel geopolitical project is premised on the maintenance of a patriarchal domestic social order.

Mleeta offers sweeping mountain views to take in while contemplating the past and future. Much like the version of the past that it commemorates, the future is cast as one of ongoing crisis, the threat of which requires a maintenance of the status quo. Rather than a place to consider paths not taken, there is a militarization of the senses and sentiments, foreclosing the geopolitical horizon with support for the Resistance as the only national option. Put in Rancière's political language, the museum is one example of how Hizbullah imagines a future in which it is possible to disagree, but where a more radical dissensus is precluded.[62] The museum genuinely strives to overcome the tensions inevitably created by narrating Hizbullah's victories as national ones, but the sectarian political order resurfaces in the disparate relations to the party that hang over the site—sometimes literally, in the shifting presence or absence of party flags. Hizbullah is unique not in its reproduction of the sectarian political order, or its embrace of capitalism and neoliberalism in the last instance, but in its self-description as the Resistance while doing so. It is certainly the case that Mleeta is one of few places dedicated to the experience of fighting for the liberation of South Lebanon, and constitutes a deeply moving experience for many. No one should be shamed for cherishing a gift shop memento—consumable sentiments are more, not less meaningful for being readily and inexpensively accessible. In a state with debilitated infrastructure and little historical attempt to truly remedy the stark inequality in the south, what other option do people have?

This chapter has also taken a step outside of Beirut's immediate geographical confines to reflect on the visual and infrastructural conditions that define it. The drive back from Mleeta to Beirut might take about ninety minutes if traffic flows smoothly, but the distance must be reckoned with on a different scale. The two are as closely linked with and as distant from each other as modern religious experience and the modern office cubicle—both of which generate value by orienting attention via techniques of perceptual management presumed on a subject who is otherwise potentially distracted.[63] At least Mleeta offers complimentary water fountains, a generosity not extended to the public by Solidere despite operating public space in the city center on the municipality's behalf, as well as open-air tours of Roman ruins. Mleeta should not be taken as stand-in for all of the south, but is better understood as one of many ways that the geography of the region is transformed by its relations with capitalism, urban centers such as Tyre and Sidon, as well as multiple transnational and regional actors (Syria, Iran, and Israel). Mleeta's deepest foreclosures on the future are not that it speaks in a secularized Shi'ite idiom or that it blends pietistic expression with consumer culture. For too long, targeting consumer sentiments has been the guise by which misogyny and Islamophobia pretend to critique. Rather, Mleeta presents the maintenance of the domestic status quo (at home and in the nation) as Resistance, while creating conditions that work to narrow other kinds of transnationalism and solidarity.

CONCLUSION

What can infrastructure tell us about images, and what can images tell us about the history of space? This book takes an infrastructural approach to media and visual culture so as to explore these questions in Beirut. It does so in two phases. The first two chapters constitute the first phase, examining how imaging—and notions about the meaning of making images of the city—became important to regimes of power. These attempts were frequently less than successful in effecting the total change and stability suggested by the ontology of the map, or in the accurate targeting suggested by their corollary aerial photographs. As I examine in chapter 1, the most important transformations were often in the temporal and institutional forms of images that systems of power became invested in. The trajectory of this history of mapping was ultimately realized in the use of spectacular images of before/after, which originated to aid the financialization of postwar real estate ventures, and the reformulation of urban space to accord with this visual form. As images of before/after proliferated, so too did a way of seeing and knowing the space in the manner of a citizen-investor, born of the corporate idealism of globalization, and relishing in the profit that could be extracted by enacting inequality in urban form and in naturalizing the political status quo.

The second part of the book refocuses on concealment—an infrastructural modality whose importance is hinted at by the historical record examined in the first chapter. In both the circulation of images and the mobility of bodies, concealment is a visual relation of deliberate non-appearance. It can both enable continued infrastructural functioning when targeted by countervailing forces, as in the practices of shooting live, or it can keep people from ever appearing at all. The materiality of the Al Manar satellite feed, particularly in the 2006 war, demonstrates the crucial role of concealment, and the importance of an eventful understanding of infrastructure. Concealment is built on knowing when and what to hide, and a sense of why things remain hidden—and so analyzing it requires a precise understanding of the stakes and the context in which it operates. This is not to say that concealment is inherently unproblematic, and the Mleeta museum demonstrates how recreations, reenactments, and records of past occurrences can be remobilized in commodified form. Much as a consideration of infrastructure opens up our understanding of the media geographies of Beirut's borders, so does a consideration of Mleeta open up our understanding of how other regions within the country are bound to the capital's political orbit. Beirut's peripheries are multiple and composed of internal frontiers, as well as deepening national inequalities. Concealment makes only a minimal appearance in the first half of the book, and none at all in chapter 2. This is not to say that concealment was not an important phenomenon in those periods. This book charts a path intended to interrogate the nature of spectacular media forms—especially live televisuality—as shaped by the history of the visualization of the city. As concealment gives little into evidence, it creates the methodological challenge of only being able to analyze the records left behind. In the case of Lebanon and Beirut, this means considering the specific nature of the media and urban landscape. Other research into concealment, drawing on other archives or contexts, embodied experiences, or other philosophies of the event and sensation, would surely extend this line of inquiry. Perhaps this might lead to a political appreciation of the powers of concealment, and an ethical relationship to visual culture not so directly tied to the practices of targeting, or the promises of looking and of making things (and people) visible.

Taken together, these chapters demonstrate the productivity of considering media infrastructure in terms of its incompleteness. This shift in perspective is greatly needed to make sense of the duration of infrastructure, perhaps particularly because infrastructural imaginaries and their corollary felt experience are often figured in terms of permanence, totality, and stability—or on the other side of the temporal binary, total collapse. Media infrastructure in Beirut suggests taking at least one conceptual step further. The collective experiences and public forms that infrastructure enables are bound up with the spaces they are a part of, and making and contesting those spaces and infrastructure are bound up with images. As demonstrated by the archives of maps in Beirut, the lives of those images are at least provisionally a part of the space they presumably shape. The archives in the city demonstrate how the media processes of storage and retrieval are conditioned by the city. A parallel insight can be drawn from the decidedly different media form of live satellite broadcasting, in which the act of circulating images generated either before or at the time of their viewing becomes bound up with their meaning. On the one hand, the contradictions of Al Manar during the 2006 war and the demonstration that followed dramatizes the recursivity of the image—we are always watching the actuality of the circulation of the image, and the uncertainty of the live feed's continuity. On the other hand, the specific ideology and political project of the infrastructure comes to matter quite deeply—not because seeing is believing, but because the manner in which one believes Nasrallah depends on his facility with the form of the televised pitch. However, Nasrallah's televisual performance of authority and sovereign martial capacity demonstrates not an attempt to make media over in religious terms, or the erosion of sacred viewing experiences by new technology. Rather, this particular facet of Al Manar's programming demonstrates that in the contemporary moment in the global media landscape, geopolitical imaginaries and infrastructure become more rather than less tightly bound together.

If infrastructure is always incomplete, then we can find this to be the case not just in what content ends up on which streaming platforms, or where Netflix's servers are placed, but also the repurposing of livestreaming for a range of geopolitical goals. Those visual forms also come back to Earth; the proliferation of the means of making and circulating images from and to the spaces of the city deepens the general tendency. This is why two of the visual forms of the early portion of the October 2019 revolution mirrored each other—the vox populi person-on-the-street interviews by reporters on the scene by channels such as MTV and Al Jadeed, and livestreaming on social media platforms.

I have struggled to find a satisfying ending point for this story that isn't bleak. As such, this book is haunted by the unfulfilled past possibilities for undoing the ruling order in Beirut, and has worked to show how things might have been otherwise. I have sought do so via a critique of the gendered order that the sectarian system presumes, examining how it inheres in the structures of feeling and the political economic order that underpins it. The epistemic subordination of space suggested by the coloniality of these maps is part and parcel of the emerging gendered spaces they sought to foster. The before/after image beckons to the masculinist gaze of the citizen-investor while reinforcing the patriarchal order of citizenship reinscribed by the post–Civil War consensus. The valorization of guerrilla masculinity and the attentive viewer/listener of Nasrallah speeches fostered by Al Manar and Mleeta suggest that concealment and spectacle can become bound together in a manner that sediments their place in the geopolitical order.

There is a strange attachment to the political consensus that inheres in the political structures, media institutions, and subject formations of sectarianism— one which imagines that there is no alternative because capitalism and its racial and ethno-religious structures cannot be challenged. Yet the images and phenomena examined in this book (taken separately or all together) also suggest a very different set of contradictions—that the incompleteness of infrastructure and the collectivities it creates tie political regimes ever closer to the people they dominate. It is in this sense that the revolution that began October 17, 2019, is the flip side of the Hizbullah-led 2006 sit-in demonstration. If 2006 staged the demands of a status quo political party as though they were the demand of the people opposed to the government, then 2019 was an absolute shattering of the façade of coherence performed by the ruling order. This book was already in production at the time of the port explosion.

The idea for this book began with a visit to the 2006 demonstration, and the sense that a new politics of images in the spaces of the city was emerging, and I have argued for opening up the question of the eventfulness of infrastructure. At the time I hadn't yet hoped for something like the revolution of October 2019. Revolutions are at best uncertain, and at worst, coopted and put down by counterrevolutionary forces. The velvet fist of the interests of the banking class showed itself to be directly tied to the bare-knuckle counterrevolutionary force of Hizbullah and Amal. The manifestation of this latent synergy should not have been a surprise, lest anti-US and Israeli geopolitics wash away any other political consideration or frame of analysis. Many remain skeptical of the possibility of radical change, at least if that change is thought to occur in a short time-span in the realm of formal politics. Prediction is a game best left to oracles, and one that is only won by placing bets that are collected in hindsight. Some sought to congratulate the protesters for acting on the desperate conditions they found themselves in, others satisfied themselves with skepticism. Neither of these modes of naming and claiming intellectual mastery of such events are adequate to the multiple potentialities they open up. Perhaps, though, it becomes more possible to imagine a media infrastructure of the people, one in which the unknowability of who the people are becoming is held open.

History's contingencies can make people uneasy, and in Lebanon, this uneasiness has often been reassured by images of strong men who promise to lead.

It was precisely the visual culture of admiration and adulation of party leaders that led to an iconoclastic impulse toward all symbols of parties and images of party leaders. The revolution made manifest the hollowness of the before/after image and its urban outcomes in Downtown. If the citizen-investor probes and appropriates urban space so as to better plug it into systems of financialization, then the revolution countered this by a rediscovery of the space as one belonging to the people. It is not a stretch to say that, well before the revolution, there was a commonly felt intuition that there was something wrong about Solidere and therefore the entire edifice that made it possible. Yet this sense was accompanied by not having a way to direct that feeling—by the sense that there was no alternative, the construction was complete, and the shape of the city was a fait accompli. Yet what kind of double tragedy would it be, for example, to nationalize Solidere and its profits without challenging the autophagic mechanism by which it extracts profits and delineates what buildings and spaces are of value? Or to try to undo the sectarian political system but leave the patriarchal order and its racializations untouched? What kind of optimism would one need to smash these and replace them with something better? The equality of all with all has always reemerged, if only as an aspirational form. In October 2019 Beirut finally appeared as merely one of many centers of concentrated political sentiment, relieved of the myopia of being synonymous with the nation, politics, and public culture.

NOTES

Introduction

1 Given the passage's connection to downtown Beirut, it is worth reproducing here in full: "On a visit to Beirut during the terrible Civil War of 1975–1976 a French journalist wrote regretfully of the gutted downtown area. . . . He was right about the place, of course, especially so far as a European was concerned. The Orient was almost a European invention, and had been since antiquity a place of romance, exotic beings, haunting memories and landscapes, remarkable experiences. Now it was disappearing; in a sense it had happened, its time was over. Perhaps it seemed irrelevant that Orientals themselves had something at stake in the process, that even in the time of Chateaubriand and Nerval Orientals had lived there, and that now it was they who were suffering; the main thing for the European visitor was a European representation of the Orient and its contemporary fate, both of which had a privileged communal significance for the journalist and his French readers" (Said 1978, 1).

2 There have been an exceptional number of studies of infrastructure in cities in India (Anand 2017; Chattopadhyay 2012; Sundaram 2010) and Africa (B. Larkin 2008; Mbembe 2001; Simone 2004). In the Arab world, notable work includes Elyachar (2010); Menoret (2014); and Nucho (2016). Works by such as Easterling (2014) and Harvey and Knox (2015) move beyond the limits of the city.

3 As demonstrated by Mbembe (2001).

4 For example, see Chirumamilla (2019); Chu (2014); Graham and Thrift (2007); Steven Jackson (2014); and Rosner and Ames (2014).

5 See Farman (2012); Kraidy (2016); Mankekar (2015); Moores (2012); Morley (2017); and Packer and Wiley (2011).

6 Hall says: "We have to acknowledge the real indeterminancy of the political—the level which condenses all the other levels of practice and secures their functioning in a particular system of power" (1986, 43). Much is to be gained by transposing his discussion of ideology in Marxist thought to media infrastructure.

7 Essays reviewing the multidisciplinary conversations in which the study of infrastructure has unfolded have become a genre unto themselves, part of the materialist turn in media and communication studies (Gillespie et al. 2014; Packer and Wiley 2011). Parks and Starosielski (2015) offer a useful reconstruction of these debates, and what they have to offer to these fields. This recent attention to media infrastructure is exemplified in work such as Hu (2015); Plantin et al. (2018); Sandvig (2013); and Starosielski (2015). Some of its antecedents may be found in Bowker and Star (1999); Innis (1994); and Mayntz and Hughes (1988). Lobato (2019, 73–81) also offers a useful entry point into what he terms the "infrastructural optic" in the context of a consideration of the political economy of television distribution.

8 In this sense, the renewed attention to questions of media distribution are not that distant from the concerns presented here. Some examples of work that interrogate digital distribution include Holt and Sanson (2013); Lobato and Meese (2016); and Lotz (2018).

9 The essays gathered in Anand, Gupta, and Appel (2018) fruitfully build on the possibilities inherent to studying the lived tensions of infrastructure, particularly in the Global South. Two useful entry points to discussions in geography are Amin and Thrift (2017); and Graham and MacFarlane (2015).

10 Stamatopoulou-Robbins (2020) gives a compelling account of how the politics of repair and destruction of waste infrastructure in Palestine becomes a politics of life itself.

11 See Chalcraft's (2009) account of the role of Syrian labor in postwar Lebanon, and Kassamali's (2017) consideration of the racialization of migrant and domestic workers in Beirut.

12 W. J. T. Mitchell (2005) shows how the formulation *visual media* first imagines, in ocularcentric fashion, a sensory purification and isolation that fundamentally misunderstands the visual in culture, and then nominates it for critical attention on confused grounds.

13 See Sheehi's (2016) account of the place of portrait photography in modern self-fashioning in the region circa the end of the nineteenth century, and Scheid's (2010) contextualization of the debates surrounding nude painting in the 1920s and 1930s.

14 Rancière argues: "The political begins precisely when one stops balancing profits and losses and worries instead about distributing common lots and evening out communal shares and entitlements to these shares, the *axiai* entitling one to community. For the political community to be more than a contract between those exchanging goods and services, the reigning equality needs to be radically different from that according to which merchandise is exchanged and wrongs redressed" (1999, 5). I select this passage as the language employed reminds of

the Marxism underpinning Rancière's work but that is sometimes forgotten in Anglophone reception.

15 Rancière clarifies: "consensus, before becoming the reasonable virtue of individuals and groups who agree to discuss their problems and build up their interests, is a determined regime of the perceptible, a particular mode of visibility of *right* as *arkhê* of the community. Before problems can be settled by well-behaved social partners, the rule of conduct of the dispute has to be settled, as a specific structure of community. The identity of the community with itself must be posited, along with the rule of right as identical to the elimination of wrong" (1999, 107–8). This understanding of the political contrasts with liberal sensibilities, and a Habermasian conception of communicative action, which presumes a minimum degree of agreement as to what it means to speak and what there is to speak about.

16 Mirzoeff is in dialog with Chakrabarty's (2000) conception of the modes of history under capitalism, divided into History 1 (the worldview of imperial authority) and History 2 (that which is the precondition of but necessarily excluded by History 1). Neither of these are what Mirzoeff theorizes as countervisuality, "the performative claim of a right to look where none exists" (2011, 24). See also Rancière (2001).

17 The question of recognition in relation to Rancière's thought is taken up in his encounter with Axel Honneth (Honneth and Rancière 2016).

18 See Graham's (2016) critique of the spatiality of verticality.

19 Browne argues: "We can think of the lantern as a prosthesis made mandatory after dark, a technology that made it possible for the black body to be constantly illuminated from dusk to dawn, made knowable, locatable, and contained within the city. The black body, technologically enhanced by way of a simple device made for a visual surplus where technology met surveillance . . . and encoded white supremacy, as well as black luminosity, in law" (2015, 79). Browne's writing is a much richer elaboration of sousveillance and fugitivity than my limited engagement with the technique of power highlighted here.

20 Drawing on Bachelard's (1994) interpretation of candlelight, Schivelbusch argues that carrying lanterns in an otherwise dark public space leads to a visual antagonism: "Someone who feels observed in this way tries to turn the tables. He extinguishes his own lantern so that he is not exposed defenceless to the gaze of the other, whom he can now observe without himself being observed" (1995, 95).

21 See also Mirzoeff's (2011, 84) discussion of the appropriation of the symbol of the lamp post in revolutionary France, as a popular call to summary execution by using them as makeshift gallows.

22 On the history of electrification in Beirut, see Abu-Rish (2014) and Pascoe (2019).

23 Wark argues that Guy Debord described two kinds of spectacle: the integrated spectacle, concentrated on images focused on and emanating from the fascist leader, and the diffuse spectacle, one spread throughout all capitalist social relations. Wark does so to propose a third kind—the disintegrated spectacle, a fusing of the integrated and the diffuse, ". . . in which the spectator gets to watch the

withering away of the old order, ground down to near nothingness by a steady divergence from any apprehension of itself" (2013, 3). Unlike the Hizbullah protest, Wark proposes a way past the social relations mediated by images, principally via a reading of the legacies of the Situationists.

24 One may notice a family resemblance to the dynamic found in J. Scott's (1990) notion of the "hidden transcript"—those forms of dissimulation by the oppressed that result from deeply stratified and established hierarchies. In Scott's account, the transcript becomes hidden (from the oppressor) through the performance of feigned acquiescence to the social theater of domination, often to delay or lessen punishment, or to secure better reward or preferential treatment for work completed just enough to be satisfactory. Concealment may at times be the end result of the negotiation of complex social relations and cultural codes such as these.

25 For example, see Coulthard's (2014) critique of settler liberalism and its strategies of accumulation.

26 As De Villiers (2012) argues, this involves a very different set of relations from the silencing of the closet. However, as Mourad (2011) shows, the Western discourse of the closet and implied rituals of individual coming-out fail to account for Lebanese queer media practices that contest the form and stakes of visibility. These conceptual resonances are explored in greater depth in chapter 3.

27 As explored in Geroulanos (2017).

28 See El-Ariss's (2018) theorization of the scandalous politics of the leak in the Arab world, which tellingly opens on the hacking of the Lebanese electric company's website.

29 Hizbullah are frequently referred to in shorthand as *al-muqawama*, or simply as "The Resistance" or "The Islamic Resistance." For a closer examination of the rapidly transforming valences of the political discourse of this period, see Arsan (2018).

30 For example, the Lebanese Marxist Mahdi 'Amil (1986) argued some three decades ago that to equate class with a specific sect would only serve to obscure class relations within a sect, reinforcing domination within the confessional system. See Frangie's (2012) framing of 'Amil's thought on the periphery, and Frangie (2016) in terms of the history of the notion of "crisis" in Arab left thought in context of the divisions prompted by contemporary Syria. See also Abu-Rabi' (2003, 318–43).

31 See U. Makdisi's (2000) seminal account of the emergence of sectarianism in this period.

32 Prior to this, non-Muslims were distinctly second-class citizens in legal terms.

33 As U. Makdisi (2000, 166) shows, these new politicized identities are better understood as the *product* of the violence rather than its cause. For example, the term "sectarian" only appears many decades later in the twentieth century, when Arab nationalists dealing with the realities of multi-ethnic societies needed to differentiate the nature of their project from this previous violence. The history of Arab nationalism, especially in its secular variants, was marked by these contradictions. On the emergence of Arab nationalism and its relationship to

Beirut, see Khalidi et al. (1991); see Provence (2017) for an account of the historical continuities and disjunctures between the Ottoman and Mandate periods' relationship to the Arab nationalist movement.

34 As L. Fawaz (1983) shows, prior to this period Beirut was a small town, relatively unimportant when compared with its eastern Mediterranean neighbors. For an examination of the reformation of the Levant more broadly, see Schayegh (2017).

35 See Mikdashi (2014).

36 See Mikdashi and Puar (2016). Puar's (2017) critical extension of the language of biopolitics is particularly important.

37 S. Collier's (2009) examination of Foucault's lecture courses *Security, Territory, Population* (2007) and *The Birth of Biopolitics* (2008) shows how this conceptual and methodological shift plays out. For a close reading contextualizing this period of Foucault's work, see Elden (2016).

38 As Campbell (2011) argues, this reading of technology (and subjectification) is an influence that takes pronounced form in Agamben, but can also be found in the work of Foucault and Peter Sloterdijk. Campbell holds out Roberto Esposito's work as an alternative.

39 S. Collier's (2011) study of post-Soviet cities and economies exemplifies this approach. Stoler (1995; 2009) demonstrates the usefulness of rereading Foucault through the colonial archive.

40 There is a robust literature that details the uneven social, political, and economic processes by which felt communal belonging is made sectarian. See Bou Akar (2018); Cammett (2014); Daher (2016); Hermez (2017); Hourani (2010; 2015); Joseph (1975; 1983; 2008); Kingston (2013); Picard (2000); Safieddine (2015); Salloukh et al. (2015); and Weiss (2010a).

41 The oversimplification presented here temporarily sidelines the relationship of television to other media industries and cultural histories to give an illustrative broad sweep. More detailed versions of this picture painted in fine and broad brushstrokes can be found in Alhassan and Chakravartty (2011); Chakravartty and Roy (2013); Miller and Kraidy (2016); Straubhaar (2007); and Thussu (2006). Shome (2019) outlines the ongoing importance of attending to postcolonial difference within media studies.

42 See Abu-Lughod (2005). However, as Khazaal (2018) shows, this is not to say that ideas about proper citizenship and how to broadcast to it did not inform programming.

43 French Vichy forces later destroyed the station to prevent it from falling into the Allies' hands; it would then be rebuilt by the Lebanese government in 1946 (Dajani 1979).

44 Stanton's (2014) history of the Palestine Broadcasting Service usefully contextualizes the polyphony and division that characterized radio listening in the pre-1948 period.

45 These included the pro-Arabist Voice of Arabism, the Christian Phalange Party's Voice of Lebanon, and Voice of the People's Resistance, associated with the politician Rashid Karami (Dajani 1992). The stabilization of the political situation ended their operation.

46 For example, Dajani (2005) notes that before satellite broadcasting, "Egyptian, Lebanese, and Syrian television signals could be picked up in neighboring countries, particularly during the warm weather conditions that were characteristic for nine months of the year. It was a common sight to see Arab television homes displaying tall rotating antenna towers that were not necessary to receive local television; they were there to receive signals from regional neighbors" (583).

47 See Kraidy (1998).

48 See Boyd (1991) for a more detailed account of how the structure of the advertising industry affected this process.

49 See Kraidy (1998).

50 See Dajani (1992, 105).

51 See Khazaal (2018) on the gendered valences of the transformations of this relationship.

52 See Kraidy (1998).

53 See El-Richani's (2016) detailed explanation of the tendency to crisis in the postwar media landscape as a whole.

54 As Parks (2005) shows, the combination of satellites with televisuality created a cultural form that played a crucial role in this period of globalization. One of the first satellite television channel to operate from an Arab country was the satellite service of the Egyptian armed forces in Iraq. The channel was launched with the intention of inoculating Egyptian troops against the risk of exposure to Iraqi propaganda (Kraidy 2010, 79).

55 See Sakr (2001; 2007)

56 See Sakr (2001, 9).

57 Kraidy (2010) aptly calls this dynamic the "Saudi-Lebanese connection."

58 For example, there is a history within cultural diplomacy aligned with the idea that the Arab world (or culture, or media landscape) is one composed of an essential cultural unity or center. This cultural sphere does at times experience itself as part of a single conversation, however fragmented. There are conceptions of this that can be found, for example, in post-9/11 attempts by the United States to shape public opinion (Sienkiewicz 2016), often complicated by two other wandering metaphors—the Middle East and the Muslim world. As Youmans (2017) has shown, there are numerous blockages and complications that can arise in the global counterflow of Al Jazeera English.

59 This history has been examined by Z. Harb (2011; 2016); Khatib, Matar, and Alshaer (2014); and Lamloum (2009a; 2009b).

60 As Buonanno (2008) shows, television's domestication is an uneven process wherever it has been adopted. In the case of Lebanon, the transition to a wide range of channels was also a transition to transnational viewing.

61 Khalil (2013) makes the case for examining the media industry in relation to media capitals.

62 Some seminal works that explicitly theorize media and the everyday include Armbrust (1996); Sabry (2010); Salamandra (2004); and Zayani (2015).

63 See Fahmy (2011); and Hirschkind (2006).

64 Some useful points of entry into these conversations can be found in Brunsdon (2012); Chattopadhyay (2012); Couldry, Hepp, and Krotz (2010); Mattern (2017); McCarthy (2001); McQuire (2008); and Morley (2006). I engage these literatures in greater depth in the chapters that follow.

65 Mapping can be an optimistic and pessimistic trope for modern ways of knowing. As P. Mitchell (2008) has shown, the map has an outsized role in critical theory in the second half of the twentieth century, much of it detached from critical study of the history of cartography, and premised on a forgetting of the metaphors that enable mapping itself as a practice. A different sensibility is possible when we examine mapping practice *in situ*.

66 This concept is elaborated in chapter 2, and builds on critical study of finance found in work such as Appadurai (2016); Callon, Millo, and Muniesa (2007); MacKenzie (2006); and Martin (2002).

67 This is demonstrated by Bou Akar (2018); Haugbolle (2010); Hermez (2017); and Sawalha (2010).

Chapter One: The Social Life of Maps of Beirut

1 Raymond Williams's (1989) essay "Culture Is Ordinary" opens on a scene of the author waiting at a bus stop outside a cathedral, looking at a Mappa Mundi, and then noticing a movie theater across the street—an ordinariness in tension with the structuring forces that create it.

2 While Haraway (2016) uses the term "staying with the trouble" to rethink interspecies and ecological relations, I aim to tap into the resonance of the term for consideration of mapping as an entangled technological practice and episteme.

3 Sparke (1998, 466) refers to mapping's "recursive proleptic effect" in considering the role of maps in indigenous land claims mobilized against the Canadian state. For useful entry points into the literature on critical cartography, foundational for any consideration of maps as media, see Kitchin, Perkins, and Dodge (2009); Kitchin, Lauriault, and Wilson (2017); Pickles (2004); Wood (2010). Wilson (2017) offers a conceptually rich engagement with these questions related to the debates surrounding critical GIS and computation.

4 See U. Makdisi (2000) for a thorough contextualization of this event.

5 Renan conducted a number of archaeological excavations at the time. See Kaufman (2015).

6 See Akerman (2009); Craib (2017); Ramaswamy (2010); Winichakul (1994).

7 In this sense, maps are akin to writing, which as Peters (2015) argues, "is not simply a storage device for words and data; it is also, like all media, a power technology. Its raw power is less its content than its leverage" (279).

8 My formulation is indebted to Appadurai's (1986) approach to material culture and commodity exchange, although I shift the focus to mapping and archives, and maps as part of the remaking of circulation in the city.

9 See Kitchin, Gleeson, and Dodge (2013).

10 In particular, see Ghorayeb (2014); Hanssen (2005); Verdeil (2010).

11 Urban planning in the late Ottoman period was influenced by French approaches, and many of the objectives of the Ottoman period were continued under the French. See Hanssen (2005).

12 See Wilson's (2017, 45–66) treatment of this period. Rankin (2016) explores in greater depth the American influence on the post–World War II international organizations that standardized mapping practices. These texts both offer useful overviews of the secondary literature on the debates in critical cartography.

13 See Burke (1973); Khalili (2013); Neep (2012).

14 For a more extended treatment of Gallieni, see Boisfleury (2010); Rid (2010); Singer and Langdon (2004).

15 See Dodge (2012); and Khalili (2010; 2013).

16 Gottman (1943) offers an early contextualization of Gallieni and Lyautey's move.

17 Khalili's (2013) analysis offers a close reading of these conversations.

18 See Wright (1991).

19 Henni's (2017) account give a sense of how these objectives in French Algeria responded to historically specific crises of rule. See Wright (1991) on the relationship between the social sciences and the colonies.

20 Wright (1991) offers a broader history in which Lyautey's views can be situated. Rabinow's (1989) account of the governmental modes remains indispensable to placing the colonial encounter in perspective. Abu-Lughod's (1980) seminal account of Rabat notes the impact of this period on the city's geography.

21 It is perhaps not surprising that Lyautey admired Mussolini.

22 T. Mitchell's often-cited *Rule of Experts* (2002b), which includes a detailed examination of the importance of the British land survey of Egypt, is often read for its analysis of techniques of economic calculation. The Callon-inspired discussion of technology in this section is less often read for the insight it holds for media theory. The "divide between reality and representation" (T. Mitchell 2002b, 88) did not simply create new forms of economic rule, but in Mitchell's vivid reading, the moisture-absorbing and then drying qualities of the paper, and the uncooperative tools of measurement such as the feddan comb, made accuracy an elusive epistemic virtue.

23 See Buisseret (1998); Cosgrove (2001); Cosgrove and Fox (2010).

24 In the first years after World War I, the British and French militaries primarily used air power for reconnaissance, and only gave it a supplementary role in combat. This would change in the interwar period, particularly via the increased willingness to utilize aerial bombardment on civilians in the overseas empire. See Chasseaud (2002); Finnegan (2011); Kaplan (2018); Neep (2012); Rankin (2016, 23–64, 119–62). See Bagley (1922) for a review of French work on aerial survey. Some other examples of work that assesses the potentials of the technology in geographic journals at the time are Dowson (1921); Salmon (1922); H. Thomas (1920); Winterbotham (1920).

25 For example, Gavish (1987) highlights (in a not unproblematic manner) the contingencies that limited the implementation of an aerial cadastral survey in Mandatory Palestine.

26　Photogrammetry is the technique of creating reliably precise depictions of space from photographs. As Monmonier (1985, 63–86) highlights, although it was much simpler to transfer details from an aerial photo to a map than from data gathered via land survey, given the difficulties and perspectival distortions inherent to placing a camera (or more accurately, a series of cameras) on a plane, the level of precision continued to require extensive land surveying. Although popular accounts and some critical traditions hold that the aerial view from above is equivalent to Haraway's (2016) view from nowhere God-trick, the cartographers trying to make use of aerial photography were all too aware of the specificity of perspective introduced by the difficulty of flying a plane perfectly level to the uneven surface of the earth, and the small degrees of camera tilt needed. This is part of what necessitated multiple cameras placed on timers—it may be a view from the heavens, but one which is far more multiple than singular. It also required technical expertise in "'air photo interpretation,' the field that became remote sensing.

27　See E. Williams (2015).

28　As discussed by Provence (2005, 1–26); this period created an uneven geography of archives. The Vichy regime played its own role in an uneven geography of a different kind—making off with approximately six million lira in gold, effectively depleting the Lebanese national reserves (Safieddine 2019, 32).

29　See the entry "Reproduction of Maps" in Monmonier (2015) for a concise overview of the intertwined histories of printing techniques, photography, and mapmaking and reproduction.

30　CERMOC (Centre d'Etudes et de Recherche sur le Moyen-Orient Contemporain) was the predecessor of IFPO (Institut Français du Proche-Orient); the organization that inherited the cartographic archive of the French embassy's cultural mission.

31　Author interview with Gregoire Serof, 2010. Serof, a Russian expatriate and lifelong resident of Ras Beirut, was eager that I note this connection.

32　See Crampton (2006; 2007; 2010).

33　Iğsız (2018) examines the formative role of population transfers between Greece and Turkey.

34　See Bawardi (2014); Gualtieri (2009).

35　The breakup of the Ottoman Empire and the making of the post–World War I order also played a complex role in the making of humanitarianism, as well as the creation of displaced groups laying claim to them, such as the Armenians. See Watenpaugh (2015) for a general overview of this literature.

36　See Schaebler (2000, 280); E. Williams (2015).

37　See Kain and Baigent (1992) on the uses of the Torrens system in settler appropriation schemes in South Australia, New South Wales, and New Zealand. As noted by Burtch (2015); as a result of identifying land with ownership and occupancy and not terrain, this system's compatibility with the needs of real estate markets also created a problem of compatibility with topographical maps and surveys.

38　Duraffourd would have also consulted with the geodetic survey conducted by the military (Fares 2002).

39 See E. Williams (2015, 171).

40 Not all interwar military practitioners believed such photomosaics to be effective to these ends. As Saint-Amour (2011) argues, "even those early partisans of the 'all-seeing lens' and its capacity to open the book of enemy tactics recognized that the accuracy of aerial photographs was a latent property that could be activated only when the medium's native disfigurements were undone" (243).

41 Unlike Syria, Lebanon was placed under a more direct military jurisdiction. For more detailed consideration of the political differentials of the Mandate and the uprising, see Burke (1973); Khoury (1982; 1987); Provence (2005).

42 For a productive theorization of ungovernability's relationship to colonial formations and how they inform the present, see Marei et al. (2018).

43 For more detailed considerations of the role of air power and intelligence gathering in the revolt, see J. Miller (1977); Neep (2012); Provence (2005); M. Thomas (2002); Young (1974). For accounts of the role of air power in colonial warfare and British Iraq, see Dodge (2003); Gregory (2006); Grosscup (2006); Kaplan (2018); Omissi (1990); Satia (2006; 2013).

44 See Provence (2008) on the role of liberal thought in the Mandate.

45 See Neep (2012); Provence (2005).

46 See Neep (2012).

47 As Rankin (2016, 119) shows, the need to aim artillery at targets that were not visible—far away and in possibly foggy conditions—informed the development of universal cartographic grid systems in World War I.

48 See Neep (2012).

49 See Provence (2005, 17). For consideration of the politics of nationalist mobilization, see Gelvin (1998).

50 See M. Thomas (2005).

51 See Hanssen (2005) on these developments during the late Ottoman period.

52 See Monmonier (1985) and P. Collier (2002; 2018). This was by no means an even process, and although most empires and Great Powers would eventually rely on a couple of standardized mathematical models and devices for photographic printing, development, and interpretation, they did so with very different beginning points.
    See Rankin (2016) for a more detailed consideration of French, British, and American approaches between 1914–39, and particularly, the turn to a universal grid in cartographic calculation.

53 See Haffner (2013).

54 The tensions of the consolidation of a new national political and economic sphere centered in Beirut found continued expression in rural areas and the agricultural sector, inflected by a sectarian marginalization of Shi'ites. For example, see Abisaab's (2009) analysis of the 1936 revolt in Bint Jubayl, and its relationship to the tobacco trade.

55 For detailed treatment and contextualization of Duraffourd's plan, see Davie (2001); Ghorayeb (2014); Verdeil (2010); Yahya (2005, 232).

56 As Monroe (2014) shows, the advent of women driving, like other new kinds of mobility, formed an important site of lived and imagined tensions. As McCormick (2016) argues, the vacation season was a crucial part of how the pleasures of mobility were imagined, whose sensory enticements and affordances were constructed and experienced across those of the limits of the city.

57 Hastaoglou-Martinidis argues that René in particular "was convinced that town planning is an affair of sanitation and circulation as well as an artistic project—the métier of a planner as well as of an artist" (2011, 169).

58 See Fries (1994) on the plans for Aleppo and Damascus.

59 See Hastaoglou-Martinidis (2011).

60 Author interviews with Gregoire Serof, July 2009 and February 2010.

61 See Verdeil (2008).

62 See Ghorayeb (1998, 107).

63 See Davie (2003).

64 See Hanssen (2005). For more on the politics of temporality in the late Ottoman Empire, see Wishnitzer (2015).

65 For useful entry points into the legal transformations around *awqaf* in the Mandate and the emergence of a sectarian legal and political order, see Moumtaz (2018) and Weiss (2010a; 2010b).

66 See Davie (2003).

67 See Thompson (2000).

68 Abisaab (2010) examines how women negotiated the transforming relationship between gender, work, kinship, and labor organizing in this period, particularly in the agricultural sectors in the south, many of whom remained suspicious of the national consolidation of the economy. This often meant contesting the meaning of what was considered acceptable for women to be and do in both the spheres of social reproduction (the home) and production (the workplace).

69 The political and military history of this conflict is recounted in Gaunson (1987).

70 See Bou Akar (2018).

71 As McGowan (2017) demonstrates with respect to the social history of cartography during British rule over the Gold Coast (Ghana); the creation of cadastral surveys and maps involved locals even while leaving their contributions undocumented. The belief was that this training inculcated a sensibility that maps and mapmaking were neutral, mathematical, and factual enterprises, even if the establishment of property rights was a highly contentious process. McGowan also shows that the "cartographic governmentality" that emerged during British rule continued in that "many postcolonial surveyors and cartographers maintained a sensibility about their work similar to that of their colonial predecessors" (2017, 225).

72 See Bou Akar (2018, 159); Verdeil (2003; 2012).

73 See Bou Akar's (2018, 160) discussion of the place of this specific plan in other proposed plans.

74 For an illuminating discussion of the political economy of this period, see Traboulsi (2007, 115–33).

75 For an account of this broader context, see Khalidi (2009); T. Mitchell (2011).
76 See Adas (2006); Gilman (2003); Latham (2000).
77 See Barney (2015, 159).
78 See Barney (2015, 136–69).
79 See Traboulsi (2007, 115–33).
80 This meant a reformulation of the social relations of financial activity between the state, the banking sector, and capital to accord a great deal of power to the banks. As Safieddine (2019) argues, "bank depositors became largely immune from any form of public prosecution, taxation or even inspection. Their monetary transactions were above the law in relation to the state, *not* the banks" (84).
81 See Gendzier (1997, 143–96).
82 See Bou Akar (2018, 150).
83 True to the times, the map indicates Anglo-Egyptian Sudan and Israel, but makes no mention of Palestine.
84 The afterlife and nature of these films is a subject that goes beyond the scope of this chapter but is worthy of more extended study. The use of these films easily fits within a history of attempts to solve social problems and advance development schemes by training modern viewers. It is likely that similar film libraries existed in other countries, and interesting comparisons could likely be drawn to African and Latin American countries. See Gharabaghi (2018).
85 The booklet's deep resonance with mid-century biopolitical social management, falling along distinct national, racial, and civilizational fault lines, makes it worth quoting at length: "In earlier civilizations, man was more concerned with individual health. Now the emphasis has shifted to *community* health [emphasis in the original]. People have begun to see health as a tangible asset to a city or country, the need for organization to improve general health and prevent sickness and unnecessary deaths through the disease, the problem of enlightenment for all people. . . . In general, the aims have been to stimulate and increase the motive for healthful living through education" (United States Operations Mission to Lebanon 1955, 69).
86 See Ostherr (2005).
87 Doxiadis Associates developed urban master plans and regional plans for a number of cities across the Arab world and developing world, perhaps most notoriously in Baghdad, Islamabad, and Riyadh. See Hull (2009); Menoret (2017); Pyla (2008).
88 See Menoret's (2014; 2017) account of how Doxiadis's approach to planning and geopolitical positioning aligned to make him a planner of choice in the 1960s and 1970s in Saudi Arabia.
89 See Sarkis (2003) for the intellectual and practical importance of the aerial view to Doxiadis's approach to planning.
90 As Bou Akar argues, the targeted areas "were the squatter settlements, refugee camps, and poor areas in Beirut's south and north peripheries (for example, Tel al-Zaatar, Qarantina, Medawar, Shatila, Bourj el-Barajneh, and Ouzaii)" (2018, 153).

91 As Sarkis (1998) has argued, the broader context for these local tensions was the demand placed on Chamoun by sympathizers of Pan-Arabism to sever his ties to the United States following its involvement in the Suez Crisis against Nasser. See Gendzier (1997) and Traboulsi (2007) for more on this episode, and its culmination in the deployment of US Marines in Lebanon in the summer of 1958. Commenting on the nature of the Doxiadis plan, Sarkis writes: "In retrospect, such projects, and the modernist urban planning that inspired them, were adopted partly to erase the highly politicized differences among selected projects and among income groups within projects; and yet they remained inexplicably underdeveloped in terms of their formal ambitions, particularly in relation to the terrain and the internal distinctions between residential and public arenas" (1998, 194).

92 As Bou Akar explains "While Doxiadis's intervention had been about construction and containment in 'problem sites,' and IRFED had been charged with developing a comprehensive national approach focused on the underdevelopment of the hinterlands, Écochard's plan firmly articulated the problem of the [urban] periphery" (2018, 161).

93 See Verdeil (2003; 2012).

94 Bou Akar's (2018) ethnographic study of planning in Beirut presents a highly nuanced treatment of the frustrations this creates for professionals whose work in the post–Civil War period is highly constrained by, if not at times totally subsumed within, a political context and social conditions they may otherwise desire to improve.

95 See Bou Akar (2018, 155) and Verdeil (2004).

96 Khuri elaborates that "the self-sufficient who are not strangled economically exercise greater freedom of action. Their political commitments, if any, are not derived from immediate economic pressure as much as from family and community pressure. The difference between economic pressure and family and community pressure is very significant socially: the former connotes social inequality between follower and leader, the latter connotes equality" (1975, 89–90).

97 See Verdeil (2003, 292).

98 See Verdeil (2003, 293–99) for a nuanced treatment of this debate, and Verdeil (2010) for a broader contextualization of the debate around the IRFED study in Lebanese urban planning circles. As Safieddine (2019, 99–106) shows, many of the laissez-faire critiques of Chehabism do not accurately reflect its fundamental commitment to conservative monetary policy, banking secrecy, and the power of the financial sector.

99 See Corm (1964).

100 See Verdeil (2012).

101 See Sarkis (2003).

102 Author interview (2010) with Gregoire Serof, a former colleague of Écochard's who worked on the plan in question.

103 See Verdeil (2012).

104 See Bou Akar (2018, 42); M. Fawaz (2004).

105 See Asseily and Asfahani (2007) and Hashimoto (2012) for great insight into the historical and transnational formation of the Lebanese intelligence apparatus of which the Deuxième Bureau was a part.

106 See Nucho's (2016) account of the urban and infrastructural formation of sectarian affiliation.

107 See Bou Akar's (2018, 94) discussion of this "ghost infrastructure" in Sahra Choueifat, and the contemporary conflict between the local priorities of Amal, PSP, and Hizbullah regarding the status of the peripheral highway. There has been the occasional attempt to build portions of this highway by cutting through urban fabric, with the original legal foundation and rationale originating in the Écochard Plan. As evidenced by the "Stop the Highway" campaign, these attempts have been met with quite vocal and expert opinion by civil society organizations opposing it. See https://stopthehighway.wordpress.com/ (last accessed November 30, 2018).

108 See Maasri (2016); Monroe (2017).

109 See Cook (2002); Montello (2002). For a useful overview of this history, and theoretical and historiographical perspectives from critical cartography, see the essays in Dodge, Kitchin, and Perkins (2009), which also reproduces important primary source material by key figures in American cartography, such as essays by Waldo Tobler and Arthur H. Robinson. See also Rankin (2016).

110 See Cloud (2001; 2002).

111 There is a great deal of concurrence on this point in the historical literature. To take just two, Bâli (2016) and Kaufman (2015) each present compelling explanations of the difference between the historical Sykes-Picot Agreement and the outsized place it occupies in contemporary imaginaries of various political stripes. There is a big difference between noting the drawing of borders and making grand sociopolitical assumptions about the realities that result, and Sykes-Picot itself didn't establish the borders of any modern state.

112 See Fregonese (2012).

113 The literature examining the factors leading up the Lebanese Civil War, and tracking the complex and shifting alliances during this period, is too large to usefully summarize here. Important accounts representing a range of intellectual stakes would be Fisk (2001); Hanf (1993); Khalaf (1987; 2002); Salibi (1976); Traboulsi (2007).

114 Fregonese borrows the term "urbicide" from the work of Coward (2006; 2007; 2008). See the special issue of *Theory and Event* 10.2 (Coole and Shapiro 2007) for a series of essays examining the concept.

115 See Beyhum (1992).

116 See Beyhum (1992, 45).

117 See Anziska's (2018) careful parsing of the documentary evidence of the massacre.

118 See Bou Akar (2018, 166). As Baumann (2017, 35) shows, this "improvement," contracted with Oger, sought to create luxury housing and tourist facilities by the sea, quite similar to the logic of the Solidere project.

119 See Norton (2014) on the emergence of Hizbullah in this period.

120 See Sarkis (1998, 196).

121 The concept of the dialectical image is at the heart of the method of *The Arcades Project* (Benjamin 1999), although it almost makes an appearance in "Paralipomena to 'On the Concept of History'" (Benjamin 2003).

Chapter Two: Images of Before/After in the Economy of Postwar Construction

1 For a useful overview of this line of argumentation, see Bou Akar (2012; 2015) and Bou Akar and Hafeda (2011).

2 For an account of this historical process in dialog with Lefebvre, see M. Fawaz (2009).

3 See Ghandour and Fawaz (2009); M. Harb (2001); Rowe and Sarkis (1998). Solidere is better understood as one example of a type of corporation formed in conjunction with and subsidized by the Lebanese state to concentrate political control and wealth in the hands of elites, and gain control of valuable real estate as compensation for remediating rubble. Other projects would include Linord and Elissar, which were formed to deal with the coast in the Metn region and South Beirut, respectively. Linord was formed in 1982, and had been used by Hariri to generate money until the Civil War reintensified. Elissar was held up by Amal and Hizbullah in the postwar period, but as shown by M. Harb el-Kak (2000), not because of any fundamental disagreement with the nature of such projects, but over a conflict as to how their own constituencies would benefit from them.

4 Haugbolle's (2010) gives an account of the discourse of memory and forgetting, especially prevalent in art and other forms of cultural production of this period.

5 Hayek (2014) demonstrates the importance that geographic imaginaries played in Lebanese literature dating at least to the middle of the twentieth, and even late nineteenth centuries.

6 Huyssen (2003) usefully historicizes, problematizes, and makes use of this intellectual gesture. For a consideration of a wider range of the varied genres, technologies, and cultural and urban histories, see the essays in Hell and Schönle (2010). See Seigneurie (2011) for a discussion of this tradition in relation to Lebanon in particular. The essays in Stoler (2013) develop the concept of ruination further, extending it by taking multiple imperial histories and formations into account.

7 C. Larkin's (2012) account makes productive use of the concept of "multidirectional memory" to analyze this condition.

8 The Council for Development and Reconstruction's *Progress Report on Reconstruction 1983-1987* (1988) details some $18.4 million paid for work in this period.

9 S. Makdisi (1997) cites Assem Salaam in an article in *Le Monde* of June 3, 1995.

10 Gordillo suggests that we "[conceive of] rubble as the lens through which to examine space negatively: by way of the places that were negated to create the geographies of the present." (2014, 11).

11 As Lim (2009) argues, "the conditions of emergence of homogeneous time [are] shaped not by the limits of 'natural' human consciousness and perception but by

global historical processes, that is, [by] the world-historical project of modernity that hinged on colonialism" (13).

12 For a Deleuzian problematization of the rationality of the figure of the rational economic actor envisioned in neoliberalism, see Massumi (2015).

13 I borrow this historical method from Buck-Morss in *Dreamworld and Catastrophe* (2000). She writes: "Although historically grounded, [this is] not history in the traditional sense . . . concerned less with how things actually were than how they appear in retrospect. [I] reshuffle the ordering of facts with the goal of informing present political concerns. [I] rescue the past, but not for nostalgic reasons. The goal is to blast holes in established interpretations of the twentieth century, liberating new lines of sight that allow for critical reappropriations of its legacy" (97). The coincidence of the end of the Lebanese Civil War with the post–Cold War moment is one of several ways that Beirut embodies the historical currents Buck-Morss analyzes, if not also some of the blast holes.

14 For example, shooting commercials and music videos typically requires the permission of the company, and that due compensation be paid.

15 As Baumann (2017, 40–55) shows, Hariri's rise can be understood to be a product of Saudi Arabia's interest in creating a conservative solution to the Arab-Israeli conflict represented by Syria's continued presence in Lebanon. Hariri's willingness to work closely with Syria was as important to his rise as was his willingness to share the proceeds of the systems of patronage corruption that he helped institutionalize.

16 Law 117 was passed on December 7, 1991, by the remaining members of Parliament who had been elected in 1972. The first election to be held since the beginning of the Civil War didn't take place until August 1992.

17 As Baumann (2017) argues, Lebanon's economy was not "'over-bureaucratic' or 'highly regulated,' but Hariri presented it in these terms in order to prevent Lebanon from ever becoming thus" (55).

18 See Schmid (2006) for a more detailed contextualization of specific episodes of this public debate.

19 Author interview, May 2010.

20 For a summary of the public debate about the legality of the transfer of land, see Leenders (2012, 108–13).

21 Sawalha's (2010) rich ethnographic account of postwar memories of pre–Civil War Beirut demonstrates that there was a great degree of both convergence and divergence over what the prewar space was exactly.

22 See Sawalha (2010).

23 This is particularly true of Zokak El Blat, which until the early postwar period was one of the oldest and most ethno-religiously mixed parts of the city. See Gebhart (2005).

24 See Becherer (2005) for a more extended treatment of the presence of this gaze in the plan.

25 For instance, Assem Salaam lamented an "inhuman effect" that the loss of older buildings and their "regional flavor" in favor high-rise apartments would have.

Jad Tabet condemned the plan in its entirety: "*Planning is reduced to the production of images* and post-modern clichés that could serve only real estate speculation" (Tabet 1993, 95). Emphasis is my own.

26 Quoted in *Al Hayat*, July 11, 1991.

27 Quoted in *Assafir*, July 21, 1991.

28 On this count, El Shalaq was in accordance with an elite consensus that emerged during the war equating the recovery of the city center with that of Beirut and in turn the rest of the country. See chapter 1.

29 As Kosmatopoulos (2011) has shown, the notion of "state failure" is better understood as an epistemic category with a social life of its own than as a value-free or critical term that can be unproblematically deployed to understand Lebanon. See also Kosmatopoulos's (2014) incisive analysis of the technopolitical work that "peace expertise" (and its favored form, the workshop) has played in Lebanon.

30 Miller and Rose (2008) offer a useful exploration of this conflation.

31 See S. Makdisi (1997).

32 For analyses of the gendered structures of Lebanese citizenship, see Allouche (2019); Hyndman-Rizk (2019); Mikdashi (2014).

33 See Beyhum, Salaam, and Tabet (1995).

34 A number of my interview subjects who worked as journalists at the time reported to me that they would on occasion poke fun at the comparative size of bribes during closed-door interviews, asking why Person A or B hadn't negotiated a higher sale price.

35 Baumann (2017, 24) interrogates the social and economic formation of a group that he evocatively terms the "contractor bourgeoisie," of which Hariri was a part and whose class interests he tended to serve. This group left during the Civil War, made their money in the Gulf, and then either returned or put their money into real estate or the financial sector in Lebanon.

36 Beyhum (1992) presciently argued: "conceived as an island of wealth and power, the city center would no longer have a centralizing role, but would instead become an island like all the other urban islands which arose during the war" (52).

37 See M. Fawaz (2017); Krijnen and Fawaz (2010). On the permutation this took in the post–2006 war reconstruction of the Haret Hreik neighborhood led by Hizbullah, see M. Fawaz (2014).

38 Perring (2009) explains how, despite the symbolic importance of archaeology in the Gavin plan, the needs of profit maximization severely curtailed the form of archaeological practice and preservation. Perring says of the Gavin plan: "These plans were not drawn up around actual discoveries, or with any reference to heritage management needs and considerations. Here, as was also to be the case in many subsequent management decisions, there was no attempt to assess and understand the value, potential and needs of either the material resource or the communities of interest in that resource. Instead *a priori* assumptions about the role of the historic past in framing the modern urban landscape were incorporated into the master-plan" (2009, 301–2).

39 Sixteen buildings in the Saifi village sector were the other primary targets of restoration.

40 Author interview, 2009, with an architect with firsthand knowledge and who requested anonymity, and that no specific deals be mentioned to avoid potentially being exposed. Many of these deals were public knowledge to a degree.

41 As Callon (1998); Callon, Millo, and Muniesa (2007); MacKenzie (2006); MacKenzie, Muniesa, and Siu (2007) explore, the technical function of market devices perform or even create the economic forms that they are often thought to merely facilitate. Following Appadurai's (2011) detailed engagement with the recent "pragmatic" or STS and actor-network theory–inspired turn in social studies of finance, understanding the design of financial techniques and economic models is key to understanding their function—but limited if one attempts to deduce the nature of the social assemblage they are a part of from the device itself. Appadurai further develops this line of thought by building on a rereading of Weber in subsequent work (Appadurai 2016), which, although addressed to the financial derivative, offers an analysis of the role of trust in contemporary financial markets that also illuminates this case.

42 Author interview, February 2010. He also expressed a weary frustration with the inability for even this close level of surveillance to guarantee total perfection. A small number of buildings that ended up using stone of an incorrect color seemed to be a source of abiding irritation.

43 Solidere, Annual Report 1997, Beirut.

44 See Baumann (2017, 68) on the context in which Hariri was forced to share in the pilfering of state money and contracts by other major political players such as Nabih Berri, the head of the Amal movement and speaker of Parliament. Berri would later install his brother on the board of the CDR.

45 The number most often agreed upon and cited is around 250,000 claimants, as found in Beyhum (1992); S. Makdisi (1997); Solidere, Annual Report 1994, Beirut.

46 Baumann (2017) highlights that diagnosing corruption can renaturalize these binaries, obscuring their origins: "the line between public and private, between state and society, is not a clear-cut demarcation but is itself constantly negotiated. Narratives of corruption thus reveal the contestation of where the line should be drawn. The reassignment of property rights inherent in capitalist development means that the economic development process is constantly open to challenges over the legitimacy of property rights, debates which engage with questions of legality and morality" (59).

47 Hourani (2012) demonstrates how the notion that the economic is what is "real" and "culture" merely the window-dressing is itself a feature of neoliberal discourse, which also informed debates about the construction of the Beirut Souks.

48 Almost all of the 1,630 lots in the area had been dealt with in this fashion by March 1997.

49 The GDR offering was lead managed by Merrill Lynch, and raised $77 million by the end of the year.

50 See Hourani (2012).

51 Hourani writes: "Of the 103 shops that participated in the grand opening in late 2009, at least 41 are owned by just five business groups, each of which is distinguished by extensive shop holdings in the [Beirut Central District]" (2012, 156).

52 See the essays in Al-Harithy (2010).

53 Sebald (2003), quoted in Vidler (2008, 29).

54 See Sturken (2004; 2015; 2016); Vidler (2008, 30).

55 von Moltke (2008) offers a useful overview of this perspective: "The cinema and the ruin plough common epistemological ground: as peculiarly modern forms of grasping contingency and temporality, they activate ways of knowing the past and its relation to the present. In this view, the century-long obsession of cinema with the image of ruins, in turn, is but the visible manifestation of cinema's and the ruin's common function to visualize time and history in modernity"(396).

56 This a very large literature, some of it specialized in particular cities, some of it drawing much broader conceptual linkages between the urban and the cinematic. See Rhodes and Gorfinkel (2011) for a useful review of this literature. AlSayyad (2006); Charney and Schwartz (1995); Clarke (1997); Dimendberg (2004); Prakash (2010) are also productive entry points into this literature.

57 For example, Braester's (2010) examination of film and urban change in China, also in this period, traces the emergence of a new set of visual practices, resembling a palimpsest (an underappreciated media technology) in their layering of memories of the past on the landscape of the new.

58 See Sobchack (2000).

59 Some important critical works on GIS methodology and software include Crampton (2010); Kwan (2008); Pickles (1995). For a consideration of the increased uncertainty that the use of algorithms and big data analytic approaches introduce into geographic knowledge, see Kwan (2016).

60 Following Chikamori's (2009) essay that puts McQuire's *The Media City* (2008) in dialog with Lefebvre and Benjamin, as well as Kittler's (1996) essay "The City Is a Medium," the before/after image expresses the logic of the material conditions governing the city, including the new capitalist vectors traversing its spaces.

61 I am grateful to Solidere's PR department for providing me with cassette copies of this archival material.

62 Solidere also produced a number of films in this period documenting the ongoing work at the site, but which go into greater detail about the technical dimensions of construction. Although they focus on the actual process of construction to a much greater extent than the three films I discuss, they also bear the imprint of the citizen-investor in the films mentioned above. This might suggest their more limited circulation and use in communicating with audiences in the contracting industry or with a greater technical fluency.

63 For notable work establishing this analytical perspective, see Acland and Wasson (2011a); Hediger and Vonderau (2009); Orgeron, Orgeron, and Streible (2012).

64 They clarify that "useful cinema" overlaps with, but is not equivalent to, similar terms such as "functional film," "educational film," "non-fictional film," and "non-theatrical film," as "the concept of useful cinema does not so much name a

mode of production, a genre, or an exhibition venue as it identifies a disposition, an outlook, and an approach toward a medium on the part of institutions and institutional agents. In this way, useful cinema has as much to do with the maintenance and longevity of institutions seemingly unrelated to cinema as it does with cinema per se" (Acland and Wasson 2011a, 5). Damluji (2013; 2016) can be understood as sharing this analytical direction in institutional film, while shifting focus to the distinct political and spatial formation that was the mid-century oil company and city in the Middle East.

65 McCarthy (2010) notes: "As an educational film technique, the onscreen discussion had shortcomings, most notably a tendency toward wooden acting styles and artificial, even preachy dialogue, which potentially diminished the technique's pedagogical effects" (398).

66 To return to the example of postwar Germany, it is entirely possible to see a predecessor to the Solidere corporate films in the films created as part of the Marshall Plan's public outreach efforts. I owe this insight to Mohamed Elshahed.

67 As Abisaab (2010) shows, the emergence of neoliberalism in Lebanon was articulated within a longer history of political contestation of patriarchy and sectarianism by women in the feminist and labor movements.

68 While I do not share Cooper's (2017) specific way of critiquing the secular and the religious, she compellingly argues that "neoliberalism and neoconservatism may be diametrically opposed on many issues, but on the question of family values, they reveal a surprising a unity" (33).

69 See Hourani (2008).

70 In addition to long shots on damaged buildings and anonymous, silent figures walking amid them, *Dialogue* also features interviews with archaeologists and architects, notably Oussama Kabbani, one of the key voices of expertise in *Which Beirut Tomorrow?* As Greg Burris pointed out to me (private communication, August 2016), the figure of characters lost in and engulfed by urban ruins also seem to distantly recall Rossellini's *Rome, Open City* (1945).

71 See Hourani (2008).

72 For a useful problematization of the trauma discourse as it pertains to cinema, see Rastegar (2015).

73 See Toufic (2003); Rastegar (2015). Hayek's (2019) analysis of the 1957 Lebanese film *Ila Ayn?* (Where To?) highlights how the recurrence of ruins ties the family anxieties of emigration to historical remains of past conflicts and "the sense of the nation as a ruined home" (189).

74 See Trigg's (2009) discussion of trauma, ruins, and spectrality.

75 Trigg (2009) argues: "Peculiar to the spatial memory of trauma is the role ruins play in housing what is absent. Such a fundamentally altered form testifies to the negative spatiality of the ruin, and ultimately to their significance. Phenomenologically, the formation and discovery of the ruin is marked by the fulfillment and embodiment of what is dynamically void. Here, the ruins of disaster paradoxically present themselves in terms of being empty of memory . . . instead

of monumentalizing what remains, the ruin brings about a non-memory, a puncturing in spatio-temporal presence" (94–95).

76 See Lim (2009) for an account of the intricacies by which these two temporal orders intertwine, as found in East Asian cinema.

77 This of course does not preclude the possibility of the complexities of postmemory, which Hirsch (1997) theorizes as the second-generation inheritance of trauma, memory, and nostalgia by people who did not themselves live the historical event. See Hayek (2011) for a productive reading of the theme of postmemory in postwar Lebanese fiction.

78 Hariri made the stabilization of national currency a priority, pegging it to the US dollar at the rate of approximately 1 to 1,500 Lebanese lira. Due to Hariri's policies, the state debt would in fact mushroom in the years to come, and Lebanese treasury bonds would eventually be downgraded to junk status. The majority of these would be owned by Lebanese banks, including those controlled by Hariri. See Becherer (2005).

79 The bird's-eye view map is only one way that this type of gaze is historically prefigured. It would also seem to be in tension with the moving panorama. See Crary (2002); Huhtamo (2013); Oettermann (1997).

80 Fregonese (2012) terms these "hybrid sovereignties."

81 As Gordillo (2014) demonstrates, it is in these continuities that rural or urban life amongst rubble and ruins persists.

82 I borrow the term neoliberal realism from Hourani (2012).

83 See Arsan (2018, 27–60) for a closer discussion of the public life of these and other related events, such as Hariri's widely televised funeral.

84 See the *Washington Post* article on March 3, 2005, also at http://www .washingtonpost.com/wp-dyn/articles/A1911-2005Mar2.html (last accessed July 25, 2016).

85 See Arsan (2018) for an analysis of the many political twists, turns, and stalemates of this period.

86 See Haugbolle (2013); Volk (2010, 154–88).

87 The Saint-George Hotel filed legal suit against Solidere, and a public battle has ensued ever since. It maintains complete documentation of its cases on its website at http://saintgeorgebeirut.com/ (last accessed January 19, 2019). The hotel has also long draped one of its most visible sides with a banner with the graphic of a stop sign that reads STOP SOLIDERE.

88 This theme was also featured on Future TV.

89 See Baumann (2017, 178). Secure Plus appears to have been meant as a counterweight to Hizbullah, and avoided the form of a centralized militia.

90 Hariri and the Future Movement helped prepare the discursive ground for this resurgent and regional sectarianism, even partnering with Islamist groups to shore up their coalition in areas such as Akkar and Tripoli in the north of the country.

91 This spatial form is documented in the "Mapping Security" project (Fawaz, Gharbieh, and Harb 2009). See Monroe (2016) on the lived experience of the new forms of securitization in this period.

92 Other than praise for the book's main benefactor, Trawi's work presents each half of the before/after opposite the other in a two-page spread.

93 My discussion of lenticular images is somewhat different from Ghassan Hage's illuminating theorization of the diasporic condition as bearing a kind of lenticularity—a mode of consciousness that oscillates between a "then and there" that coexists in the social reality of the "here and now." See Suvi P. Rautio, "Ghassan Hage: The Difficult Temporality of Diasporic Nostalgia," University of Helsinki Anthropology blog, August 29, 2019, accessed September 16, 2020, https://blogs.helsinki.fi/anthropology/2019/08/29/ghassan-hage-the-difficult-temporality-of-diasporic-nostalgia/.

Chapter Three: Concealment, Liveness, and Al Manar TV

1 See Sundaram (2010; 2015).

2 As argued by Edwards (2003).

3 Peters (2015) offers a rich reimagining of the concept of infrastructure, one which has cleared much of the ground for this book. Yet his theoretical engagements remain largely within a Euro-American sphere and its relationship to infrastructure, albeit with a civilizational historical-comparative mode as one of its many foundations.

4 I borrow the concept of a media-oriented practice from Couldry (2012, 35).

5 Nasrallah says as much in an interview with Al Jazeera on July 20.

6 See Arkin (2007, 46) for a detailed discussion of the rate of Hizbullah rocket fire by type of weapon.

7 See Moghnieh (2015a; 2015b; 2016; 2017).

8 See Naber (2009); Naber and Zaatari (2014).

9 See Hermez (2017).

10 See Hermez (2017) for a discussion of 2006 in particular, and in relation to other events.

11 See Limbrick (2012).

12 See Wilson-Goldie (2007).

13 Marks's (2015) appreciative understanding contextualizes the film's positive reception abroad but negative reception in Lebanon.

14 See Hayek (2017); Hout (2017).

15 People with a plurality of political positions were placed in this spectator role, additionally divided along the lines of those who did and did not expect (or want) to be evacuated. Anthony Bourdain's food travel show *No Reservations*, whose first visit to Lebanon coincided with the first week of the 2006 war, spends a fair amount of the episode reflecting on the complexity and relative privilege of watching war from the pool of the hotel the crew stayed at until they were evacuated by US Marines.

16 See Morag (2012); Rastegar (2015).

17 As Stewart (2007) has shown, the ordinary can be productively understood to be both affectively charged, and the categories and genres in which that charge is registered.

18 See Lambeth (2011); Matthews (2008).

19 See Arkin (2007).

20 See Halper (2015) for a detailed discussion of these tactics.

21 See Khalidi (2004) in particular.

22 See Kaplan (2018).

23 See Neep (2012); Provence (2005); Satia (2006; 2013).

24 See Khalili (2010). This is not to say that the legal regimes that are applied in Palestine are equivalent to Lebanon; Erakat (2019) demonstrates how the former has come to be treated as legally sui generis.

25 See Puar's (2017) invaluable elaboration of this logic and its techniques.

26 Elden (2009, xxii) identifies September 11 and Hizbullah's use of Katyusha rockets as two key moments in which the territorial formation of sovereignty was disrupted by aerial attack, provoking massive aerial response in kind. Parks (2018) advances this analysis further, analyzing how the vertical dimension of events like these are technologically formed.

27 See Human Rights Watch (2007).

28 See Puar (2017).

29 As argued by Human Rights Watch (2007), it is questionable whether IDF officials really believed the assumption that there were no Lebanese civilians left in southern Lebanon, or simply adopted the assumption to justify their actions (63).

30 See Deeb (2006).

31 See https://www.c-span.org/video/?193427-1/israel-hezbollah-conflict (last accessed June 15, 2018). The "personal appeal" begins a little before the thirty-eight-minute mark, following several minutes of quotations by Lebanese voices critical of Hizbullah, and evocations of Lebanon's "Golden Era" of the 1950s and 1960s, problematically equating being "Western" with not being a cancerous growth.

32 See Simon Jackson (2017); Watenpaugh (2015).

33 See chapter 1.

34 See Human Rights Watch (2007); Arkin (2007).

35 See Lambeth (2011, 79). This RAND study, which generally attempts to exonerate the professionalism of the IAF's performance, seems to ultimately find the lack of "success" lay in decision-making by the Olmert government, and a broader unwillingness to more fully commit to a more extended conflict.

36 Peters (2015) contends that "ballistics is also a key source for media theory" (243).

37 See Parks (2012).

38 For example, Packer (2013) demonstrates the centrality of sound in the technical history of automating anti-aircraft detection.

39 For a consideration of how anonymity underpins digital forms of exchange, see Pace (2017). See also Bancroft and Reid (2017) on the kinds of capitalist exchange that obtain in online drug markets.

40 The question of urban anonymity is a deep wellspring of insight and is too vast to usefully summarize here, but a consideration of the relationship to gender and sexuality is one possible entry point. Within the sociological tradition, Karp (1973) offers a discussion of the lineages that feed into

Erving Goffman's work via a discussion of hiding in the media space of the New York pornographic book store. In a very different context, Shah (2014) offers an analysis of how discretion and secrecy are necessary underpinnings of sex work, another pairing of anonymity with economic exchange. The work of Pétonnet (1987; 1994) theorizes anonymity to be of central importance for those living in conditions of social inequality.

41 See Licoppe's (2016) discussion of "pseudonymous strangers" and locative media.

42 See Bachmann et al.'s (2017) discussion of how understanding the productivity of anonymity appears more urgent when its possibility appears under threat.

43 Deseriis's (2015) history of collective pseudonyms examines how the refusal of conflating identity with individuality can become part and parcel of a political project.

44 The work of Zach Blas explores the queer productivity of the refusal of facial identification and tactics for confounding facial recognition technology, where anonymity and concealment can be understood to coincide. See Blas and Gaboury (2016).

45 See Pasquale (2015).

46 See Franklin (2015).

47 As in Brunton and Nissenbaum (2016).

48 See Shell (2012).

49 See Kaplan (2018).

50 O'Neill (2016) coins the term "narcotecture" to explain the relationship between architectural and spatial forms that markedly differ in terms of their conspicuousness—how clandestine air strips in the jungle and money-laundering high-rise condos sit alongside imagined and real drug lords' mansions. O'Neill's extension of Michel de Certeau's language of tactics and strategy to analyze the narcotics trade loosens a reading that would suggest that these tactics are inherently resistant or subaltern in and of themselves.

51 Remarking on the Situationists' theorization of secrecy, Wark (2013) writes: "The secret is not the truth of the spectacle. The division between the spectacle of appearances and the secrecy of non-appearances is itself an aspect of the falsification of the whole that the spectacle affects. . . . For Debord and Sanguinetti, it is not knowledge which is power, but secrecy. A counter-power is then not so much a counter-knowledge as a strategy that is capable of both revealing secrets when it is tactically advantageous, but also of fabricating them. Against the power of the secret as the founding power of the state, Situationists and Post-Situationists alike pose the glamour of the clandestine as a kind of counter-power" (110). This passage clarifies the danger of equating the clandestine with liberation.

52 This does not mean that no intelligible experiences or accounts can result. As detailed by Weizman (2017, 85–93), the Forensic Architecture group has worked with former detainees of the infamous Sadynaya Syrian prison to approximate the layout of the space from their accounts of and acoustic memory of the space, despite strict conditions of sensory deprivation at the prison.

53 See Khazaal's (2018) account of the visual culture of militia publications and mediated publics. See also Johnson (2002).

54 See Dajani (1992); Kraidy (1998; 1999).

55 See Khatib, Matar, and Alshaer (2014) for a more complete account of the party's political communication strategy. See Z. Harb (2011) for a historical account of how the channel's professionalization of news reporting was in part spurred by attempts to counter what the channel and party saw as Israeli disinformation.

56 van Es (2017) gives a very useful overview of the debates around liveness, clarifying that the category assumes a different role depending on whether the analysis assumes the most important element to be the moment of production and transmission, or that of transmission and reception.

57 Kraidy's (2010) discussion of the promise of liveness in Arab reality genres reveals a key reason why they have frequently become a battleground for competing political worldviews.

58 In one productive account, Turner (2011) suggests that the differences between television in different contexts destabilizes any straightforward normative reading of these contingent elements.

59 See Khazaal's (2018) discussion of LBC and its relationship to the crisis of traditional patriarchy in the Civil War posed by the emergence of militias that challenged older clientelist networks.

60 See Lamloum (2009a; 2009b) for a useful treatment of this history. Al Manar leadership later publicly expressed regret for airing a documentary about the infamously anti-Semitic "Protocols of the Elders of Zion" conspiracy theory.

61 See Feuilherade (2006).

62 "Dramatic Changes in Arab Television Ratings," Albawaba Business, August 22, 2006. https://www.albawaba.com/business/dramatic-changes-arab-television -ratings-%E2%80%98al-manar%E2%80%99-climbs-nowhere-top-10 (last accessed July 12, 2018).

63 Khalil and Kraidy (2009) usefully situate Al Manar within Arab television.

64 While quite different from it, the concealment of the camera crew emerges in the wake of an earlier generation of experimental and radical film and video work that sought to critique or destroy television as an apparatus (Boyle 1997; Goddard 2018; Stam, Porton, and Goldsmith 2015). See Dickinson (2018) on similar approaches to filmmaking in the Arab world. The most telling difference can be found in Hizbullah's status as a quasi-state actor with a media apparatus of its own.

65 While some of these are also staged after the fact (as exciting battle scenes for music video clips and other dramatizations), recordings made during combat are a better indicator of the stakes of concealment.

66 See El-Houri and Saber (2010); Z. Harb (2011).

67 The unofficial uploading of these videos in the context of Hizbullah's possession of an official satellite channel can be usefully contrasted with Fattal's (2017; 2018, 62) analysis of the FARC utilizing the internet as a primary video distribution strategy.

68 This video in particular tends to go down and come back up, but at the time of writing could be seen at https://www.dailymotion.com/video/x2w96mt (last accessed July 14, 2018).

69 Crandall (2010) suggests that in the twenty-first century, the targeting of weapons is defined by an anticipatory move that seeks to precede and prevent a potential future threat. Crandall suggests that targeting is better understood in the context of what he terms tracking, meaning the application of a combination of remote sensing and data management technologies to the planning, management, and anticipation of spaces and the range of possible movements within them.

70 This conversation continues to rapidly expand, but for a useful introduction, see Parks and Kaplan (2017).

71 See Arkin (2007, 63).

72 See Arkin (2007, 29).

73 Farocki (2004) theorizes images that are involved in doing things more than representing them as "operational images."

74 Parks (2018) has developed the concept of "reading satellite images like a state" to destabilize the appeals to expertise and precision that underpin images that might otherwise be taken to be much more ambiguous.

75 As Chandler (2016) argues: "Attempts to counter drone aircraft similarly mirror dualisms that frame their use. Critics count targets as civilians, whose lives 'we' must protect" (2).

76 See İşcen (2019); Rhee (2018).

77 For example, see Grewal (2017); Nath (2016; 2017).

78 In fairness to Baudrillard (1995), the images he discusses are missile cam and not guncam images—the former being distinguished by affixing the camera to the projectile itself. The inadequacy of the visual geography remains.

79 See Ahmed (2018).

80 The escalating use of drones has been well chronicled in the literature on drones, but see Chamayou (2015); Gusterson (2016); Parks (2018); Satia (2013); Shaw (2016).

81 On the problem of incalculability in security discourse and risk management, see Amoore (2009; 2013; 2014); Amoore and de Goede (2008). One entry point into the cultural status of calculative reason in colonial systems is Appadurai (1993).

82 For example, see Hussain (2013).

83 The transmission stations for Future TV and LBCI also came under attack (Feuilherade 2006), as did the antennas of TeleLiban and NBN (El-Khadem 2008). As chronicled in Mai Masri's *33 Days*, NewTV (later Al Jadeed) was temporarily forced underground.

84 This might be seen as a limit case of what Parks (2012) terms infrastructural concealment, which is an application or type of the modality as applied to infrastructure.

85 Doane's (1990) account highlights how this potential haunts network broadcasting in places like the United States, but is newly relevant in the case of Al Manar.

86 The clip can be viewed at https://www.youtube.com/watch?v=fUeKo672LnI (last accessed July 15, 2018).

87 The classic accounts of the gendered dynamics of family viewing in television studies in the US and UK (Morley and Brunsdon 1999; Spigel 1992) and in the Arab world (Abu-Lughod 2005; Kraidy 2010) also highlight how the unstable boundaries of the nation are reflected in those of the domestic sphere. As Feuer (1983) has argued, the ideology of liveness has often served to tighten the bonds of family, but is by no means the only framework in which television does so.

88 See Alagha (2011) and Saade (2016).

89 The essays collected in Meyer and Stordalen (2019) offer a comparative framework for these themes in Jewish, Christian, and Islamic traditions.

90 See Hirschkind (2006); Hirschkind and Larkin (2008); Houtman and Meyer (2012); Stolow (2013).

91 As B. Larkin (2009) argues, understanding the place of broadcasting in contemporary Islam requires taking media technology seriously, without reducing all historical and social change to technology. Examples of such an approach can be found in Moll (2012; 2017; 2018); Rajagopal (2001).

92 Buonanno (2008) puts it: "these diverse places do not cancel each other out, but interact within the new co-existence between nearness and distance, here and elsewhere, home and world, 'home and away'" (19).

93 What he says can be translated as "there is no doubt that the Israeli Air Force is the most powerful in the region, and there is no way we can cope with it."

94 See Adey (2010).

95 Mahnaimi, in Acosta (2007, 46).

96 See Fulghum (2006).

97 See Harik (2005, 131). While capturing the execution of high-value targets was of great political significance in this instance, Al Manar routinely broadcasted military operations recorded on the front line in this period.

98 See Harik (2005, 138).

99 See van Es (2017) on how live streaming on social media platforms reworks these promises and affordance.

100 Relying on IAF reports, Lambeth (2011) claims that Nasrallah ". . . was said to become all but completely unhinged for a brief [time]. Unlike Stalin, however, who was put out of the fight in complete psychological shock for two weeks after the Wehrmacht's surprise attack on the Soviet Union in 1941, Nasrallah pulled himself back together fairly quickly" (Lambeth 2011, 156). The equation of the IAF and the Luftwaffe might be explained by the attempt to make a historical reference to (unfavorably thought-of) leaders in bunkers.

101 See Matar (2008).

102 The IDF requested a rush-airlifted delivery of munitions from the United States to replenish a supply that was rapidly being depleted.

103 The 2010 Wikileaks release of US State Department communications would later give evidence supporting this assertion.

104 That is, relative to the escalation in overt sectarian agitation and street violence in the period that followed.

105 The number of members of parliament is apportioned according to sect, the exact number having only been renegotiated at crucial junctures such as the Taif Agreement at the end of the Lebanese Civil War and the Doha Accords of May 2008—a direct outcome of the political stalemate created by the sit-in and resolved by Hizbullah's military takeover of Beirut in clashes later that year. For a more detailed account of this political context and dynamic, see Arsan (2018, 61–98).

106 Resolution 1559 called for the end of the involvement of foreign governments, and the full disarmament of all non-state actors; 1701 was the basis for the 2006 ceasefire agreement, and explicitly called for a political solution leading to Hizbullah's disarmament.

107 The building is located adjacent to the former site of the Saudi embassy. At the time of writing, the ruin was in roughly the same condition as in 2008. Like the Saudi embassy, Future has newer offices elsewhere in Beirut.

Chapter Four: The Open Secret of Concealment at the Mleeta Museum

1 Mirzoeff develops this aspect of Rancière's thought in *The Right to Look* (2011), particularly with his elaboration of the concepts of countervisuality and Visuality 2. He argues: "the two modes of visuality are not opposed in a binary system, but operate as a relation of difference that is always deferred. So not all forms of Visuality 2 are what I am calling countervisuality, the attempt to reconfigure visuality as a whole. For example, many forms of religion might deploy some mode of Visuality 2 without seeking to change the perceived real in which that religion is practiced" (24). Mleeta exemplifies why this point is crucial.

2 The nomination of the "Western tradition" in Derrida, while designating a specific point of intervention, need not imply that other intellectual traditions are incapable of developing a reified or comparative conception of religion.

3 See Naas (2012, 67).

4 See Engelke (2011); Hirschkind (2011), on how such arguments can run aground.

5 See Engelke (2011) on the relationship between McLuhan's Catholic faith and the Catholicism of his media theory.

6 This of course is not a novel claim, and the argument that Islam and capitalism are not intrinsically incompatible has a long history. Rodinson's classic study *Islam and Capitalism* (1974) and T. Mitchell's argument about "McJihad" (2002a) are two illustrative examples, with quite different premises and points of intervention. For closer analysis of the historical overlap and conflict between Shi'ite movements and communism in Lebanon, see Abisaab and Abisaab (2014). See also Bardawil (2016) on how this Marxist tradition can be misread in retrospect.

7 Jordan's (2014) careful reading of the place of religion in Foucault puts it this way: "the forms of power under which many of us now live count on capturing bodies in approved records, not least by training bodies to speak themselves through set scripts" (4). Jordan then gets at the kernel of religion in a way that is

even more evocative of Mleeta: "religion is distinguished . . . by how it arranges languages and practices—teachings and rituals—to control this world and the bodies very much in it" (9).

8 The Arab intellectual debates about the politically committed aesthetic (*iltizām*) in literature have arguably always been concerned with the barely contained potentialities of the reader, listener, or viewer at risk of losing commitment. The essays gathered in Pannewick, Khalil, and Albers (2015) explore the trajectories of this debate as it pertains to literature in the second half of the twentieth century. See also Al-Musawi (2003); Klemm (2000). El-Ariss's (2018) account of the "leaking subject" examines the literary practices that are the result of the cracks in the political project of the committed aesthetic as much as they are of digital media.

9 See Cammett's (2014) account of the relationship between the state, welfare and political sectarianism, and ethno-religious groups. As Volk (2009) puts it: "This official illegibility of Lebanon's marginal regions creates a vacuum to be filled by unofficial competitive documentary practices that accomplish a head-count of a different kind: the faces of martyrs, which appear on billboards, lampposts, walls of residential homes, and special commemorative structures (ac)count (for) the individual sacrifices of the residents in the borderlands" (266). This in part explains why it is often political parties that claim martyrs on behalf of the nation, and not exclusively the state.

10 See Deeb and Harb (2009) for more on the institutional resources and intellectual work underlying these cultural policies.

11 The term "actually existing neoliberalism," as used by Brenner and Theodore (2002), is useful in avoiding the pitfall of neoliberalism becoming a floating signifier rather than a historically and geographically specific set of policies and projects.

12 See Marei (2016).

13 For a close conceptual and historical parsing of the concept of pious neoliberalism in relation to Hizbullah, see Marei (2016). M. Harb's (2008) analysis also examines the place of Hizbullah as an agent of development and urban planning.

14 Larkin and Parry-Davies (2019) comment on this turn within Lebanon, noting that Mleeta's head architect visited and studied other war memorials around the world.

15 See Deeb and Harb (2013); Harb and Deeb (2011), for an illuminating discussion of these spaces of religiously acceptable fun.

16 For more on the political context, institutional structure, and planning challenges associated with the post–2006 war period, see the essays in Al-Harithy (2010).

17 See Volk's (2007) account of this dynamic at the two incarnations of the Qana memorial. See Volk (2010) for a broader historical contextualization of the valences of sectarianism and inter-communal memorial practices. On the rise of memorial museums and memory, see Gómez-Barris (2008); Sodaro (2018); Violi (2012); P. Williams (2007).

18 See Schwenkel (2009) for an account of the politics of memory and museums in Vietnam pertaining to the "American War" and their relationship to postwar tourism.

19 See Bajoghli (2019).

20 Bajoghli writes of the Sacred Defense Garden and Museum that "the museum moved from celebrating martyrs—like the ubiquitous yet empty martyrs' museums that dot the map of Iran—to offering a narrative of nationalism, dignity, and pride" (2019, 103).

21 The website is available in the standard Lebanese linguistic trio of Arabic, English, and French.

22 I have only visited the site with a group of more than four or five people on one occasion, but the guides worked to maintain a conversational style in even that circumstance.

23 Toscano's (2010) discussion of the history of overcharged dismissals of figures of the fanatic do much to rescue antagonistic and uncompromising political affinity. Toscano can also be read as a critique of the pitfalls of valorizing all such political stances.

24 All names such as "the Abyss" reflect the English names given by the site.

25 Joseph (1993) defines patriarchal connectivity as "the production of selves with fluid boundaries organized for gendered and aged domination in a culture valorizing kin structures, morality, and idiom" (1993, 453).

26 The melodramatic mode found in this film is widespread in Hizbullah's broader televisual and cinematic corpus. It is worth noting that Nasrallah is widely known to have lost a son in the fight against Israel, giving a particular resonance to his being moved at this point.

27 This speech, from February 16, 2011, actually spends a fair amount of time discussing the comparative condition of Lebanese and Israeli industrial, energy, and transportation infrastructure, claiming that the large disparity in terms of development makes Israel's infrastructure a much higher-value target. Nasrallah even claims that were the power to go out in Lebanon, the resulting darkness would only make it easier to hide.

28 In an imploring tone, Nasrallah's voiceover describes "A link that is made of light, and hope, and passion, and love, and trust," superimposed over scenes of fighters in the field, and mournful vocals and violin.

29 El-Ariss's (2018, 63–69) theorization of the "Equality in Insult" examines the relationship between post-1967 defeat and humor from a different but productive angle.

30 Mughniyah's ingenuity as a field tactician is also mentioned on a number of the placards around Mleeta. Mughniyah was assassinated by Israel in 2008, and is one of the few individuals mentioned by name at Mleeta.

31 See Parks (2018).

32 See Shell (2012) on the technological, scientific, military, and artistic confluences that shaped twentieth-century camouflage, particularly in its formative early decades.

33 Near the entrance of the Bunker, visitors are also asked to discern which of a number of nearly identical rocks are fake, and thus admire the skill of the party's combat engineers.

34 One of the feature's official names is "the Tunnel."

35 Nasrallah wasn't the leader of the party at the time.

36 As Elden (2013) outlines, this way of relating to space is implicated in the deepened logic of securitization that emerged in the wake of September 11, and which bunkers like the one in Mleeta are a response to.

37 See Pike (2005; 2007) on the place of the figure of the underground in modern Euro-American cultural imaginaries, particularly when figured in relation to urban space.

38 Cadava (2012) notes that in Nadar's reflections, "much of his account of this work details the difficulties and challenges he encountered while experimenting with electric light. Among other things, Nadar's underground work literalizes the relation between photography and death that he understands to belong to photography's signature. . . . Nadar emphasizes the palimpsest-like relation between the underground network of tunnels and the above ground network of streets" (70–71). Mleeta, however, is a very rural location, and is better understood in relation to the visual vantage points of the sky and other nearby mountaintops.

39 For example, see Garrett (2016).

40 See H. Scott (2008), who explains how "in using the underground as a resource to defend their pre-colonial religious practices, indigenous populations [in Peru] played an active role in producing Spanish anxieties about the connections between the visible landscapes and the realms that lay beneath" (1863).

41 See Schwenkel (2009), although the comparison merits a number of qualifications—unlike Vietnam, the landscape of South Lebanon is part of an ongoing military conflict—and is only meant to illustrate an example of one kind of underground installation meant to accommodate a small-ish outpost of fighters.

42 Llamas-Rodriguez (2016) theorizes the relationship between technologies meant to bypass the exercise of national sovereignty and the geographies of media markets alongside the subterranean subversion of the US-Mexico border. The Bunker at Mleeta doesn't cross a border, but in its original use, it did facilitate guerrilla movements against an occupation force that had crossed one.

43 In this respect, the discovery of the hidden underground space resonates with the longer cinematic history of underground command/control center and bomb shelters that are almost always discovered or breached, often figured narratively as a climactic moment. See Pike (2009).

44 Searching #mleeta or #mlita on any given day will pretty reliably turn up images of the Bunker, the Abyss, and views of the landscape.

45 See Kaplan (2015).

46 See Weizman (2007).

47 It is telling that the counterinsurgency techniques of the Vietnam War eventually led to the use of Agent Orange to remove places to hide, and the frustrating

inability to visualize the enemy was to become a feature of much of the cultural output following in its wake.

48 To begin to unpack the normative ableism here, one could note that this walk down the mountain would potentially preclude many wounded Hizbullah veterans, whose numbers greatly increased as the Syrian Civil War wore on.

49 I draw on the insights developed by Butler (2009), who develops a general framework in response to the War on Terror in general, and Abu Ghraib and Guantánamo in particular. I do so not to suggest an equivalence between those bodies and images and that of the Israeli soldiers presented, but to draw attention to the ways such ethical encounters can go awry. Butler argues: "Encountering a life as precarious is not a raw encounter, one in which life is stripped bare of all its usual interpretations, appearing to us outside all relations of power. . . . on the contrary, it is only by challenging the dominant media that certain kinds of lives may become visible or knowable in their precariousness. It is not only or exclusively the visual apprehension of a life that forms a necessary precondition for an understanding of the precariousness of life" (2009, 51).

50 Butler (2009) traces the gendered and sexualized twists and turns that such situations require of certain kinds of militarized masculinities. Writing of the Abu Ghraib photographs of sexualized torture, Butler argues that "the torturer, though debasing homosexuality, can only act by becoming implicated in a version of homosexuality in which the torturer acts as the 'top' who only penetrates and who coercively requires that penetrability be located in the body of the tortured" (2009, 98). The images at the exhibition hall are different in a few key ways: they are not premised on an explicit sexualization of pain, the person or persons inflicting pain do not appear in the images, the ones inflicting the pain are assumed to be capable of being similarly targeted and hurt, and all the people who appear are men.

51 Most of the ads are approximately forty seconds long, with a few as short as fifteen or as long as sixty seconds. One of the other videos on the channel documents a visit by a group of AUB students and professor, all of whom proclaim that visiting the site is important for all kinds of people, not just party members.

52 The joke in the title of Neil MacFarquhar's (2009) book *The Media Relations Department of Hizbollah Wishes You a Happy Birthday: Unexpected Encounters in the Changing Middle East* is one example.

53 As Joseph (1997) explains, "family relations have flowed into the state and political relationships have become familial. The political leader has been seen as a family member, an honorary family patriarch" (87).

54 Joseph's (1997; 2000) analysis is indispensable in tracing how the Lebanese state has long depended on patriarchal family relations and forms of selfhood, particularly when it is reproduced in practices of kinship and sectarian institutions, where the state is often perceived not to be present.

55 See Deeb's (2008) discussion of Hizbullah's creation of dioramas depicting nearly current events prior to the construction of the Mleeta museum.

56 Derrida's term is that the concept of "religion" is already a confusion of how "tele-technoscience" takes its own history as being that of reason as an article of faith, and of those social and cultural experiences we call "religions" to be part of an "auto-immune disorder of modernity, themselves largely indistinguishable from the media cultures they are a part of, itself understood through a teleological understanding of Christianity (Derrida's term is "globalatinization").

57 Lofton (2017) articulates this inner duality: "religion manifests in efforts to mass-produce relations of value" (2) and "much of consumer life is itself a religious enterprise, religious in the sense of enshrining certain commitments stronger than almost any other acts of social participation" (6).

58 As shown by Banet-Weiser (2012).

59 See Fattal (2018) on the role of advertising agencies in attempts to demobilize the FARC in Colombia.

60 Banet-Weiser (2012) argues: "Branding religious lifestyles represents an open-ended marketing and business *opportunity*, where there are no discrete products to commodify but rather politically-diffused identities. These identities are reimagined and reframed not only within and as consumer items but also in the ways in which religion is organized, insititutionalized, and experienced in everyday life" (171). Banet-Weiser's analysis is geared primarily to religious groups in the United States, which have a very different relationship to the state and market than does Hizbullah. For example, Hizbullah receives financial support from Iran, wealthy benefactors, and its involvement in the Lebanese economy (official and unofficial). But the resonances between brand Mleeta and those that Banet-Weiser diagnoses are numerous.

61 Islamic traditions have long and varied histories of negotiating the meaning of sound reproduction technology, appropriate recording techniques, and modes of listening. See Eisenlohr (2018); Hirschkind (2006).

62 I explore this theoretical point in greater depth in El-Hibri (2017).

63 As Lofton (2017) has shown, the Protestantism of the Herman Melville corporation was instrumental and not incidental to the design of the "action office" or office cubicle. Mirroring the contemporary doxa about open office plans as the antidote to the deadening cubicle, Mleeta offers plenty of wide open spaces and vistas for contemplation of exhibits, the Path, and the Bunker.

REFERENCES

Abisaab, Malek. 2009. "Shiite Peasants and a New Nation in Colonial Lebanon: The Intifada of Bint Jubayl, 1936." *Comparative Studies of South Asia, Africa and the Middle East* 29, no. 3: 483–501. https://doi.org/10.1215/1089201X-2009-033.

Abisaab, Malek. 2010. *Militant Women of a Fragile Nation*. Syracuse, NY: Syracuse University Press.

Abisaab, Rula Jurdi, and Malek Hassan Abisaab. 2014. *The Shiites of Lebanon: Modernism, Communism, and Hizbullah's Islamists*. Syracuse, NY: Syracuse University Press.

Abu Lughod, Janet L. 1980. *Rabat: Urban Apartheid in Morocco*. Princeton, NJ: Princeton University Press.

Abu-Lughod, Lila. 2005. *Dramas of Nationhood: The Politics of Television in Egypt*. Chicago: University of Chicago Press.

Abu-Rabi', Ibrahim M. 2003. *Contemporary Arab Thought: Studies in Post-1967 Arab Intellectual History*. London: Pluto Press.

Abu-Rish, Ziad. 2014. "On Power Cuts, Protests, and Institutions: A Brief History of Electricity in Beirut (Part One)." Jadaliyya. April 22, 2014. https://www.jadaliyya.com/Details/30564.

Acland, Charles R., and Haidee Wasson. 2011a. "Introduction: Utility and Cinema." In *Useful Cinema*, edited by Charles R. Acland and Haidee Wasson. Durham, NC: Duke University Press.

Acland, Charles R., and Haidee Wasson, eds. 2011b. *Useful Cinema*. Durham, NC: Duke University Press.

Acosta, David A. 2007. "The Makara of Hizballah: Deception in the 2006 Summer War." Master's thesis, Naval Postgraduate School, Monterey, CA.

Adas, Michael. 2006. *Dominance by Design: Technological Imperatives and America's Civilizing Mission*. Cambridge, MA: Belknap Press of Harvard University Press.

Adey, Peter. 2010. "Vertical Security in the Megacity: Legibility, Mobility and Aerial Politics." *Theory, Culture and Society* 27, no. 6: 51–67.

Ahmed, Sabeen. 2018. "From Threat to Walking Corpse: Spatial Disruption and the Phenomenology of 'Living under Drones.'" *Theory and Event* 21, no. 2: 382–410.

Akerman, James R., ed. 2009. *The Imperial Map: Cartography and the Mastery of Empire.* Chicago: University of Chicago Press.

Akerman, James R., ed. 2017. *Decolonizing the Map: Cartography from Colony to Nation.* Chicago: University of Chicago Press.

Alagha, Joseph. 2011. *Hizbullah's Identity Construction.* Amsterdam: Amsterdam University Press.

Al-Harithy, Howaida, ed. 2010. *Lessons in Post-War Reconstruction: Case Studies from Lebanon in the Aftermath of the 2006 War.* New York: Routledge.

Alhassan, Amin, and Paula Chakravartty. 2011. "Postcolonial Media Policy under the Long Shadow of Empire." In *The Handbook of Global Media and Communication Policy,* edited by Robin Mansell and Marc Raboy. Oxford, UK: Wiley-Blackwell.

Allouche, Sabiha. 2019. "Queering Heterosexual (Intersectarian) Love in Lebanon." *International Journal of Middle East Studies* 51, no. 4: 547–65. https://doi.org/10.1017/S0020743819000655.

Al-Musawi, Muhsin. 2003. *The Postcolonial Arabic Novel: Debating Ambivalence.* Boston: Brill.

AlSayyad, Nezar. 2006. *Cinematic Urbanism: A History of the Modern from Reel to Real.* New York: Routledge.

'Amil, Mahdi. 1986. *Fi Al-Dawla al-Ta'ifiyya [On the Sectarian State].* Beirut: Dar Al Farabi.

Amin, Ash, and Nigel Thrift. 2017. *Seeing Like a City.* Cambridge, UK: Polity Press.

Amoore, Louise. 2009. "Lines of Sight: On the Visualization of Unknown Futures." *Citizenship Studies* 13, no. 1: 17–30. https://doi.org/10.1080/13621020802586628.

Amoore, Louise. 2013. *The Politics of Possibility: Risk and Security beyond Probability.* Durham, NC: Duke University Press.

Amoore, Louise. 2014. "Security and the Incalculable." *Security Dialogue* 45, no. 5: 423–39. https://doi.org/10.1177/0967010614539719.

Amoore, Louise, and Marieke de Goede, eds. 2008. *Risk and the War on Terror.* New York: Routledge.

Anand, Nikhil. 2017. *Hydraulic City: Water and the Infrastructures of Citizenship in Mumbai.* Durham, NC: Duke University Press.

Anand, Nikhil, Akhil Gupta, and Hannah Appel, eds. 2018. *The Promise of Infrastructure.* Durham, NC: Duke University Press.

Anziska, Seth. 2018. *Preventing Palestine: A Political History from Camp David to Oslo.* Princeton, NJ: Princeton University Press.

Appadurai, Arjun, ed. 1986. *The Social Life of Things: Commodities in Cultural Perspective.* Cambridge, UK: Cambridge University Press.

Appadurai, Arjun. 1993. "Number in the Colonial Imagination." In *Orientalism and the Postcolonial Predicament: Perspectives on South Asia,* edited by Carol Breckenridge and Peter van der Veer. Philadelphia: University of Pennsylvania Press.

Appadurai, Arjun. 2011. "The Ghost in the Financial Machine." *Public Culture* 23, no. 3: 517–39.

Appadurai, Arjun. 2016. *Banking on Words: The Failure of Language in the Age of Derivative Finance*. Chicago: University of Chicago Press.

Aractingi, Phillippe, dir. 2008. *Under the Bombs*. Santa Monica, CA: Lions Gate Films.

Arkin, William M. 2007. *Divining Victory: Airpower in the 2006 Israel-Hezbollah War*. Maxwell Air Force Base, AL: Air University Press.

Armbrust, Walter. 1996. *Mass Culture and Modernism in Egypt*. New York: Cambridge University Press.

Arsan, Andrew. 2018. *Lebanon: A Country in Fragments*. London: Hurst.

Asseily, Youmna, and Ahmad Asfahani, eds. 2007. *A Face in the Crowd: The Secret Papers of Emir Farid Chehab, 1942-1972*. London: Stacey International.

Atia, Mona. 2012. "A Way to Paradise: Pious Neoliberalism, Islam, and Faith-Based Development." *Annals of the Association of American Geographers* 102, no. 4: 808-27. https://doi.org/10.1080/00045608.2011.627046.

Bachelard, Gaston. 1994. *The Poetics of Space: The Classical Look at How We Experience Intimate Places*. Translated by Maria Jolas. Boston: Beacon Press.

Bachmann, Götz, Michi Knecht, and Andreas Wittel. 2017. "The Social Productivity of Anonymity." *Ephemera: Theory and Politics in Organization* 17, no. 2: 241-58.

Bagley, James W. 1922. "Concerning Aerial Photographic Mapping: A Review." *Geographical Review* 12, no. 4: 628-35. https://doi.org/10.2307/208595.

Bajoghli, Narges. 2019. *Iran Reframed: Anxieties of Power in the Islamic Republic*. Stanford, CA: Stanford University Press.

Bâli, Aslı. 2016. "Sykes-Picot and 'Artificial' States." *AJIL Unbound* 110: 115-19. https://doi.org/10.1017/S2398772300002919.

Bancroft, Angus, and Peter Scott Reid. 2017. "Challenging the Techno-Politics of Anonymity: The Case of Cryptomarket Users." *Information, Communication and Society* 20, no. 4: 497-512. https://doi.org/10.1080/1369118X.2016.1187643.

Banet-Weiser, Sarah. 2012. *Authentic™: Politics and Ambivalence in a Brand Culture*. New York: New York University Press.

Bardawil, Fadi A. 2016. "Dreams of a Dual Birth: Socialist Lebanon's World and Ours." *Boundary 2* 43, no. 3: 313-35. https://doi.org/10.1215/01903659-3572854.

Barney, Timothy. 2015. *Mapping the Cold War: Cartography and the Framing of America's International Power*. Chapel Hill: University of North Carolina Press.

Baudrillard, Jean. 1995. *The Gulf War Did Not Take Place*. Translated by Paul Patton. Bloomington: Indiana University Press.

Baumann, Hannes. 2017. *Citizen Hariri: Lebanon's Neo-Liberal Reconstruction*. New York: Oxford University Press.

Bawardi, Hani J. 2014. *The Making of Arab Americans: From Syrian Nationalism to U.S. Citizenship*. Austin: University of Texas Press.

Becherer, Richard. 2005. "A Matter of Life and Debt: The Untold Costs of Rafiq Hariri's New Beirut." *Journal of Architecture* 10, no. 1: 1-41.

Benjamin, Walter. 1999. *The Arcades Project*. 2nd ed. Edited by Rolf Tiedemann. Translated by Howard Eiland and Kevin McLaughlin. Cambridge, MA: Belknap Press of Harvard University Press.

Benjamin, Walter. 2003. "Paralipomena to 'On the Concept of History.'" In *Walter Benjamin: Selected Writings. Vol. 4, 1938–1940*, edited by Howard Eiland and Michael W Jennings. Translated by Edmund Jephcott and Howard Eiland. Cambridge, MA: Belknap Press f Harvard University Press.

Beyhum, Nabil. 1992. "The Crisis of Urban Culture: The Three Reconstruction Plans for Beirut." *Beirut Review* 4 (fall): 43–62.

Beyhum, Nabil, Assem Salaam, and Jad Tabet. 1995. *Beyrouth: Construire l'avenir, Reconstruire Le Passe?* Beirut: Dossiers de l'Urban Research Institute.

Blas, Zach, and Jacob Gaboury. 2016. "Biometrics and Opacity: A Conversation." *Camera Obscura: Feminism, Culture, and Media Studies* 31, no. 2 (92): 155–65. https://doi.org/10.1215/02705346-3592510.

Boisfleury, Grégoire Potiron de. 2010. "The Origins of Marshal Lyautey's Pacification Doctrine in Morocco from 1912 to 1925." Fort Leavenworth, KS: US Army Command and General Staff College.

Bou Akar, Hiba. 2012. "Contesting Beirut's Frontiers." *City and Society* 24, no. 2: 150–72.

Bou Akar, Hiba. 2015. "From Poor Peripheries to Sectarian Frontiers: Planning, Development, and the Spatial Production of Sectarianism in Beirut." In *Territories of Poverty: Rethinking North and South*, edited by Ananya Roy and Emma Crane. Athens: University of Georgia Press.

Bou Akar, Hiba. 2018. *For the War Yet to Come: Planning Beirut's Frontiers*. Stanford, CA: Stanford University Press.

Bou Akar, Hiba, and Mohamad Hafeda. 2011. *Narrating Beirut from Its Borderlines*. Lebanon: Heinrich Böll Foundation.

Bowker, Geoffrey C., and Susan Leigh Star. 1999. *Sorting Things Out: Classification and Its Consequences*. Cambridge, MA: MIT Press.

Boyd, Douglas A. 1991. "Lebanese Broadcasting: Unofficial Electronic Media During a Prolonged Civil War." *Journal of Broadcasting and Electronic Media* 35, no. 3 (summer): 269–87.

Boyle, Deirdre. 1997. *Subject to Change: Guerrilla Television Revisited*. New York: Oxford University Press.

Braester, Yomi. 2010. *Painting the City Red: Chinese Cinema and the Urban Contract*. Durham, NC: Duke University Press.

Brenner, Neil, and Nik Theodore. 2002. "Cities and the Geographies of 'Actually Existing Neoliberalism.'" *Antipode* 34, no. 3: 349–79.

Browne, Simone. 2015. *Dark Matters: On the Surveillance of Blackness*. Durham, NC: Duke University Press.

Brunsdon, Charlotte. 2012. "The Attractions of the Cinematic City." *Screen* 53, no. 3: 209–27. https://doi.org/10.1093/screen/hjs021.

Brunsdon, Charlotte. 2018. *Television Cities: Paris, London, Baltimore*. Durham, NC: Duke University Press.

Brunton, Finn, and Helen Nissenbaum. 2016. *Obfuscation: A User's Guide for Privacy and Protest*. Cambridge, MA: MIT Press.

Buck-Morss, Susan. 2000. *Dreamworld and Catastrophe: The Passing of Mass Utopia in East and West*. Cambridge, MA: MIT Press.

Buisseret, David, ed. 1998. *Envisioning the City: Six Studies in Urban Cartography*. Chicago: University of Chicago Press.

Buonanno, Milly. 2008. *The Age of Television: Experiences and Theories*. Translated by Jennifer Radice. Bristol, UK: Intellect.

Burke, Edmund, III. 1973. "A Comparative View of French Native Policy in Morocco and Syria, 1912–1925." *Middle Eastern Studies* 9, no. 2: 175–86.

Burtch, Robert C. 2015. "Property Mapping." In *The History of Cartography, Volume 6: Cartography in the Twentieth Century*, edited by Mark Monmonier. Chicago: University of Chicago Press.

Butler, Judith. 2009. *Frames of War: When Is Life Grievable?* New York: Verso.

Cadava, Eduardo. 2012. "Nadar's Photographopolis." *Grey Room* 48 (July): 56–77. https://doi.org/10.1162/GREY_a_00080.

Callon, Michel. 1998. *The Laws of the Markets*. Oxford, UK: Blackwell.

Callon, Michel, Yuval Millo, and Fabian Muniesa, eds. 2007. *Market Devices*. Malden, MA: Blackwell.

Cammett, Melani Claire. 2014. *Compassionate Communalism: Welfare and Sectarianism in Lebanon*. Ithaca, NY: Cornell University Press.

Campbell, Timothy C. 2011. *Improper Life: Technology and Biopolitics from Heidegger to Agamben*. Minneapolis: University of Minnesota Press.

Chakrabarty, Dipesh. 2000. *Provincializing Europe: Postcolonial Thought and Historical Difference*. Princeton, NJ: Princeton University Press.

Chakravartty, Paula, and Srirupa Roy. 2013. "Media Pluralism Redux: Towards New Frameworks of Comparative Media Studies 'Beyond the West.'" *Political Communication* 30, no. 3: 349–70. https://doi.org/10.1080/10584609.2012.737429.

Chalcraft, John. 2009. *The Invisible Cage: Syrian Migrant Workers in Lebanon*. Stanford, CA: Stanford University Press.

Chamayou, Grégoire. 2015. *A Theory of the Drone*. Translated by Janet Lloyd. New York: New Press.

Chandler, Katherine Fehr. 2016. "A Drone Manifesto: Re-Forming the Partial Politics of Targeted Killing." *Catalyst: Feminism, Theory, Technoscience* 2, no. 1: 1–23. https://doi.org/10.28968/cftt.v2i1.28832.

Charney, Leo, and Vanessa R. Schwartz, eds. 1995. *Cinema and the Invention of Modern Life*. Berkeley: University of California Press.

Chasseaud, Peter. 2002. "British, French and German Mapping and Survey on the Western Front in the First World War." In *Fields of Battle: Terrain in Military History*, edited by Peter Doyle and Matthew R. Bennett. GeoJournal Library. Dordrecht: Springer Netherlands.

Chattopadhyay, Swati. 2012. *Unlearning the City: Infrastructure in a New Optical Field*. Minneapolis: University of Minnesota Press.

Chikamori, Takaaki. 2009. "Between the 'Media City' and the 'City as a Medium.'" *Theory, Culture and Society* 26, no. 4: 147–54. https://doi.org/10.1177/0263276409104972.

Chirumamilla, Padma. 2019. "Remaking the Set: Innovation and Obsolescence in Television's Digital Future." *Media, Culture and Society* 41, no. 4: 433–48. https://doi.org/10.1177/0163443718781993.

Chow, Rey. 2006. *The Age of the World Target: Self-Referentiality in War, Theory, and Comparative Work*. Durham, NC: Duke University Press.

Chu, Julie Y. 2014. "When Infrastructures Attack: The Workings of Disrepair in China." *American Ethnologist* 41, no. 2: 351–67. https://doi.org/10.1111/amet.12080.

Clarke, David B., ed. 1997. *The Cinematic City*. New York: Routledge.

Cloud, John. 2001. "Imaging the World in a Barrel: CORONA and the Clandestine Convergence of the Earth Sciences." *Social Studies of Science* 31, no. 2: 231–51.

Cloud, John. 2002. "American Cartographic Transformations during the Cold War." *Cartography and Geographic Information Science* 29, no. 3: 261–82. https://doi.org/10.1559/152304002782008422.

Collier, Peter. 2002. "The Impact on Topographic Mapping of Developments in Land and Air Survey: 1900–1939." *Cartography and Geographic Information Science* 29, no. 3: 155–74. https://doi.org/10.1559/152304002782008440.

Collier, Peter. 2018. "The Development of Photogrammetry in World War I." *International Journal of Cartography* 4, no. 3: 285–95. https://doi.org/10.1080/23729333.2018.1497439.

Collier, Stephen J. 2009. "Topologies of Power: Foucault's Analysis of Political Government beyond 'Governmentality.'" *Theory, Culture and Society* 26, no. 6: 78–108.

Collier, Stephen J. 2011. *Post-Soviet Social: Neoliberalism, Social Modernity, Biopolitics*. Princeton, NJ: Princeton University Press.

Cook, Karen Severud. 2002. "The Historical Role of Photomechanical Techniques in Map Production." *Cartography and Geographic Information Science* 29, no. 3: 137–54. https://doi.org/10.1559/152304002782008495.

Coole, Diana, and Michael J. Shapiro, eds. 2007. *Theory and Event* 10, no. 2.

Cooper, Melinda. 2017. *Family Values: Between Neoliberalism and the New Social Conservatism*. New York: Zone Books.

Corm, Georges. 1964. *Politique Économique et Planification Au Liban: 1953-1963*. Beirut: Imprimerie universelle.

Cosgrove, Denis E. 2001. *Apollo's Eye: A Cartographic Genealogy of the Earth in the Western Imagination*. Baltimore: Johns Hopkins University Press.

Cosgrove, Denis E., and William L. Fox. 2010. *Photography and Flight*. London: Reaktion.

Couldry, Nick. 2012. *Media, Society, World: Social Theory and Digital Media Practice*. Malden, MA: Polity Press.

Couldry, Nick, Andreas Hepp, and Friedrich Krotz, eds. 2010. *Media Events in a Global Age*. New York: Routledge.

Coulthard, Glen Sean. 2014. *Red Skin, White Masks: Rejecting the Colonial Politics of Recognition*. Minneapolis: University of Minnesota Press.

Coward, Martin. 2006. "Against Anthropocentrism: The Destruction of the Built Environment as a Distinct Form of Political Violence." *Review of International Studies* 32, no. 3: 419–37. https://doi.org/10.1017/S0260210506007091.

Coward, Martin. 2007. "'Urbicide' Reconsidered." *Theory and Event* 10, no. 2. https://doi.org/10.1353/tae.2007.0056.

Coward, Martin. 2008. *Urbicide: The Politics of Urban Destruction*. New York: Routledge.

Craib, Raymond B. 2017. "Cartography and Decolonization." In *Decolonizing the Map: Cartography from Colony to Nation*, edited by James R. Akerman. Chicago: University of Chicago Press.

Crampton, Jeremy W. 2006. "The Cartographic Calculation of Space: Race Mapping and the Balkans at the Paris Peace Conference of 1919." *Social and Cultural Geography* 7, no. 5: 731–52. https://doi.org/10.1080/14649360600974733.

Crampton, Jeremy W. 2007. "Maps, Race and Foucault: Eugenics and Territorialization." In *Space, Knowledge and Power: Foucault and Geography*, edited by Jeremy W. Crampton and Stuart Elden. Burlington, VT: Ashgate.

Crampton, Jeremy W. 2010. *Mapping: A Critical Introduction to Cartography and GIS*. Malden, MA: Wiley-Blackwell.

Crandall, Jordan. 2010. "The Geospatialization of Calculative Operations: Tracking, Sensing and Megacities." *Theory, Culture and Society* 27, no. 6: 68–90.

Crary, Jonathan. 2002. "Géricault, the Panorama, and Sites of Reality in the Early Nineteenth Century." *Grey Room* 9: 5–25.

Daher, Joseph. 2016. *Hezbollah: The Political Economy of Lebanon's Party of God*. London: Pluto Press.

Dajani, Nabil H. 1979. *Lebanon: Studies in Broadcasting*. London: International Institute of Communications.

Dajani, Nabil H. 1992. *Disoriented Media in a Fragmented Society: The Lebanese Experience*. Beirut: American University of Beirut Press.

Dajani, Nabil H. 2005. "Television in the Arab East." In *A Companion to Television*, edited by Janet Wasko. Malden, MA: Blackwell.

Damluji, Mona. 2013. "The Oil City in Focus: The Cinematic Spaces of Abadan in the Anglo-Iranian Oil Company's Persian Story." *Comparative Studies of South Asia, Africa and the Middle East* 33, no. 1: 75–88.

Damluji, Mona. 2016. "Visualizing Iraq: Oil, Cinema, and the Modern City." *Urban History* 43, no. 4: 641. https://doi.org/10.1017/S0963926815000851.

Davie, Mae. 2001. *Beyrouth 1825–1975: Un Siècle et Demi d'urbanisme*. Beirut: Publications de l'Ordre des Ingénieurs et Architectes de Beyrouth.

Davie, Mae. 2003. "Beirut and the Étoile Area: An Exclusively French Project?" In *Urbanism: Imported or Exported?*, edited by Joe Nasr and Mercedes Volait, 206–29. New York: Wiley-Academy.

Deeb, Lara. 2006. *An Enchanted Modern: Gender and Public Piety in Shi'i Lebanon*. Princeton, NJ: Princeton University Press.

Deeb, Lara. 2008. "Exhibiting the Just-Lived Past: Hizbullah's Nationalist Narratives in Transnational Political Context." *Comparative Studies in Society and History* 50, no. 2: 369–99. https://doi.org/10.1017/s0010417508000170.

Deeb, Lara, and Mona Harb. 2009. "Politics, Culture, Religion: How Hizbullah Is Constructing an Islamic Milieu in Lebanon." *Review of Middle East Studies* 43, no. 2: 198–206.

Deeb, Lara, and Mona Harb. 2013. *Leisurely Islam: Negotiating Geography and Morality in Shi'ite South Beirut*. Princeton, NJ: Princeton University Press.

Derrida, Jacques. 1996. "Faith and Knowledge: The Two Sources of 'Religion' at the Limits of Reason Alone." In *Religion*, edited by Jacques Derrida and Gianni Vattimo. Stanford, CA: Stanford University Press.

Derrida, Jacques. 2001. "Above All No Journalists!" In *Religion and Media*, edited by Hent de Vries and Samuel Weber. Stanford, CA: Stanford University Press.

Deseriis, Marco. 2015. *Improper Names: Collective Pseudonyms from the Luddites to Anonymous*. Minneapolis: University of Minnesota Press.

De Villiers, Nicholas. 2012. *Opacity and the Closet: Queer Tactics in Foucault, Barthes, and Warhol*. Minneapolis: University of Minnesota Press.

Dickinson, Kay. 2018. *Arab Film and Video Manifestos: Forty-Five Years of the Moving Image amid Revolution*. New York: Palgrave Pivot.

Dimendberg, Edward. 2004. *Film Noir and the Spaces of Modernity*. Cambridge, MA: Harvard University Press.

Doane, Mary Ann. 1990. "Information, Crisis, Catastrophe." In *Logics of Television: Essays in Cultural Criticism*, edited by Patricia Mellencamp. Bloomington: Indiana University Press.

Dodge, Toby. 2003. *Inventing Iraq: The Failure of Nation Building and a History Denied*. New York: Columbia University Press.

Dodge, Toby. 2012. "Iraq, US Policy and the Rebirth of Counter-Insurgency Doctrine." *Adelphi Series* 52, nos. 434-35: 75-114. https://doi.org/10.1080/19445571.2012.758339.

Dodge, Martin, Rob Kitchin, and Chris Perkins, eds. 2009. *Rethinking Maps: New Frontiers in Cartographic Theory*. New York: Routledge.

Dowson, E. M. 1921. "Further Notes on Aeroplane Photography in the Near East." *Geographical Journal* 58, no. 5: 359-70. https://doi.org/10.2307/1780883.

Easterling, Keller. 2014. *Extrastatecraft: The Power of Infrastructure Space*. New York: Verso.

Edwards, Paul N. 2003. "Infrastructure and Modernity: Force, Time, and Social Organization in the History of Sociotechnical Systems." In *Modernity and Technology*, edited by Thomas J. Misa, Philip Brey, and Andrew Feenberg. Cambridge, MA: MIT Press.

Eisenlohr, Patrick. 2018. *Sounding Islam: Voice, Media, and Sonic Atmospheres in an Indian Ocean World*. Oakland: University of California Press.

El-Ariss, Tarek. 2018. *Leaks, Hacks, and Scandals: Arab Culture in the Digital Age*. Princeton, NJ: Princeton University Press.

Elden, Stuart. 2009. *Terror and Territory: The Spatial Extent of Sovereignty*. Minneapolis: University of Minnesota Press.

Elden, Stuart. 2013. "Secure the Volume: Vertical Geopolitics and the Depth of Power." *Political Geography* 34: 35-51. https://doi.org/10.1016/j.polgeo.2012.12.009.

Elden, Stuart. 2016. *Foucault's Last Decade*. Malden, MA: Polity Press.

El-Hibri, Hatim. 2017. "Disagreement without Dissensus: The Contradictions of Hizbullah's Mediatized Populism." *International Journal of Communication* 11: 4239-55.

El-Houri, Walid, and Dima Saber. 2010. "Filming Resistance: A Hezbollah Strategy." *Radical History Review* 106 (winter): 70-85.

El-Khadem, Samir. 2008. *The War of Surprises and Deceptions*. 2nd ed. Beirut: Arab Institute for East and West Studies.

El-Richani, Sarah. 2016. *The Lebanese Media: Anatomy of a System in Perpetual Crisis*. New York: Palgrave Macmillan.

Elyachar, Julia. 2010. "Phatic Labor, Infrastructure, and the Question of Empowerment in Cairo." *American Ethnologist* 37, no. 3: 452–64.

Engelke, Matthew. 2011. "Response to Charles Hirschkind: Religion and Transduction." *Social Anthropology* 19, no. 1: 97–102. https://doi.org/10.1111/j.1469-8676.2010 .00140_2.x.

Erakat, Noura. 2019. *Justice for Some: Law and the Question of Palestine*. Stanford, CA: Stanford University Press.

Fahmy, Ziad. 2011. *Ordinary Egyptians: Creating the Modern Nation through Popular Culture*. Stanford, CA: Stanford University Press.

Fares, Adib. 2002. "The Cadastral System in Lebanon Comparing to the Other International Systems." *FIG International Congress* XXII.

Farman, Jason. 2012. *Mobile Interface Theory: Embodied Space and Locative Media*. New York: Routledge.

Farocki, Harun. 2004. "Phantom Images." Translated by Brian Poole. *Public* 29: 12–24.

Fattal, Alexander L. 2017. "Uploading the News after Coming Down from the Mountain: The FARC's Experiment with Online Television in Cuba, 2012–2016." *International Journal of Communication* 11: 3832–56.

Fattal, Alexander L. 2018. *Guerrilla Marketing: Counterinsurgency and Capitalism in Colombia*. Chicago: University of Chicago Press.

Fawaz, Leila Tarazi. 1983. *Merchants and Migrants in Nineteenth-Century Beirut*. Cambridge, MA: Harvard University Press.

Fawaz, Mona. 2004. "Strategizing for Housing: An Investigation of the Production and Regulation of Low-Income Housing in the Suburbs of Beirut." PhD diss., Massachusetts Institute of Technology. http://dspace.mit.edu/handle/1721.1 /28789.

Fawaz, Mona. 2009. "Neoliberal Urbanity and the Right to the City: A View from Beirut's Periphery." *Development and Change* 40, no. 5: 827–52.

Fawaz, Mona. 2014. "The Politics of Property in Planning: Hezbollah's Reconstruction of Haret Hreik (Beirut, Lebanon) as Case Study." *International Journal of Urban and Regional Research* 38, no. 3: 922–34. https://doi.org/10.1111/1468-2427.12114.

Fawaz, Mona. 2017. "Exceptions and the Actually Existing Practice of Planning: Beirut (Lebanon) as Case Study." *Urban Studies* 54, no. 8: 1938–55. https://doi.org/10.1177 /0042098016640453.

Fawaz, Mona, Ahmad Gharbieh, and Mona Harb. 2009. *Beirut: Mapping Security*. Beirut: Diwan.

Feuer, Jane. 1983. "The Concept of Live Television: Ontology as Ideology." In *Regarding Television: Critical Approaches—An Anthology*, edited by E. Ann Kaplan. Frederick, MD: University Publications of America.

Feuilherade, Peter. 2006. "Israel Steps Up 'Psy-Ops' in Lebanon." *BBC Monitoring*, July 26, 2006. http://news.bbc.co.uk/2/hi/middle_east/5217484.stm.

Finnegan, Terrence. 2011. *Shooting the Front: Allied Aerial Reconnaissance in the First World War*. Stroud, UK: History Press.

Fisk, Robert. 2001. *Pity the Nation: Lebanon at War*. Oxford, UK: Oxford University Press.

Foucault, Michel. 2007. *Security, Territory, Population: Lectures at the Collège de France, 1977–1978*. Edited by Michel Senellart. Translated by Graham Burchell. New York: Palgrave Macmillan.

Foucault, Michel. 2008. *The Birth of Biopolitics: Lectures at the Collège de France, 1978–79*. Edited by Michel Senellart. Translated by Graham Burchell. New York: Palgrave Macmillan.

Frangie, Samer. 2012. "Theorizing from the Periphery: The Intellectual Project of Mahdi 'Amil." *International Journal of Middle East Studies* 44, no. 3: 465–82.

Frangie, Samer. 2016. "The Anatomy of a Crisis: On Mahdi 'Amil's Naqd Al-Fikr Al-Yawmi." *Arab Studies Journal* 24, no. 1: 144–67.

Franklin, Seb. 2015. *Control: Digitality as Cultural Logic*. Cambridge, MA: MIT Press.

Fregonese, Sara. 2009. "The Urbicide of Beirut? Geopolitics and the Built Environment in the Lebanese Civil War (1975–1976)." *Political Geography* 28, no. 5: 309–18.

Fregonese, Sara. 2012. "Beyond the 'Weak State': Hybrid Sovereignties in Beirut." *Environment and Planning D: Society and Space* 30, no. 4: 655–74.

Fries, Franck. 1994. "Les plans d'Alep et de Damas, un banc d'essai pour l'urbanisme des frères Danger (1931–1937)." *Revue du monde musulman et de la Méditerranée* 73, no. 1: 311–25. https://doi.org/10.3406/remmm.1994.1684.

Fulghum, David. 2006. "Doubt as a Weapon." *Aviation Week and Space Technology*, November 27, 2006.

Garrett, Bradley L. 2016. "Picturing Urban Subterranea: Embodied Aesthetics of London's Sewers." *Environment and Planning A: Economy and Space* 48, no. 10: 1948–66. https://doi.org/10.1177/0308518X16652396.

Gaunson, A. B. 1987. *The Anglo-French Clash in Lebanon and Syria, 1940–45*. New York: St. Martin's Press.

Gavin, Angus, and Ramez Maluf. 1996. *Beirut Reborn: The Restoration and Development of the Central District*. London: Academy Editions.

Gavish, Dov. 1987. "An Account of an Unrealized Aerial Cadastral Survey in Palestine under the British Mandate." *Geographical Journal* 153, no. 1: 93–98. https://doi.org/10.2307/634475.

Gebhart, Hans, ed. 2005. *History, Space and Social Conflict in Beirut: The Quarter of Zokak El-Blat*. Würzburg: Ergon.

Gelvin, James L. 1998. *Divided Loyalties: Nationalism and Mass Politics in Syria at the Close of Empire*. Berkeley: University of California Press.

Gendzier, Irene L. 1997. *Notes from the Minefield: United States Intervention in Lebanon and the Middle East, 1945–1958*. New York: Columbia University Press.

Geroulanos, Stefanos. 2017. *Transparency in Postwar France: A Critical History of the Present*. Stanford, CA: Stanford University Press.

Ghandour, Marwan, and Mona Fawaz. 2009. "Spatial Erasure: Reconstruction Projects in Beirut." *ArteEast* (winter). http://www.arteeast.org/pages/artenews/extra-territoriality/254/.

Gharabaghi, Hadi. 2018. "'American Mice Grow Big!': The Syracuse Audiovisual Mission in Iran and the Rise of Documentary Diplomacy." PhD diss., New York University.

Ghorayeb, Marlene. 1998. "The Work and Influence of Michel Ecochard in Lebanon." In *Projecting Beirut: Episodes in the Construction and Reconstruction of a Modern City*, edited by Peter Rowe and Hashim Sarkis. New York: Prestel.

Ghorayeb, Marlène. 2014. *Beyrouth Sous Mandat Français: Construction d'une Ville Moderne*. Paris: Karthala.

Gillespie, Tarleton, Pablo J. Boczkowski, and Kirsten A. Foot, eds. 2014. *Media Technologies: Essays on Communication, Materiality, and Society*. Cambridge, MA: MIT Press.

Gilman, Nils. 2003. *Mandarins of the Future: Modernization Theory in Cold War America*. Baltimore: Johns Hopkins University Press.

Goddard, Michael. 2018. *Guerrilla Networks: An Anarchaeology of 1970s Radical Media Ecologies*. Amsterdam: Amsterdam University Press.

Gómez-Barris, Macarena. 2008. *Where Memory Dwells: Culture and State Violence in Chile*. Berkeley: University of California Press.

Gordillo, Gastón. 2014. *Rubble: The Afterlife of Destruction*. Durham, NC: Duke University Press.

Gottmann, Jean. 1943. *Bugeaud, Galliéni, Lyautey: The Development of French Colonial Warfare*. Princeton, NJ: Princeton University Press.

Graham, Stephen. 2016. *Vertical: The City from Satellites to Bunkers*. London: Verso Books.

Graham, Stephen, and Colin MacFarlane, eds. 2015. *Infrastructural Lives: Urban Infrastructure in Context*. New York: Routledge.

Graham, Stephen, and Nigel Thrift. 2007. "Out of Order: Understanding Repair and Maintenance." *Theory, Culture and Society* 24, no. 3: 1–25. https://doi.org/10.1177/0263276407075954.

Gregory, Derek. 2006. "'In Another Time-Zone, the Bombs Fall Unsafely . . .': Targets, Civilians, and Late Modern War." *Arab World Geographer* 9, no. 2: 88–111 [published 2007].

Grewal, Inderpal. 2017. *Saving the Security State: Exceptional Citizens in Twenty-First-Century America*. Durham, NC: Duke University Press.

Grosscup, Beau. 2006. *Strategic Terror: The Politics and Ethics of Aerial Bombardment*. New York: Zed Books.

Gualtieri, Sarah. 2009. *Between Arab and White: Race and Ethnicity in the Early Syrian American Diaspora*. Berkeley: University of California Press.

Gunning, Tom. 1986. "The Cinema of Attractions: Early Film, Its Spectator and the Avant-Garde." *Wide Angle* 8, no. 3–4: 63–70.

Gusterson, Hugh. 2016. *Drone: Remote Control Warfare*. Cambridge, MA: MIT Press.

Hadjithomas, Joana, and Khalil Joreige, dirs. 2011. *Je Veux Voir* [*I Want to See*]. Typecast Releasing.

Haffner, Jeanne. 2013. *The View from Above: The Science of Social Space*. Cambridge, MA: MIT Press.

Hage, Ghassan. 2015. *Alter-Politics: Critical Anthropology and the Radical Imagination*. Carlton, Victoria: Melbourne University Press.

Hall, Stuart. 1986. "The Problem of Ideology-Marxism without Guarantees." *Journal of Communication Inquiry* 10, no. 2: 28–44. https://doi.org/10.1177/019685998601000203.

Halper, Jeff. 2015. *War against the People: Israel, the Palestinians and Global Pacification.* London: Pluto Press.

Hanf, Theodor. 1993. *Coexistence in Wartime Lebanon: Decline of a State and Rise of a Nation.* London: I. B. Tauris.

Hanssen, Jens. 2005. *Fin de Siècle Beirut: The Making of an Ottoman Provincial Capital.* Oxford, UK: Oxford University Press.

Haraway, Donna J. 2016. *Staying with the Trouble: Making Kin in the Chthulucene.* Durham, NC: Duke University Press.

Harb el-Kak, Mona. 2000. "Post-War Beirut: Resources, Negotiations, and Contestations in the Elyssar Project." *Arab World Geographer* 3, no. 4: 272–88.

Harb, Mona. 2001. "Urban Governance in Post-War Beirut: Resources, Negotiations, and Contestations in the Elyssar Project." In *Capital Cities: Ethnographies of Urban Governance in the Middle East,* edited by Seteney Shami. Toronto: University of Toronto Press.

Harb, Mona. 2008. "Faith-Based Organizations as Effective Development Partners? Hezbollah and Post-War Reconstruction in Lebanon." In *Development, Civil Society and Faith-Based Organizations,* edited by Gerard Clarke and Michael Jennings. London: Palgrave Macmillan.

Harb, Mona, and Lara Deeb. 2011. "Culture as History and Landscape: Hizballah's Efforts to Shape an Islamic Milieu in Lebanon." *Arab Studies Journal* 19, no. 1: 10–41.

Harb, Zahera. 2011. *Channels of Resistance in Lebanon: Liberation Propaganda, Hezbollah and the Media.* London: I. B. Tauris.

Harb, Zahera. 2016. "Hezbollah, Al-Manar, and the Arab Revolts: Defiance or Survival?" In *Bullets and Bulletins: Media and Politics in the Wake of the Arab Uprisings,* edited by Mohamed Zayani and Suzi Mirgani. Oxford, UK: Oxford University Press.

Harik, Judith Palmer. 2005. *Hezbollah: The Changing Face of Terrorism.* London: I. B. Tauris.

Harvey, Penny, and Hannah Knox. 2015. *Roads: An Anthropology of Infrastructure and Expertise.* Ithaca, NY: Cornell University Press.

Hashimoto, Chikara. 2012. "British Security Liaison in the Middle East: The Introduction of Police/Security Advisers and the Lebanon–Iraq–Jordan 'Anti-Communist Triangle' from 1949 to 1958." *Intelligence and National Security* 27, no. 6: 848–74. https://doi.org/10.1080/02684527.2012.722763.

Hastaoglou-Martinidis, Vilma. 2011. "Urban Aesthetics and National Identity: The Refashioning of Eastern Mediterranean Cities between 1900 and 1940." *Planning Perspectives* 26, no. 2: 153–82. https://doi.org/10.1080/02665433.2011.550442.

Haugbolle, Sune. 2010. *War and Memory in Lebanon.* New York: Cambridge University Press.

Haugbolle, Sune. 2013. "'History' and 'Memory' in Lebanon since 2005: Blind Spots, Emotional Archives and Historiographic Challenges." In *Lebanon: After the Cedar*

Revolution, edited by Are Knudsen and Michael Kerr. New York: Oxford University Press.

Hayek, Ghenwa. 2011. "Rabī' Jābir's Bayrūt Trilogy: Recovering an Obscured Urban History." *Journal of Arabic Literature* 42, no. 2–3: 183–204. https://doi.org/10.1163/157006411x596140.

Hayek, Ghenwa. 2014. *Beirut, Imagining the City: Space and Place in Lebanese Literature.* New York: I. B. Tauris.

Hayek, Ghenwa. 2017. "Making Ordinary: Recuperating the Everyday in Post-2005 Beirut Novels." *Arab Studies Journal* 25, no. 1: 8–28.

Hayek, Ghenwa. 2019. "Where To? Filming Emigration Anxiety in Prewar Lebanese Cinema." *International Journal of Middle East Studies* 51, no. 2: 183–201. https://doi.org/10.1017/S0020743819000011.

Hediger, Vinzenz, and Patrick Vonderau, eds. 2009. *Films That Work: Industrial Film and the Productivity of Media.* Amsterdam: Amsterdam University Press.

Hell, Julia, and Andreas Schönle, eds. 2010. *Ruins of Modernity.* Durham, NC: Duke University Press.

Henni, Samia. 2017. *Architecture of Counterrevolution: The French Army in Northern Algeria.* Zurich: GTA.

Hermez, Sami. 2017. *War Is Coming: Between Past and Future Violence in Lebanon.* Philadelphia: University of Pennsylvania Press.

Hirsch, Marianne. 1997. *Family Frames: Photography, Narrative, and Postmemory.* Cambridge, MA: Harvard University Press.

Hirschkind, Charles. 2006. *The Ethical Soundscape: Cassette Sermons and Islamic Counterpublics.* New York: Columbia University Press.

Hirschkind, Charles. 2011. "Media, Mediation, Religion." *Social Anthropology* 19, no. 1: 90–97. https://doi.org/10.1111/j.1469-8676.2010.00140_1.x.

Hirschkind, Charles, and Brian Larkin. 2008. "Media and the Political Forms of Religion." *Social Text* 26, no. 3: 1–9. https://doi.org/10.1215/01642472-2000-001.

Holt, Jennifer, and Kevin Sanson, eds. 2013. *Connected Viewing: Selling, Streaming, and Sharing Media in the Digital Age.* New York: Routledge.

Honneth, Axel, and Jacques Rancière. 2016. *Recognition or Disagreement: A Critical Encounter on the Politics of Freedom, Equality, and Identity.* Edited by Katia Genel and Jean-Philippe Deranty. New York: Columbia University Press.

Hourani, Najib. 2008. "The Militiaman Icon: Cinema, Memory, and the Lebanese Civil War." *Centennial Review* 8, no. 2: 287–307.

Hourani, Najib. 2010. "Transnational Pathways and Politico-Economic Power: Globalization and the Lebanese Civil War." *Geopolitics* 15, no. 2: 290–311.

Hourani, Najib. 2012. "From National Utopia to Elite Enclave: The Selling of the Beirut Souqs." In *Global Downtowns*, edited by Gary W. McDonogh and Marina Peterson. Philadelphia: University of Pennsylvania Press.

Hourani, Najib. 2015. "Post-Conflict Reconstruction and Citizenship Agendas: Lessons from Beirut." *Citizenship Studies* 19, no. 2: 184–99. https://doi.org/10.1080/13621025.2015.1005949.

Hout, Syrine. 2017. "Artistic Fallout from the July 2006 War: Momentum, Mediation, and Mediatization." *Arab Studies Quarterly* 39, no. 2: 793–814.

Houtman, Dick, and Birgit Meyer, eds. 2012. *Things: Religion and the Question of Materiality*. New York: Fordham University Press.

Hu, Tung-Hui. 2015. *A Prehistory of the Cloud*. Cambridge, MA: MIT Press.

Huhtamo, Erkki. 2013. *Illusions in Motion: Media Archaeology of the Moving Panorama and Related Spectacles*. Cambridge, MA: MIT Press.

Hull, Matthew. 2009. "Uncivil Politics and the Appropriation of Planning in Islamabad." In *Beyond Crisis: Re-Evaluating Pakistan*, edited by Naveeda Khan. New York: Routledge.

Human Rights Watch. 2007. "Why They Died: Civilian Casualties in Lebanon during the 2006 War." *Human Rights Watch* 19, no. 5(E). https://www.hrw.org/reports/2007/lebanon0907/.

Hussain, Nasser. 2013. "The Sound of Terror: Phenomenology of a Drone Strike." *Boston Review*, October 14, 2013. http://bostonreview.net/world/hussain-drone-phenomenology.

Huyssen, Andreas. 2003. *Present Pasts: Urban Palimpsests and the Politics of Memory*. Stanford, CA: Stanford University Press.

Hyndman-Rizk, Nelia. 2019. "A Question of Personal Status: The Lebanese Women's Movement and Civil Marriage Reform." *Journal of Middle East Women's Studies* 15, no. 2: 179–98. https://doi.org/10.1215/15525864-7490967.

Iğsız, Aslı. 2018. *Humanism in Ruins: Entangled Legacies of the Greek-Turkish Population Exchange*. Stanford, CA: Stanford University Press.

Innis, Harold. 1994. *Empire and Communications*. Lanham, MD: Rowman & Littlefield.

İşcen, Özgün. 2019. "Forensic Aesthetics for Militarized Drone Strikes: Affordances for Whom, and for What Ends?" *Media Theory* 3, no. 1: 239–68.

Jackson, Simon. 2017. "Transformative Relief: Imperial Humanitarianism and Mandatory Development in Syria-Lebanon, 1915–1925." *Humanity: An International Journal of Human Rights, Humanitarianism, and Development* 8, no. 2: 247–68. https://doi.org/10.1353/hum.2017.0018.

Jackson, Steven J. 2014. "Rethinking Repair." In *Media Technologies: Essays on Communication, Materiality, and Society*, edited by Tarleton Gillespie, Pablo J. Boczkowski, and Kirsten A. Foot. Cambridge, MA: MIT Press.

Johnson, Michael. 2002. *All Honourable Men: The Social Origins of War in Lebanon*. London: I. B. Tauris.

Jordan, Mark D. 2014. *Convulsing Bodies: Religion and Resistance in Foucault*. Stanford, CA: Stanford University Press.

Joseph, Suad. 1975. "The Politicization of Religious Sects in Borj Hammoud, Lebanon." PhD diss., Columbia University.

Joseph, Suad. 1983. "Working-Class Women's Networks in a Sectarian State: A Political Paradox." *American Ethnologist* 10, no. 1: 1–22. https://doi.org/10.1525/ae.1983.10.1.02a00010.

Joseph, Suad. 1993. "Connectivity and Patriarchy among Urban Working-Class Arab Families in Lebanon." *Ethos* 21, no. 4: 452–84. https://doi.org/10.1525/eth.1993.21.4.02a00040.

Joseph, Suad. 1997. "The Public/Private—The Imagined Boundary in the Imagined Nation/State/Community: The Lebanese Case." *Feminist Review* 57, no. 1: 73–92. https://doi.org/10.1080/014177897339669.

Joseph, Suad. 2000. "Civic Myths, Citizenship, and Gender in Lebanon." In *Gender and Citizenship in the Middle East*, edited by Suad Joseph. Syracuse, NY: Syracuse University Press.

Joseph, Suad. 2008. "Pensée 2: Sectarianism as Imagined Sociological Concept and as Imagined Social Formation." *International Journal of Middle East Studies* 40, no. 4: 553–54. http://dx.doi.org/10.1017/S0020743808081464.

Kain, Roger J. P., and Elizabeth Baigent. 1992. *The Cadastral Map in the Service of the State: A History of Property Mapping*. Chicago: University of Chicago Press.

Kaplan, Caren. 2015. "Air Power's Visual Legacy: Operation Orchard and Aerial Reconnaissance Imagery as Ruses de Guerre." *Critical Military Studies* 1, no. 1: 61–78.

Kaplan, Caren. 2018. *Aerial Aftermaths: Wartime from Above*. Durham, NC: Duke University Press.

Karp, David A. 1973. "Hiding in Pornographic Bookstores: A Reconsideration of the Nature of Urban Anonymity." *Urban Life and Culture* 1, no. 4: 427–51.

Kassamali, Sumayya. 2017. "Migrant Worker Lifeworlds of Beirut." PhD diss., Columbia University.

Kaufman, Asher. 2015. "Colonial Cartography and the Making of Palestine, Lebanon, and Syria." In *The Routledge Handbook of the History of the Middle East Mandates*, edited by Cyrus Schayegh and Andrew Arsan. New York: Routledge.

Khalaf, Samir. 1987. *Lebanon's Predicament*. New York: Columbia University Press.

Khalaf, Samir. 2002. *Civil and Uncivil Violence: A History of the Internationalization of Communal Conflict*. New York: Columbia University Press.

Khalidi, Rashid. 2004. *Resurrecting Empire: Western Footprints and America's Perilous Path in the Middle East*. Boston: Beacon Press.

Khalidi, Rashid. 2009. *Sowing Crisis: The Cold War and American Dominance in the Middle East*. Boston: Beacon Press.

Khalidi, Rashid, Lisa Anderson, Muhammad Muslih, and Reeva Simon, eds. 1991. *The Origins of Arab Nationalism*. New York: Columbia University Press.

Khalil, Joe F. 2013. "Towards a Supranational Analysis of Arab Media: The Role of Cities." In *National Broadcasting and State Policy in Arab Countries*, edited by Tourya Guaaybess. New York: Palgrave Macmillan.

Khalil, Joe F., and Marwan M. Kraidy. 2009. *Arab Television Industries*. London: Palgrave Macmillan.

Khalili, Laleh. 2010. "The New (and Old) Classics of Counterinsurgency." *Middle East Report* 255. http://www.merip.org/mer/mer255/khalili.html.

Khalili, Laleh. 2013. *Time in the Shadows: Confinement in Counterinsurgencies*. Berkeley: University of California Press.

Khatib, Lina, Dina Matar, and Atef Alshaer. 2014. *The Hizbullah Phenomenon: Politics and Communication*. New York: Oxford University Press.

Khazaal, Natalie. 2018. *Pretty Liar: Television, Language, and Gender in Wartime Lebanon*. Syracuse, NY: Syracuse University Press.

Khoury, Phillip S. 1982. "The Tribal Shaykh, French Tribal Policy, and the Nationalist Movement in Syria between Two World Wars." *Middle Eastern Studies* 18, no. 2: 180–93.

Khoury, Phillip S. 1987. *Syria and the French Mandate: The Politics of Arab Nationalism, 1920–1945*. Princeton, NJ: Princeton University Press.

Khuri, Fuad. 1975. *From Village to Suburb: Order and Change in Greater Beirut*. Chicago: University of Chicago Press.

Kingston, Paul W. T. 2013. *Reproducing Sectarianism: Advocacy Networks and the Politics of Civil Society in Postwar Lebanon*. Albany: State University of New York Press.

Kitchin, Rob, Justin Gleeson, and Martin Dodge. 2013. "Unfolding Mapping Practices: A New Epistemology for Cartography." *Transactions of the Institute of British Geographers* 38, no. 3: 480–96. https://doi.org/10.1111/j.1475-5661.2012 .00540.x.

Kitchin, Rob, Tracey P. Lauriault, and Matthew W. Wilson, eds. 2017. *Understanding Spatial Media*. Thousand Oaks, CA: Sage Publications.

Kitchin, Rob, Chris Perkins, and Martin Dodge. 2009. "Thinking about Maps." In *Rethinking Maps: New Frontiers in Cartographic Theory*, edited by Martin Dodge, Rob Kitchin, and Chris Perkins. New York: Routledge.

Kittler, Friedrich. 1996. "The City Is a Medium." Translated by Matthew Griffin. *New Literary History* 27, no. 4: 717–30.

Klemm, Verena. 2000. "Different Notions of Commitment (Iltizam) and Committed Literature (Al-adab Al-multazim) in the Literary Circles of the Mashriq." *Arabic and Middle Eastern Literature* 3, no. 1: 51–62. https://doi.org/10.1080 /13666160008718229.

Kosmatopoulos, Nikolas. 2011. "Toward an Anthropology of 'State Failure': Lebanon's Leviathan and Peace Expertise." *Social Analysis* 55, no. 3. https://doi.org/10.3167/sa .2011.550307.

Kosmatopoulos, Nikolas. 2014. "The Birth of the Workshop: Technomorals, Peace Expertise, and the Care of the Self in the Middle East." *Public Culture* 26, no. 3: 529–58. https://doi.org/10.1215/08992363-2683657.

Kraidy, Marwan M. 1998. "Broadcasting Regulation and Civil Society in Postwar Lebanon." *Journal of Broadcasting and Electronic Media* 42, no. 3: 387–400. https://doi .org/10.1080/08838159809364457.

Kraidy, Marwan M. 1999. "State Control of Television News in 1990s Lebanon." *Journalism and Mass Communication Quarterly* 76, no. 3: 485–98.

Kraidy, Marwan M. 2010. *Reality Television and Arab Politics: Contention in Public Life*. New York: Cambridge University Press.

Kraidy, Marwan M. 2016. *The Naked Blogger of Cairo: Creative Insurgency in the Arab World*. Cambridge, MA: Harvard University Press.

Krijnen, Marieke, and Mona Fawaz. 2010. "Exception as the Rule: High-End Developments in Neoliberal Beirut." *Built Environment* 36, no. 2: 245–59.

Kwan, Mei-Po. 2008. "Feminist Perspectives on Geographic Information Systems: Implications for Geographic Research." In *Gendered Innovations in Science and Engineering*, edited by Londa Schieberger. Stanford, CA: Stanford University Press.

Kwan, Mei-Po. 2016. "Algorithmic Geographies: Big Data, Algorithmic Uncertainty, and the Production of Geographic Knowledge." *Annals of the American Association of Geographers* 106, no. 2: 274–82.

Lambeth, Benjamin S. 2011. *Air Operations in Israel's War against Hezbollah: Learning from Lebanon and Getting It Right in Gaza*. Santa Monica, CA: RAND Corporation.

Lamloum, Olfa. 2009a. "Hezbollah and the 'al-Manâr Affaire.'" Presented at Journalism Testing Legal Boundaries Conference, London, 2008. London: University of Westminster. http://halshs.archives-ouvertes.fr/halshs-00373560.

Lamloum, Olfa. 2009b. "Hezbollah's Media: Political History in Outline." *Global Media and Communication* 5, no. 3: 353–67.

Larkin, Brian. 2008. *Signal and Noise: Media, Infrastructure, and Urban Culture in Nigeria*. Durham, NC: Duke University Press.

Larkin, Brian. 2009. "Islamic Renewal, Radio, and the Surface of Things." In *Aesthetic Formations: Media, Religion, and the Senses*, edited by Birgit Meyer. New York: Palgrave Macmillan.

Larkin, Brian. 2013. "The Politics and Poetics of Infrastructure." *Annual Review of Anthropology* 42, no. 1: 327–43. https://doi.org/10.1146/annurev-anthro-092412-155522.

Larkin, Craig. 2012. *Memory and Conflict in Lebanon: Remembering and Forgetting the Past*. New York: Routledge.

Larkin, Craig, and Ella Parry-Davies. 2019. "War Museums in Postwar Lebanon: Memory, Violence, and Performance." *Nationalism and Ethnic Politics* 25, no. 1: 78–96. https://doi.org/10.1080/13537113.2019.1565182.

Latham, Michael E. 2000. *Modernization as Ideology: American Social Science and "Nation Building" in the Kennedy Era*. Chapel Hill: University of North Carolina Press.

Leenders, Reinoud. 2012. *Spoils of Truce: Corruption and State-Building in Postwar Lebanon*. Ithaca, NY: Cornell University Press.

Licoppe, Christian. 2016. "Mobilities and Urban Encounters in Public Places in the Age of Locative Media. Seams, Folds, and Encounters with 'Pseudonymous Strangers.'" *Mobilities* 11, no. 1: 99–116. https://doi.org/10.1080/17450101.2015.1097035.

Lim, Bliss Cua. 2009. *Translating Time: Cinema, the Fantastic, and Temporal Critique*. Durham, NC: Duke University Press.

Limbrick, Peter. 2012. "'After-Effects' in 'Militarism, a Mini Forum.'" *Society and Space* (blog). September 5, 2012. https://societyandspace.org/2012/09/05/after-effects-peter-limbrick/.

Llamas-Rodriguez, Juan. 2016. "Tunnelling Media: Geoblocking and Online Border Resistance." In *Geoblocking and Global Video Culture*, edited by Ramon Lobato and James Meese. Amsterdam: Institute of Network Cultures.

Lobato, Ramon. 2019. *Netflix Nations: The Geography of Digital Distribution*. New York: New York University Press.

Lobato, Ramon, and James Meese, eds. 2016. *Geoblocking and Global Video Culture*. Amsterdam: Institute of Network Cultures.

Lofton, Kathryn. 2017. *Consuming Religion*. Chicago: University of Chicago Press.

Lotz, Amanda D. 2018. *We Now Disrupt This Broadcast: How Cable Transformed Television and the Internet Revolutionized It All*. Cambridge, MA: MIT Press.

Maasri, Zeina. 2016. "Troubled Geography: Imagining Lebanon in 1960s Tourist Promotion." In *Designing Worlds: National Design Histories in an Age of Globalization*, edited by Kjetil Fallan and Grace Lees-Maffei. New York: Berghahn Books.

MacFarquhar, Neil. 2009. *The Media Relations Department of Hizbollah Wishes You a Happy Birthday: Unexpected Encounters in the Changing Middle East*. New York: Public Affairs.

MacKenzie, Donald. 2006. *An Engine, Not a Camera: How Financial Models Shape Markets*. Cambridge, MA: MIT Press.

MacKenzie, Donald, Fabian Muniesa, and Lucia Siu, eds. 2007. *Do Economists Make Markets? On the Performativity of Economics*. Princeton, NJ: Princeton University Press.

Makdisi, Saree. 1997. "Laying Claim to Beirut: Urban Narrative and Spatial Identity in the Age of Solidere." *Critical Inquiry* 23, no. 3: 661–705.

Makdisi, Ussama. 2000. *The Culture of Sectarianism: Community, History, and Violence in Nineteenth-Century Ottoman Lebanon*. Berkeley: University of California Press.

Mankekar, Purnima. 2015. *Unsettling India: Affect, Temporality, Transnationality*. Durham, NC: Duke University Press.

Marei, Fouad. 2016. "Preaching Development: Shi'i Piety and Neoliberalism in Beirut." In *Religious Activism in the Global Economy: Promoting, Reforming or Resisting Neoliberal Globalization?*, edited by Sabine Dreher and Peter J. Smith. Lanham, MD: Rowman & Littlefield International.

Marei, Fouad Gehad, Mona Atia, Lisa Bhungalia, and Omar Dewachi. 2018. "Interventions on the Politics of Governing the 'Ungovernable.'" *Political Geography* 67 (November): 176–86. https://doi.org/10.1016/j.polgeo.2018.01.003.

Marks, Laura U. 2015. *Hanan Al-Cinema: Affections for the Moving Image*. Cambridge, MA: MIT Press.

Martin, Randy. 2002. *Financialization of Daily Life*. Philadelphia: Temple University Press.

Masri, Mai, dir. 2007. *33 Days*. Doha, Qatar: Al Jazeera Documentary Channel.

Massey, Doreen B. 1994. *Space, Place, and Gender*. Minneapolis: University of Minnesota Press.

Massumi, Brian. 1987. "Realer than Real: The Simulacrum According to Deleuze and Guattari." *Copyright* 1: 64–73.

Massumi, Brian. 2015. *The Power at the End of the Economy*. Durham, NC: Duke University Press.

Matar, Dina. 2008. "The Power of Conviction: Nasrallah's Rhetoric and Mediated Charisma in the Context of the 2006 July War." *Middle East Journal of Culture and Communication* 1, no. 2: 122–37.

Mattern, Shannon. 2017. *Code and Clay, Data and Dirt: Five Thousand Years of Urban Media*. Minneapolis: University of Minnesota Press.

Matthews, Matt. 2008. *We Were Caught Unprepared: The 2006 Hezbollah-Israeli War*. Occasional Paper 26. Fort Leavenworth, KS: Combat Studies Institute Press.

Mayntz, Renate, and Thomas P. Hughes, eds. 1988. *The Development of Large Technical Systems*. Boulder, CO: Westview Press.

Mbembe, Achille. 2001. *On the Postcolony*. Berkeley: University of California Press.

McCarthy, Anna. 2001. *Ambient Television: Visual Culture and Public Space*. Durham, NC: Duke University Press.

McCarthy, Anna. 2010. *The Citizen Machine: Governing by Television in 1950s America*. New York: New Press.

McCormick, Jared S. 2016. "Creating a Season: Tourism, Sexuality, and Imaginations of Beirut." PhD diss., Harvard University.

McGowan, Jamie. 2017. "Uncovering the Roles of African Surveyors and Draftsmen in Mapping the Gold Coast, 1874–1957." In *Decolonizing the Map: Cartography from Colony to Nation*, edited by James R. Akerman. Chicago: University of Chicago Press.

McPherson, Larry E. 2006. *Beirut City Center*. Göttingen: Steidl.

McQuire, Scott. 2008. *The Media City: Media, Architecture and Urban Space*. London: Sage Publications.

Menoret, Pascal. 2014. *Joyriding in Riyadh: Oil, Urbanism, and Road Revolt*. New York: Cambridge University Press.

Menoret, Pascal. 2017. "The Suburbanization of Islamic Activism in Saudi Arabia." *City and Society* 29, no. 1: 162–86. https://doi.org/10.1111/ciso.12117.

Meyer, Birgit, and Terje Stordalen, eds. 2019. *Figurations and Sensations of the Unseen in Judaism, Christianity and Islam: Contested Desires*. New York: Bloomsbury Academic.

Mikdashi, Maya. 2014. "Sex and Sectarianism: The Legal Architecture of Lebanese Citizenship." *Comparative Studies of South Asia, Africa and the Middle East* 34, no. 2: 279–93. https://doi.org/10.1215/1089201X-2773851.

Mikdashi, Maya, and Jasbir K. Puar. 2016. "Queer Theory and Permanent War." *GLQ: A Journal of Lesbian and Gay Studies* 22, no. 2: 215–22. https://doi.org/10.1215/10642684-3428747.

Miller, Joyce L. 1977. "The Syrian Revolt of 1925." *International Journal of Middle East Studies* 8, no. 4: 545–63.

Miller, Peter, and Nikolas Rose. 2008. *Governing the Present: Administering Economic, Social and Personal Life*. Cambridge, UK: Polity Press.

Miller, Toby, and Marwan M. Kraidy. 2016. *Global Media Studies*. Malden, MA: Polity Press.

Mirzoeff, Nicholas. 2011. *The Right to Look: A Counterhistory of Visuality*. Durham, NC: Duke University Press.

Mitchell, Peta. 2008. *Cartographic Strategies of Postmodernity: The Figure of the Map in Contemporary Theory and Fiction*. New York: Routledge.

Mitchell, Timothy. 1988. *Colonising Egypt*. Cambridge: Cambridge University Press.

Mitchell, Timothy. 2002a. "McJihad: Islam in the U.S. Global Order." *Social Text* 20, no. 4: 1–18.

Mitchell, Timothy. 2002b. *Rule of Experts: Egypt, Techno-politics, Modernity*. Berkeley: University of California Press.

Mitchell, Timothy. 2011. *Carbon Democracy: Political Power in the Age of Oil*. New York: Verso.

Mitchell, William J. T. 2002. "Showing Seeing: A Critique of Visual Culture." *Journal of Visual Culture* 1, no. 2: 165–81.

Mitchell, William J. T. 2005. "There Are No Visual Media." *Journal of Visual Culture* 4, no. 2: 257–66.

Moghnieh, Lamia M. 2015a. "Humanitarian Therapeutics of War and the Politics of Trauma and Violence in Lebanon." Civil Society Knowledge Centre. January 8, 2015. https://civilsociety-centre.org/paper/humanitarian-therapeutics-war-and-politics-trauma-and-violence-lebanon.

Moghnieh, Lamia M. 2015b. "Local Expertise and Global Packages of Aid: The Transformative Role of Volunteerism and Locally Engaged Expertise of Aid during the 2006 July War in Lebanon." Civil Society Knowledge Centre. July 29, 2015. http://cskc.daleel-madani.org/paper/local-expertise-and-global-packages-aid-transformative-role-volunteerism-and-locally-engaged.

Moghnieh, Lamia M. 2016. "Humanitarian Psychology in War and Postwar Lebanon: Violence, Therapy and Suffering." PhD diss., University of Michigan.

Moghnieh, Lamia M. 2017. "'The Violence We Live In': Reading and Experiencing Violence in the Field." *Contemporary Levant* 2, no. 1: 24–36. https://doi.org/10.1080/20581831.2017.1318804.

Moll, Yasmin. 2012. "Storytelling, Sincerity, and Islamic Televangelism in Egypt." In *Global and Local Televangelism*, edited by Pradip Ninan Thomas and Philip Lee. London: Palgrave Macmillan.

Moll, Yasmin. 2017. "Subtitling Islam: Translation, Mediation, Critique." *Public Culture* 29, no. 2 (82): 333–61. https://doi.org/10.1215/08992363-3749093.

Moll, Yasmin. 2018. "Television Is Not Radio: Theologies of Mediation in the Egyptian Islamic Revival." *Cultural Anthropology* 33, no. 2: 233–65. https://doi.org/10.14506/ca33.2.07.

Monmonier, Mark. 1985. *Technological Transition in Cartography*. Madison: University of Wisconsin Press.

Monmonier, Mark, ed. 2015. *The History of Cartography, Volume 6: Cartography in the Twentieth Century*. Chicago: University of Chicago Press.

Monroe, Kristin V. 2014. "Automobility and Citizenship in Interwar Lebanon." *Comparative Studies of South Asia, Africa and the Middle East* 34, no. 3: 518–31. https://doi.org/10.1215/1089201X-2826073.

Monroe, Kristin V. 2016. *The Insecure City: Space, Power, and Mobility in Beirut*. New Brunswick, NJ: Rutgers University Press.

Monroe, Kristin V. 2017. "Circulation, Modernity, and Urban Space in 1960s Beirut." *History and Anthropology* 28, no. 2: 188–210. https://doi.org/10.1080/02757206.2017.1279613.

Montello, Daniel R. 2002. "Cognitive Map-Design Research in the Twentieth Century: Theoretical and Empirical Approaches." *Cartography and Geographic Information Science* 29, no. 3: 283–304. https://doi.org/10.1559/152304002782008503.

Moores, Shaun. 2012. *Media, Place and Mobility*. New York: Palgrave Macmillan.

Morag, Raya. 2012. "Perpetrator Trauma and Current Israeli Documentary Cinema." *Camera Obscura: Feminism, Culture, and Media Studies* 27, no. 2: 93–133. https://doi.org/10.1215/02705346-1597222.

Morley, David. 2006. *Media, Modernity and Technology: The Geography of the New*. New York: Routledge.

Morley, David. 2017. *Communications and Mobility: The Migrant, the Mobile Phone, and the Container Box*. Hoboken, NJ: Wiley-Blackwell.

Morley, David, and Charlotte Brunsdon. 1999. *The Nationwide Television Studies*. New York: Routledge.

Moumtaz, Nada. 2018. "'Is the Family Waqf a Religious Institution?' Charity, Religion, and Economy in French Mandate Lebanon." *Islamic Law and Society* 25, no. 1–2: 37–77.

Mourad, Sara. 2011. "Beyond the Closet: Lebanese Queer (In)Visibilities Online." Paper presented at IAMCR 2011—Istanbul. https://iamcr-ocs.org/index.php/2011/2011 /paper/view/1918.

Naas, Michael. 2012. *Miracle and Machine: Jacques Derrida and the Two Sources of Religion, Science, and the Media*. New York: Fordham University Press.

Naber, Nadine. 2009. "Transnational Families under Siege: Lebanese Shi'a in Dearborn, Michigan, and the 2006 War on Lebanon." *Journal of Middle East Women's Studies* 5, no. 3: 145–74. https://doi.org/10.2979/MEW.2009.5.3.145.

Naber, Nadine, and Zeina Zaatari. 2014. "Reframing the War on Terror: Feminist and Lesbian, Gay, Bisexual, Transgender, and Queer (LGBTQ) Activism in the Context of the 2006 Israeli Invasion of Lebanon." *Cultural Dynamics* 26, no. 1: 91–111. https:// doi.org/10.1177/0921374013510803.

Nath, Anjali. 2016. "Touched from Below: On Drones, Screens and Navigation." *Visual Anthropology* 29, no. 3: 315–30. https://doi.org/10.1080/08949468.2016.1154769.

Nath, Anjali. 2017. "Stoners, Stones and Drones: Transnational South Asian Visuality from Above and Below." In *Life in the Age of Drone Warfare*, edited by Lisa Parks and Caren Kaplan. Durham, NC: Duke University Press.

Neep, Daniel. 2012. *Occupying Syria under the French Mandate: Insurgency, Space and State Formation*. Cambridge: Cambridge University Press.

Norton, Augustus R. 2014. *Hezbollah: A Short History*. Princeton, NJ: Princeton University Press.

Nucho, Joanne Randa. 2016. *Everyday Sectarianism in Urban Lebanon: Infrastructures, Public Services, and Power*. Princeton, NJ: Princeton University Press.

Oettermann, Stephan. 1997. *The Panorama: History of a Mass Medium*. New York: Zone Books.

Omissi, David E. 1990. *Air Power and Colonial Control: The Royal Air Force 1919-1939*. Manchester, UK: Manchester University Press.

O'Neill, Kevin Lewis. 2016. "Narcotecture." *Environment and Planning D: Society and Space* 34, no. 4: 672–88. https://doi.org/10.1177/0263775816637873.

Orgeron, Devin, Marsha Orgeron, and Dan Streible, eds. 2012. *Learning with the Lights Off: Educational Film in the United States*. New York: Oxford University Press.

Ostherr, Kirsten. 2005. *Cinematic Prophylaxis: Globalization and Contagion in the Discourse of World Health*. Durham, NC: Duke University Press.

Pace, Jonathan. 2017. "Exchange Relations on the Dark Web." *Critical Studies in Media Communication* 34, no. 1: 1–13. https://doi.org/10.1080/15295036.2016.1243249.

Packer, Jeremy. 2013. "Screens in the Sky: SAGE, Surveillance, and the Automation of Perceptual, Mnemonic, and Epistemological Labor." *Social Semiotics* 23, no. 2: 173–95. https://doi.org/10.1080/10350330.2013.777590.

Packer, Jeremy, and Stephen B. Crofts Wiley, eds. 2011. *Communication Matters: Materialist Approaches to Media, Mobility and Networks*. New York: Routledge.

Pannewick, Friederike, Georges Khalil, and Yvonne Albers, eds. 2015. *Commitment and Beyond: Reflections on/of the Political in Arabic Literature since the 1940s*. Wiesbaden: Reichert.

Parks, Lisa. 2005. *Cultures in Orbit: Satellites and the Televisual*. Durham, NC: Duke University Press.

Parks, Lisa. 2012. "Technostruggles and the Satellite Dish: A Populist Approach to Infrastructure." In *Cultural Technologies: The Shaping of Culture in Media and Society*, edited by Göran Bolin. New York: Routledge.

Parks, Lisa. 2018. *Rethinking Media Coverage: Vertical Mediation and the War on Terror*. New York: Routledge.

Parks, Lisa, and Caren Kaplan, eds. 2017. *Life in the Age of Drone Warfare*. Durham, NC: Duke University Press.

Parks, Lisa, and Nicole Starosielski. 2015. "Introduction." In *Signal Traffic: Critical Studies of Media Infrastructures*, edited by Lisa Parks and Nicole Starosielski. Chicago: University of Illinois Press.

Pascoe, Stephen. 2019. "A 'Weapon of the Weak': Electric Boycotts in the Arab Levant and the Global Contours of Interwar Anti-Imperialism." *Radical History Review* 2019, no. 134: 116–41. https://doi.org/10.1215/01636545-7323432.

Pasquale, Frank. 2015. *The Black Box Society: The Secret Algorithms That Control Money and Information*. Cambridge, MA: Harvard University Press.

Perring, Dominic. 2009. "Archaeology and the Post-War Reconstruction of Beirut." *Conservation and Management of Archaeological Sites* 11, no. 3–4: 296–314. https://doi .org/10.1179/175355210X12747818485529.

Peters, John Durham. 2015. *The Marvelous Clouds: Toward a Philosophy of Elemental Media*. Chicago: University of Chicago Press.

Pétonnet, Colette. 1987. "L'anonymat ou La Pellicule Protectrice." In *Le Temps de La Réflexion: La Ville Inquiète*. Paris: Gallimard.

Pétonnet, Colette. 1994. "L'anonymat Urbain." In *Penser la Ville de Demain: Qu'est-Ce Qui Institue La Ville?*, edited by Cynthia Ghorra-Gobin. Paris: L'Hartmann.

Picard, Elizabeth. 2000. "The Political Economy of Civil War in Lebanon." In *War, Institutions, and Social Change in the Middle East*, edited by Steven Heydemann, 1st ed. Berkeley: University of California Press.

Pickles, John, ed. 1995. *Ground Truth: The Social Implications of Geographic Information Systems*. New York: Guilford Press.

Pickles, John. 2004. *A History of Spaces: Cartographic Reason, Mapping, and the Geo-Coded World*. New York: Routledge.

Pike, David L. 2005. *Subterranean Cities: The World beneath Paris and London, 1800–1945*. Ithaca, NY: Cornell University Press.

Pike, David L. 2007. *Metropolis on the Styx: The Underworlds of Modern Urban Culture, 1800–2001*. Ithaca, NY: Cornell University Press.

Pike, David L. 2009. "Hiding in Plain Sight: Cinematic Undergrounds." In *Strange Spaces: Explorations into Mediated Obscurity*, edited by André Jansson and Amanda Lagerkvist. New York: Ashgate.

Plantin, Jean-Christophe, Carl Lagoze, Paul N. Edwards, and Christian Sandvig. 2018. "Infrastructure Studies Meet Platform Studies in the Age of Google and Facebook." *New Media and Society* 20, no. 1: 293–310. https://doi.org/10.1177/1461444816661553.

Prakash, Gyan, ed. 2010. *Noir Urbanisms: Dystopic Images of the Modern City*. Princeton, NJ: Princeton University Press.

Provence, Michael. 2005. *The Great Syrian Revolt and the Rise of Arab Nationalism*. Austin: University of Texas Press.

Provence, Michael. 2008. "'Liberal Colonialism' and Martial Law in French Mandate Syria." In *Liberal Thought in the Eastern Mediterranean: Late Nineteenth Century until the 1960s*, edited by Christoph Schumann. Boston: Brill.

Provence, Michael. 2017. *The Last Ottoman Generation and the Making of the Modern Middle East*. New York: Cambridge University Press.

Puar, Jasbir K. 2017. *The Right to Maim: Debility, Capacity, Disability*. Durham, NC: Duke University Press.

Pyla, Panayiota. 2008. "Back to the Future: Doxiadis's Plans for Baghdad." *Journal of Planning History* 7, no. 1: 3–19. https://doi.org/10.1177/1538513207304697.

Rabinow, Paul. 1989. *French Modern: Norms and Forms of the Social Environment*. Cambridge, MA: MIT Press.

Rajagopal, Arvind. 2001. *Politics after Television: Hindu Nationalism and the Reshaping of the Public in India*. Cambridge: Cambridge University Press.

Ramaswamy, Sumathi. 2010. *The Goddess and the Nation: Mapping Mother India*. Durham, NC: Duke University Press.

Rancière, Jacques. 1999. *Disagreement: Politics and Philosophy*. Translated by Julie Rose. Minneapolis: University of Minnesota Press.

Rancière, Jacques. 2001. "Ten Theses on Politics." Translated by Davide Panagia and Rachel Bowlby. *Theory and Event* 5, no. 3. https://doi.org/10.1353/tae.2001.0028.

Rankin, William. 2016. *After the Map: Cartography, Navigation, and the Transformation of Territory in the Twentieth Century*. Chicago: University of Chicago Press.

Rastegar, Kamran. 2015. *Surviving Images: Cinema, War, and Cultural Memory in the Middle East*. New York: Oxford University Press.

Rhee, Jennifer. 2018. *The Robotic Imaginary: The Human and the Price of Dehumanized Labor*. Minneapolis: University of Minnesota Press.

Rhodes, John David, and Elena Gorfinkel, eds. 2011. *Taking Place: Location and the Moving Image*. Minneapolis: University of Minnesota Press.

Rid, Thomas. 2010. "The Nineteenth Century Origins of Counterinsurgency Doctrine." *Journal of Strategic Studies* 33, no. 5: 727–58. https://doi.org/10.1080/01402390.2010.498259.

Rodinson, Maxime. 1974. *Islam and Capitalism*. New York: Pantheon Books.

Rosner, Daniela K., and Morgan Ames. 2014. "Designing for Repair?: Infrastructures and Materialities of Breakdown." In *Proceedings of the 17th ACM Conference on Computer Supported Cooperative Work and Social Computing*, 319–31. CSCW '14. New York: ACM. https://doi.org/10.1145/2531602.2531692.

Rowe, Peter, and Hashim Sarkis, eds. 1998. *Projecting Beirut: Episodes in the Construction and Reconstruction of a Modern City*. New York: Prestel.

Saade, Bashir. 2016. *Hizbullah and the Politics of Remembrance: Writing the Lebanese Nation*. New York: Cambridge University Press.

Sabry, Tarik. 2010. *Cultural Encounters in the Arab World: On Media, the Modern and the Everyday*. New York: I. B. Tauris.

Safieddine, Hicham. 2015. "Economic Sovereignty and the Fetters of Finance: The Making of Lebanon's Central Bank." PhD diss., University of Toronto.

Safieddine, Hicham. 2019. *Banking on the State: The Financial Foundations of Lebanon*. Stanford, CA: Stanford University Press.

Said, Edward W. 1978. *Orientalism*. New York: Pantheon Books.

Saint-Amour, Paul K. 2011. "Applied Modernism: Military and Civilian Uses of the Aerial Photomosaic." *Theory, Culture and Society* 28, no. 7–8: 241–69. https://doi.org /10.1177/0263276411423938.

Sakr, Naomi. 2001. *Satellite Realms: Transnational Television, Globalization and the Middle East*. London: I. B. Tauris.

Sakr, Naomi. 2007. *Arab Television Today*. New York: I. B. Tauris.

Salamandra, Christa. 2004. *A New Old Damascus: Authenticity and Distinction in Urban Syria*. Bloomington: Indiana University Press.

Salhab, Ghassan, dir. 2007. *Posthumous*. Radical Closure.

Saliba, Robert. 2004. *Beirut City Center Recovery: The Foch-Allenby and Étoile Conservation Area*. Gottingen: Steidl.

Salibi, Kamal. 1976. *Crossroads to Civil War: Lebanon, 1958–1976*. London: Ithaca Press.

Salloukh, Bassel F., Rabie Barakat, Jinan S. Al-Habbal, Lara W. Khattab, and Shoghig Mikaelian. 2015. *The Politics of Sectarianism in Postwar Lebanon*. London: Pluto Press.

Salmon, F. J. 1922. "Air Photography as an Aid to Survey." *Transactions of the Engineering Association of Ceylon*: 60–80.

Sandvig, Christian. 2013. "The Internet as Infrastructure." In *The Oxford Handbook of Internet Studies*, edited by William H. Dutton. Oxford, UK: Oxford University Press.

Sarkis, Hashim. 1998. "Dances with Margaret Mead: Planning Beirut since 1958." In *Projecting Beirut: Episodes in the Construction and Reconstruction of a Modern City*, edited by Peter Rowe and Hashim Sarkis. New York: Prestel.

Sarkis, Hashim. 2003. *Circa 1958: Lebanon in the Pictures and Plans of Constantin Doxiadis*. Beirut: Dar An-Nahar.

Satia, Priya. 2006. "The Defense of Inhumanity: Air Control and the British Idea of Arabia." *American Historical Review* 111, no. 1: 16–51. https://doi.org/10.1086/ahr.111.1.16.

Satia, Priya. 2013. "The Pain of Love: The Invention of Aerial Surveillance in British Iraq." In *From Above: War, Violence, and Verticality*, edited by Peter Adey, Mark Whitehead, and Alison Williams. New York: Oxford University Press.

Sawalha, Aseel. 2010. *Reconstructing Beirut: Memory and Space in a Postwar Arab City*. Austin: University of Texas Press.

Schaebler, Brigit. 2000. "Practicing 'Musha': Common Lands and the Common Good in Southern Syria under the Ottomans and the French (1812–1942)." In *New Perspectives on Property and Land in the Middle East*, edited by Roger Owen. Cambridge, MA: Harvard University Press.

Schayegh, Cyrus. 2017. *The Middle East and the Making of the Modern World*. Cambridge, MA: Harvard University Press.

Scheid, Kirsten. 2010. "Necessary Nudes: Ḥadātha and Muʿāṣira in the Lives of Modern Lebanese." *International Journal of Middle East Studies* 42, no. 2: 203–30.

Schivelbusch, Wolfgang. 1995. *Disenchanted Night: The Industrialization of Light in the Nineteenth Century*. Berkeley: University of California Press.

Schmid, Heiko. 2006. "Privatized Urbanity or a Politicized Society? Reconstruction in Beirut after the Civil War." *European Planning Studies* 14, no. 3: 365–81. https://doi.org/10.1080/09654310500420859.

Schwenkel, Christina. 2009. *The American War in Contemporary Vietnam: Transnational Remembrance and Representation*. Bloomington: Indiana University Press.

Scott, Heidi V. 2008. "Colonialism, Landscape and the Subterranean." *Geography Compass* 2, no. 6: 1853–69. https://doi.org/10.1111/j.1749-8198.2008.00164.x.

Scott, James C. 1990. *Domination and the Arts of Resistance: Hidden Transcripts*. New Haven, CT: Yale University Press.

Sebald, W. G. 2003. *On the Natural History of Destruction*. New York: Random House.

Seigneurie, Ken. 2011. *Standing by the Ruins: Elegiac Humanism in Wartime and Postwar Lebanon*. New York: Fordham University Press.

Shah, Svati P. 2014. *Street Corner Secrets: Sex, Work, and Migration in the City of Mumbai*. Durham, NC: Duke University Press.

Shaw, Ian. 2016. *Predator Empire: Drone Warfare and Full Spectrum Dominance*. Minneapolis: University of Minnesota Press.

Sheehi, Stephen. 2016. *The Arab Imago: A Social History of Portrait Photography, 1860–1910*. Princeton, NJ: Princeton University Press.

Shell, Hanna Rose. 2012. *Hide and Seek: Camouflage, Photography, and the Media of Reconnaissance*. New York: Zone Books.

Shome, Raka. 2019. "When Postcolonial Studies Interrupts Media Studies." *Communication, Culture and Critique* 12, no. 3: 305–22. https://doi.org/10.1093/ccc/tcz020.

Sienkiewicz, Matt. 2016. *The Other Air Force: U.S. Efforts to Reshape Middle Eastern Media since 9/11*. New Brunswick, NJ: Rutgers University Press.

Simone, AbdouMaliq. 2004. *For the City Yet to Come: Changing African Life in Four Cities*. Durham, NC: Duke University Press.

Singer, Barnett, and John W. Langdon. 2004. *Cultured Force: Makers and Defenders of the French Colonial Empire*. Madison: University of Wisconsin Press.

Sobchack, Vivian Carol. 2000. "'At the Still Point of the Turning World': Meta-Morphing and Meta-Stasis." In *Meta-Morphing: Visual Transformation and the Culture of Quick-Change*, edited by Vivian Carol Sobchack. Minneapolis: University of Minnesota Press.

Sodaro, Amy. 2018. *Exhibiting Atrocity: Memorial Museums and the Politics of Past Violence*. New Brunswick, NJ: Rutgers University Press.

Sparke, Matthew. 1998. "A Map That Roared and an Original Atlas: Canada, Cartography, and the Narration of Nation." *Annals of the Association of American Geographers* 88, no. 3: 463–95.

Spigel, Lynn. 1992. *Make Room for TV: Television and the Family Ideal in Postwar America*. Chicago: University of Chicago Press.

Stam, Robert, Richard Porton, and Leo Goldsmith. 2015. *Keywords in Subversive Film / Media Aesthetics*. Malden, MA: Wiley-Blackwell.

Stamatopoulou-Robbins, Sophia. 2019. *Waste Siege: The Life of Infrastructure in Palestine*. Stanford, CA: Stanford University Press.

Stanton, Andrea L. 2014. *"This Is Jerusalem Calling": State Radio in Mandate Palestine*. Austin: University of Texas Press.

Starosielski, Nicole. 2015. *The Undersea Network*. Durham, NC: Duke University Press.

Stewart, Kathleen. 2007. *Ordinary Affects*. Durham, NC: Duke University Press.

Stoler, Ann Laura. 1995. *Race and the Education of Desire: Foucault's History of Sexuality and the Colonial Order of Things*. Durham, NC: Duke University Press.

Stoler, Ann Laura. 2009. *Along the Archival Grain: Epistemic Anxieties and Colonial Common Sense*. Princeton, NJ: Princeton University Press.

Stoler, Ann Laura, ed. 2013. *Imperial Debris: On Ruins and Ruination*. Durham, NC: Duke University Press.

Stolow, Jeremy, ed. 2013. *Deus in Machina: Religion, Technology, and the Things in Between*. New York: Fordham University Press.

Straubhaar, Joseph D. 2007. *World Television: From Global to Local*. Thousand Oaks, CA: Sage Publications.

Sturken, Marita. 2004. "The Aesthetics of Absence: Rebuilding Ground Zero." *American Ethnologist* 31, no. 3: 311–25.

Sturken, Marita. 2015. "The 9/11 Memorial Museum and the Remaking of Ground Zero." *American Quarterly* 67, no. 2: 471–90. https://doi.org/10.1353/aq.2015.0022.

Sturken, Marita. 2016. "The Objects That Lived: The 9/11 Museum and Material Transformation." *Memory Studies* 9, no. 1: 13–26. https://doi.org/10.1177/1750698015613970.

Sundaram, Ravi. 2010. *Pirate Modernity: Delhi's Media Urbanism*. New York: Routledge.

Sundaram, Ravi. 2015. "Post-Postcolonial Sensory Infrastructure." *E-Flux Journal* 64 (April).

Tabet, Jad. 1993. "Towards a Master Plan for Post-War Lebanon." In *Recovering Beirut: Urban Design and Post-War Reconstruction*, edited by Samir Khalaf and Philip S. Khoury. Leiden, Netherlands: Brill.

Thomas, H. Hamshaw. 1920. "Geographical Reconnaissance by Aeroplane Photography, with Special Reference to the Work Done on the Palestine Front." *Geographical Journal* 55, no. 5: 349–70. https://doi.org/10.2307/1780446.

Thomas, Martin C. 2002. "French Intelligence-Gathering in the Syrian Mandate, 1920–40." *Middle Eastern Studies* 38, no. 1: 1–32.

Thomas, Martin C. 2005. *The French Empire between the Wars: Imperialism, Politics and Society*. Manchester, UK: Manchester University Press.

Thompson, Elizabeth. 2000. *Colonial Citizens: Republican Rights and Paternal Privilege in French Syria and Lebanon*. New York: Columbia University Press.

Thussu, Daya Kishan, ed. 2006. *Media on the Move: Global Flow and Contra-Flow*. New York: Routledge.

Toscano, Alberto. 2010. *Fanaticism: On the Uses of an Idea*. New York: Verso.

Toufic, Jalal. 2003. *Vampires: An Essay on the Undead in Film*. Sausalito, CA: Post-Apollo.

Traboulsi, Fawwaz. 2007. *A History of Modern Lebanon*. London: Pluto Press.

Trawi, Ayman. 2002. *Beirut's Memory*. Beirut: Banque de la Méditerranée.

Trigg, Dylan. 2009. "The Place of Trauma: Memory, Hauntings, and the Temporality of Ruins." *Memory Studies* 2, no. 1: 87–101. https://doi.org/10.1177/1750698008097397.

Turner, Graeme. 2011. "Convergence and Divergence: The International Experience of Digital Television." In *Television as Digital Media*, edited by James Bennett and Nikki Strange. Durham, NC: Duke University Press.

United States Operations Mission to Lebanon. 1955. *Lebanon, 1955. Progress Report, Technical Cooperation Assistance Program*. Beirut.

van Es, Karin. 2017. *The Future of Live*. Malden, MA: Polity Press.

Verdeil, Eric. 2003. "Politics, Ideology and Professional Interests: Foreign versus Local Planners in Lebanon under President Chehab." In *Urbanism: Imported or Exported?*, edited by Joe Nasr and Mercedes Volait. New York: Wiley-Academy.

Verdeil, Eric. 2004. "Methodological and Political Issues in the Lebanese Planning Experiences." In *City Debates—The Lebanese National Master Plan, City Debates 2003 Proceedings*, edited by Mona Harb. Beirut: American University of Beirut.

Verdeil, Eric. 2008. "State Development Policy and Specialised Engineers: The Case of Urban Planners in Post-War Lebanon." *Knowledge Work Society* 5, no. 1: 29–51.

Verdeil, Eric. 2010. *Beyrouth et ses urbanistes Une ville en plans (1946–1975)*. Beirut: Presses de l'Ifpo. http://books.openedition.org/ifpo/2101.

Verdeil, Eric. 2012. "Michel Ecochard in Lebanon and Syria (1956–1968): The Spread of Modernism, the Building of the Independent States and the Rise of Local Professionals of Planning." *Planning Perspectives* 27, no. 2: 243–60. http://dx.doi.org/10.1080/02665433.2012.646774.

Vidler, Anthony. 2008. "Air War and Architecture." In *Ruins of Modernity*, edited by Julia Hell and Andreas Schönle. Durham, NC: Duke University Press.

Violi, Patrizia. 2012. "Trauma Site Museums and Politics of Memory: Tuol Sleng, Villa Grimaldi and the Bologna Ustica Museum." *Theory, Culture and Society* 29, no. 1: 36–75. https://doi.org/10.1177/0263276411423035.

Volk, Lucia. 2007. "Re-Remembering the Dead: A Genealogy of a Martyrs Memorial in South Lebanon." *Arab Studies Journal* 15, no. 1: 44–69.

Volk, Lucia. 2009. "Martyrs at the Margins: The Politics of Neglect in Lebanon's Borderlands." *Middle Eastern Studies* 45, no. 2: 263–82. https://doi.org/10.1080/00263200802697365.

Volk, Lucia. 2010. *Memorials and Martyrs in Modern Lebanon*. Bloomington: Indiana University Press.

von Moltke, Johannes. 2008. "Ruin Cinema." In *Ruins of Modernity*, edited by Julia Hell and Andreas Schönle. Durham, NC: Duke University Press.

Wark, McKenzie. 2013. *The Spectacle of Disintegration: Situationist Passages out of the Twentieth Century*. New York: Verso.

Watenpaugh, Keith David. 2015. *Bread from Stones: The Middle East and the Making of Modern Humanitarianism*. Berkeley: University of California Press.

Weiss, Max. 2010a. *In the Shadow of Sectarianism: Law, Shi'ism, and the Making of Modern Lebanon*. Cambridge, MA: Harvard University Press.

Weiss, Max. 2010b. "Practicing Sectarianism in Mandate Lebanon: Shi'i Cemeteries, Religious Patrimony, and the Everyday Politics of Difference." *Journal of Social History* 40, no. 3: 707–33.

Weizman, Eyal. 2007. *Hollow Land: Israel's Architecture of Occupation*. New York: Verso.

Weizman, Eyal. 2017. *Forensic Architecture: Violence at the Threshold of Detectability*. New York: Zone Books.

White, Mimi. 2004. "The Attractions of Television: Reconsidering Liveness." In *MediaSpace: Place, Scale, and Culture in a Media Age*, edited by Anna McCarthy and Nick Couldry. New York: Routledge.

Williams, Elizabeth. 2015. "Mapping the Cadastre, Producing the Fellah: Technologies and Discourses of Rule in French Mandate Syria and Lebanon." In *The Routledge Handbook of the History of the Middle East Mandates*, edited by Cyrus Schayegh and Andrew Arsan. New York: Routledge.

Williams, Paul. 2007. *Memorial Museums: The Global Rush to Commemorate Atrocities*. Oxford, UK: Berg Publishers.

Williams, Raymond. 1973. *The Country and the City*. New York: Oxford University Press.

Williams, Raymond. 1989. "Culture Is Ordinary." In *Resources of Hope: Culture, Democracy, Socialism*. New York: Verso.

Wilson, Matthew W. 2017. *New Lines: Critical GIS and the Trouble of the Map*. Minneapolis: University of Minnesota Press.

Wilson-Goldie, Kaelen. 2007. "The War Works: Videos under Siege, Online and in the Aftermath, Again." *Art Journal* 66, no. 2: 68–82. https://doi.org/10.1080/00043249.2007.10791255.

Winichakul, Thongchai. 1994. *Siam Mapped: A History of the Geo-Body of a Nation*. Honolulu: University of Hawaii Press.

Winterbotham, H. S. L. 1920. "The Economic Limits of Aeroplane Photography for Mapping, and Its Applicability to Cadastral Plans." *Geographical Journal* 56, no. 6: 481–83. https://doi.org/10.2307/1780470.

Wishnitzer, Avner. 2015. *Reading Clocks, Alla Turca: Time and Society in the Late Ottoman Empire*. Chicago: University of Chicago Press.

Wood, Denis. 2010. *Rethinking the Power of Maps*. New York: Guilford Press.

Wright, Gwendolyn. 1991. *The Politics of Design in French Colonial Urbanism*. Chicago: University of Chicago Press.

Yahya, Maha. 2005. "Unnamed Modernisms: National Ideologies and Historical Imaginaries in Beirut's Urban Architecture." PhD diss., MIT.

Youmans, William. 2017. *An Unlikely Audience: Al Jazeera's Struggle in America*. New York: Oxford University Press.

Young, Robert J. 1974. *The Strategic Dream: French Air Doctrine in the Inter-War Period, 1919–39*. London: Sage.

Zayani, Mohamed. 2015. *Networked Publics and Digital Contention: The Politics of Everyday Life in Tunisia*. New York: Oxford University Press.

INDEX

Page numbers in italics refer to figures.

Banet-Weiser, Sarah, 215n60
Baudrillard, Jean, 125, 208n78
Baumann, Hannes, 198n15, 199n35
Beaux-Arts architecture, 36–37
beer pong, 60
before/after images, 18–19, 64–69, *65*;
    citizen-investor and, 80–98, *81–83*,
    88–93, 178; lenticular effect and, 103–4,
    204n93; in postwar Germany, 82–83;
    Solidere's use of, 80–98, *81–83*, *88–93*.
    See also images
Beirut airport, 102–4, 110
Beirut City Center (McPherson), 95, 97–98
Beirut City Center Recovery (Saliba), 95–97
Beirut Reborn (Gavin & Maluf), 95–96
Beirut's Memory (Trawi), 102
Benjamin, Walter, 68; *Arcades Project*, 62,
    64, 197n121
Berri, Nabih, 14, 140, 200n44
Beyhum, Nabil, 72, 199n36
Beyrouth: Le Dialogue des Ruines (film), 89
Bin Laden, Osama, 136
biopolitics, 30–31; of population manage-
    ment, 12; of self-government, 111; of
    War on Terror, 111
Blas, Zach, 206n44
blueprints, 29–30
Bou Akar, Hiba, 194n90, 195n94; on
    Écochard plan, 195n92; on "ghost
    infrastructure," 196n107
Bourdain, Anthony, 204n15
Browne, Simone, 7–8, 185n19
Brunsdon, Charlotte, 16, 84
Buck-Morss, Susan, 198n13
Buonanno, Milly, 209n92
Burtch, Robert C., 191n37
Butler, Judith, 214nn49–50

cadastral maps, 28–32, *29*, 193n71
Cadava, Eduardo, 213n38
camouflage, 7, 115, 145–46, 163, *164*, 212n32
Campbell, Timothy C., 187n38
cartography, 24–30; counterinsurgency
    theory and, 26–27; critical, 17, 22,

189n3, 190n12; ethnographic, 30–31,
    49–50, 60; McGowan on, 193n71;
    Mitchell on, 189n65; universal grid
    system of, 192n47, 192n52. *See also*
    mapping
Catholic Church, 148; McLuhan's theo-
    ries and, 148, 210n5; social movements
    of, 48–49; Télé Lumière and, 14
Cedar Revolution, 98–99
CERMOC (Centre d'Études et de Recher-
    che sur le Moyen-Orient Contempo-
    rain), 30, 191n30
Chakrabarty, Dipesh, 185n16
Chamaa, Nasser, 97–98
Chamayou, Grégoire, 160–61
Chamoun, Camille, 44–45, 47, 195n91
Chandler, Katherine Fehr, 208n75
Chehab, Fuad, 47, 48; Écochard and,
    50–52; Safieddine on, 195n98
Chow, Rey, 124
Christian Broadcasting Network (CBN),
    14
Christian Lebanese Forces, 14
CIAM (Congrès Internationaux
    d'Architecture Moderne), 42–43, 51
cinema: of attractions, 16; ruins and, 83,
    89–90, 201n55; "useful," 86
cinema/city studies, 84, 201n56
citizen-investor, 68, 182; before/after im-
    ages and, 80–98, *81–83*, *88–93*, 178
Civil War (1975–90), 55–64, *59*, *61*, *62*, 116,
    170; broadcasting during, 13–14; Cold
    War and, 14–15, 18; Solidere and, 95;
    Taif Agreement of, 14, 60–61
"civilizing mission," 27, 39, 111
clientelism, 77, 207n59
cluster bombs, 107, 111, 120
CNN, 14, 118, 125
"co-habitability," 56
Cold War, 14–15, 18, 44–45, *45*; city plan-
    ning and, 47; US archives of, 24
Collier, Stephen, 11–12, 187n37
commodification, 20, 143, 172–76,
    215n60

power outages, 106, 126–128
press freedom, 13
Project as Grand as Hope, A (film), 85, 91–94, *92*, *93*
Protestantism, 148, 215n63

Qatar, 142
queer aesthetic opacity, 9
queer media practices, 186n26

Rabinow, Paul, 43
radio, 13
Raisz, Erwin, 30
Rancière, Jacques, 146, 176; on consensus, 69, 185n15; on dissensus, 6–7, 9; Mirzoeff on, 210n1; on political community, 184n14
Rankin, William, 190n12
"re-Beirut" development program, 67–68
Renan, Ernest, 22
Robertson, Pat, 14
Robinson, Arthur H., 196n109
Rodinson, Maxime, 210n6
Rossellini, Roberto, 202n70
ruins, 66; cinema and, 83, 89–90, 201n55

Sabra refugee camp massacre, 58
Sacred Defense Garden and Museum (Tehran), 153, 212n20
Sadynaya prison (Syria), 206n52
Safieddine, Hicham, 194n80, 195n98
Said, Edward, 3, 171–72, 183n1
Saint-Amour, Paul K., 192n40
Salaam, Assem, 52, 72, 198n25
Saliba, Robert, 97, 98
Sarkis, Hashim, 195n91
satellite broadcasting, 15, 17, 118, 179
Saudi Arabia, 146; Arabsat and, 15; Iranian conflicts with, 12
Scheid, Kirsten, 184n13
Schivelbusch, Wolfgang, 8, 185n20
Schwenkel, Christina, 213n41
Scott, Heidi V., 213n40
Scott, James C., 186n24

Sebald, W. G., 82
sectarianism, 10–12, 41, 49–50, 181; Abisaab on, 202n67; Chehab on, 47; Doha Accords and, 142; Hariri on, 203n90; Taif Agreement and, 60–61, 87; Volk on, 211n9, 211n17
September 11th attacks, 83, 213n36
Serof, Gregoire, 191n31, 195n102
Shah, Svati P., 206n40
Shatila refugee camp massacre, 58
Sheehi, Stephen, 184n13
Shell, Hanna Rose, 212n32
signal jamming/hacking, 131–34
Siniora, Fouad, 140–42
sit-in of December 2006, 1, 138–42
Situationism, 185n23, 186n23, 206n51
Social Catholic movement, 48–49
social media platforms, 180
Solidere (Société Libanaise pour le Développement et la Reconstruction de Beyrouth), 18, 64–66, 142, 177, 182; before/after images used by, 80–98, *81–83*, *88–93*; birth of, 69–80; books published by, 95–96; Civil War period and, 95; eminent domain laws and, 74; films produced by, 85–95; licensed photographs of, 69; photograph licensing by, 69; profitability of, 75; regional offices of, 68; as state-subsidized corporation, 197n3; stock of, 78; zoning plan of, 70–74, *71*
souks (Beirut), 79, 87–88, 90, 200n47, 200n51
Sparke, Matthew, 189n3
spectacle, 7, 172; concealment and, 181; Debord on, 185n23; Wark on, 8–9, 186n23
spectatorship, 16, 106, 169, 204n15
Stalin, Joseph, 137, 209n100
Stamatopoulou-Robbins, Sophia, 184n10
"state failure," 55, 199n29
Stewart, Kathleen, 204n17
street lighting, 8
Suez Crisis, 195n91

surveillance, 3, 145; aerial photography for, 28; concealment and, 112–24; lantern laws and, 7–8, 185n19; satellite, 54, 160

Sykes-Picot Agreement (1916), 55, 196n111

Syria, 98; Civil War in, 151; Danger brothers' projects in, 36; French intervention in, 22–25; during Lebanese Civil War, 58; refugees from, 5

Tabet, Jad, 72, 79, 199n25
Tabet, Rayyane, 60
Taif Agreement (1989), 14, 60–61, 98, 210n105
tanzimat modernization plan, 11
"Target Nasrallah" (video clip), 132–34
Télé-Liban broadcaster, 13, 14
Télé Lumière (Catholic broadcaster), 14
Télé-Orient television broadcaster, 13
televisual liveness, 106, 117, 134–38, 140; definition of, 134; Feuer on, 209n87
33 Days (film), 108
Tobler, Waldo, 196n109
"topology of power," 12
Torrens system, 31, 191n37
Toscano, Alberto, 212n23
traffic patterns, 36, 40, 43, 50–54, 193n56
Trawi, Ayman, 102
Trigg, Dylan, 202n75
Truman, Harry S., 44
Tueni, Jibran, 101
Turner, Graeme, 207n58
24 (TV show), 123
2006 war, 117–21, 154, 179; casualties in, 107, 117; ceasefire agreement for, 107; context for, 106–12; drones used in, 110, 122–26, 160–61, *168*, 171; hit-and-run videos of, 119–22, 124; names for, 107; targeting concealment in, 122–26. *See also* Al Manar

Under the Bombs (film), 108
underground photography, 166

undocumented migrants, 116
urban planning, 25; during Civil War, 55–63, *59*, *61*, *62*; counterinsurgency theory and, 26–27; during early republic, 42–54, *43*, *45*, *52*, *54*; *ekistics* for, 47; during French Mandate, 26–41, *29*, *32*, *37*
"urbicide," 56, 196n114
US Defense Mapping Agency, 58–60, *59*
US Marine barracks bombing (Beirut, 1983), 58
US Operations Mission in Lebanon (USOM/L), 44–47, *45*, 194n85

Vichy France, 24, 29, 41, 187n43, 191n28
Vidal de la Blache, Paul, 30
Vidler, Anthony, 82–83
Vietnam War, 166, 167, 213n41, 213n47
Volk, Lucia, 211n9, 211n17
von Moltke, Johannes, 201n55

Wa'ad project, 80
war on drugs, 116, 206n50
War on Terror, 19, 27; biopolitics of, 110; discourse of, 111; Hizbullah and, 118
Wark, McKenzie, 8–9, 185n23, 206n51
weapons garden, 153, *168*, 168–71. *See also* Museum of the Resistance
Weizman, Eyal, 161, 206n52
Which Beirut Tomorrow? (film), 85, 87–91, *88–91*
White, Mimi, 16
Williams, Raymond, 17–18, 189n1
World Bank, 78
World War I, 30, 191n35; aerial photography in, 35, 116; airpower in, 33–34, 190n24
World War II, 35, 109; German reconstruction after, 82–83; Vichy France and, 24, 29, 41, 187n43, 191n28

zoning plans, *43*, 43–44, 50–53, *52*; of Solidere project, 70–74, *71*